SPACE WARRIORS:

THE ARMY SPACE SUPPORT TEAM

Prepared by:

Dr. James Walker

&

James T. Hooper

March 1999, July 2003 (rev.)

FOREWORD

In the fifteen years since the U.S. Army Space Command (USARSPACE) was activated, soldiers from this command have pioneered innovative and revolutionary ways for employing space capabilities on behalf of the warfighter. At the time this history was sent to press, Army space soldiers were deployed worldwide in support of a variety of critical missions. Army space support units were present during combat operations in Afghanistan in 2001 and Iraq in 2003, providing force enhancement, missile attack warning, and information operations support to commanders in the U.S. Central Command area of operations. Other Army space soldiers, working in both the United States and overseas, delivered the worldwide long-haul satellite communications support and other space products needed to maintain an effective military deterrent in Korea and other areas. As these examples attest, Army space soldiers are today playing an important role across the entire spectrum of operations.

This history considers the establishment and subsequent evolution of the Army Space Support Team (ARSST) organization, created to provide space products and expertise to field units, thereby enhancing their intelligence and operational planning capabilities. This history focuses on the period from 1986 to 1998, when a handful of soldiers and civilians experimenting with new technologies and concepts sought to leverage the "ultimate high ground" on behalf of the land force. The history discusses the hard-won lessons learned through repeated deployments and exercises, calling attention to their frustrations and setbacks as well as to their many successes. Ultimately, it seeks to explain how those early visionaries established a foundation for the progress that the Army has achieved over the past five years, as illustrated by the importance of space in today's land combat operations, and how these early lessons continue to provide valuable insights for the Army as it transforms for the future.

This history was originally written in 1998. We are publishing it now, with a new concluding chapter, because developments over the past five years underscore the importance of the early work accomplished by ARSST soldiers. In areas ranging from the formulation of space doctrine and operational concepts to the establishment of a new career field and Army space force structure, early experimentation by ARSST soldiers provided the foundation for subsequent Army initiatives. It is our hope that this early history of ARRST from 1986 to 1998 will contribute to a more complete understanding of the progress made since 1998, and to an informed vision of the future of Army space support.

Why should soldiers read this book? All military operations today are affected by space-based communications, imagery, positioning and location support, missile warning, and related capabilities. As the Army transforms itself for the future, space will be essential for achieving the information dominance necessary for the advanced, full-spectrum Army operations of tomorrow. An understanding of space systems and capabilities is becoming an increasingly important part of the professional soldier's craft, and we hope that this history will provide new and important insights into where we have come from and where we are going as an Army.

Joseph M. Cosumano, Jr.

Lieutenant General, U.S. Army

Commanding

PREFACE

This history of Army Space Support Team (ARSST) operations was written to support soldiers—both present and future—as they seek new and better ways to use space as a force multiplier. The original publication of this history in 1998 came just two years before a dramatic restructuring of the nation's space organizations and equally dramatic changes in the national security environment. These changes have impacted and continue to impact the organization and scope of Army space support capabilities. In such an environment of rapid and continuous change, it is both interesting and useful to examine the past to gain an understanding of the historical foundations for some of these new ideas and organizations. It is hoped that this history of the Army Space Support Team will provide the reader with such an understanding.

The history is dedicated to the soldiers of the Army Space Support Team. Since the ARSST was activated in October 1994, these soldiers have deployed to support warfighting units, experimented with new tactics and advanced technologies and, in the process, established a firm foundation for Army space initiatives extending into the next century. If, as many analysts claim, the United States is at the forefront of a 'Revolution in Military Affairs,' it is largely due to the efforts of soldiers such as these.

This history represents the efforts not only of the authors, but also of a number of soldiers and civilians whose roles must be acknowledged. Without the sponsorship of Colonel Steve Bowman [Chief of Staff, U.S. Army Space Command (USARSPACE)] and the support of the entire USARSPACE leadership, this study would never have been conducted. Both Colonel Bowman and Lieutenant Colonel Bob Simmons [Director of Current Operations, USARSPACE] provided extremely useful guidance and input. Many Army Space Support Team personnel provided exemplary support throughout the study, answering thousands of questions, helping gather data, and discussing their field experiences and space support insights in a series of oral history interviews. It is safe to say that this history would never have been completed without the assistance of Lieutenant Colonel LeRoy Maurer, Lieutenant Colonel Frankie Moore, Major Gwynne T. Burke, Major Scott Cuthbertson, Major Caesar Jaime, Major Michael McFarland, Captain Gerry Skaw, Captain David Strombeck, Sergeant First Class Howard Smith, Staff Sergeant William Bates, Staff Sergeant Mark Stroup, and Sergeant Eric Herrmann. Similarly valuable research support was provided by Mr. Gary Baumann [USARSPACE], Mr. Ed Kiker [formerly assigned to the Army Space Institute], and Mr. James Williamson [Brown International]. Finally, special thanks is due to Major Caesar Jaime who provided logistical support throughout the study process, arranged and scheduled interviews with a number of subject matter experts, and provided a conduit for the exchange of information between various elements of U.S. Army Space Command.

During the analysis and production phases of this project, assistance was rendered by a number of analysts whose efforts should also be acknowledged. Mr. Roy McCullough of Science Applications International Corporation (SAIC) made significant editorial contributions to the 2003 edition of this history. Reviews, input, advice, and guidance for the original edition of the history, prepared in 1998, were also provided by a number of personnel at SAIC, including Randy Jones [Lieutenant Colonel, USA (ret.)], Doug Brisson [Lieutenant Colonel, USA (ret.)], Chip Fackner [Colonel, USA (ret.)], Tom Molino [Colonel, USA (ret.)], and Jim Reams [Lieutenant Colonel, USA (ret.)]. In addition, research support, editorial assistance, and graphics development help were provided by Dr. Todd Clark [SAIC], Mrs. Sharon Lang [Historical Office, U.S. Army Space and Missile Defense Command (USASMDC)], Ms. Sherrye Alexander [Historical Office, USASMDC], Mr. Joe Kupsky [SAIC], Mr. Mike Gallardo [SAIC], Mr. Mark Torok [SAIC].

All ranks are given as they were at the time of the preparation of this study.

Dr. James Walker

James T. Hooper

CONTENTS

EXECUTIVE SUMMARY

In the period from 1986 to 1998, the Army experimented with a number of concepts and programs for providing space support to tactical commanders. During this period, the focus of Army efforts shifted from space systems demonstrations, to deployment support, to space analytic services. The Army Space Support Team (ARSST) spearheaded these efforts to utilize space capabilities in support of the warfighter. As the military space environment continues to evolve and the Army adapts to new and emerging Army requirements, the ARSST will continue to play an indispensable role in translating space capabilities into warfighting tools and knowledge.

The primary goal of this history of the Army Space Support Team is to support decision-making—both present and future—by outlining the organizational and conceptual evolution of the ARSST from 1986-1998, identifying trends and issues of significance, and explaining how important problems were approached and why key decisions were made.

ARSST Origins and Background

The Army Space Support Team organization represents the culmination of twelve years of Army conceptual development and field experience in applying space to support tactical units. This historical background was punctuated by six key milestones, as summarized below:

1986: The provisional activation of the Army Space Institute (ASI). As the coordinating body for the development of Army space concepts, doctrine, training, and equipment, ASI served a pivotal role in first introducing the Army to the benefits offered by space.

1987: The decision to implement the Army Space Demonstration Program. The demonstration program provided an early education to many tactical commanders on methods of using space technologies to support planning and operations. Although this program was not designed, organized, or funded to provide operational support in the field, personnel later deployed in support of Army operations in Saudi Arabia, Haiti, and Bosnia.

1988: The activation of U.S. Army Space Command (USARSPACE). This marked the end of a long evolutionary process that began with the activation of a four-man liaison element at Colorado Springs in 1984 and continued through 1988 when USARSPACE was established as the central organization for providing operational space support to the Army.

1990-1991: The DESERT SHIELD and DESERT STORM experience. In the deserts of Saudi Arabia, Kuwait, and southern Iraq, the "rank-and-file" Army was exposed to the value of multi-spectral imagery, GPS position/navigation, satellite weather, ballistic missile warning, and satellite communications. In addition, this experience also demonstrated the need for the Army to activate a dedicated space support organization capable of providing training and operational support to units deployed in a theater of operations.

1994: The Army's decision to activate a deployable space support team (Contingency Operations—Space or COPS) at Colorado Springs. The COPS team was the first Army organization explicitly designed to provide sustained operational support for units in the field.

1994-1998: The evolution and growth of the Army Space Support Team. The ARSST represented an extension of the original COPS idea for a deployable space support organization. Over the subsequent five years of ARSST operations, teams deployed worldwide to support units from battalion to theater level — and all echelons in between. Equally as important, the ARSST served as a conduit between the capabilities of USARSPACE and the needs of warfighting units.

ARSST Operations

Field units evaluated the quality and value of ARSST support highly. In a 1998 survey of Army officers who trained with an ARSST team every respondent stated that, if deployed to war, he would request assistance from the Army Space Support Team. Typical comments included: "I still firmly believe that ARSSTs are truly a force multiplier and bring a wealth of space systems support" and "I am a believer in the capabilities made available by the ARSST." ARSST personnel worked diligently to earn the trust of supported commanders and staffs, demonstrate the value of space systems and capabilities, and remain prepared to deploy within 48 hours to support the full spectrum of Army missions. In the process, the members of the ARSST averaged more than 140 deployment days per year.

1995: On 1 January 1995, the ARSST was officially activated and teams began deploying to the field to provide space support enhancement. The ARSST was initially divided into three teams, each aligned with a Combatant Command. Over the course of the year, a team was forward-deployed at Ft. Bragg to satisfy the heavy demands for support made by the XVIII Airborne Corps and special operations units.

1996: The ARSST concept of operations and organizational structure underwent significant changes in 1996. Efforts were made to restructure the ARSST to support two Major Regional Conflicts, provide new systems and technologies to the teams, and enhance space advisory and liaison capabilities.

1997: ARSST operations in 1997 were conducted under a new organizational construct, with five teams prepared to support each of the Corps Headquarters and U.S. Army Special Operations Command. The ARSST continued to explore ways to improve the level of space support, to include the forward deployment of ARSST teams and liaison personnel, the rotational deployment of teams, and the establishment of a self-sustainment capability. Additionally, USARSPACE began to experiment with the Army Space Support Cell (ASSC) concept.

1998: During this year, the ASSC concept was exercised and tested. As part of this process, the Command took steps to develop a more formalized training program for ARSST personnel. In another development, the forward-deployed ARSST team at Ft. Bragg was reassigned to Colorado Springs.

Looking to the Future: ARSST Viewpoints in 1998

By 1998, long range planning for the Army Space Support Team was based upon four key assumptions. First, the space capabilities of U.S. adversaries were expected to continue to improve. Second, the dependence of the United States upon space systems—both commercial and military—would also rise. Third, commercial space capabilities would expand, with a number of implications for military operations. Finally, a revolution in satellite communication systems would introduce new considerations for military command and control. Given these trends, ARSST personnel in 1998 strongly believed that the Army needed to be closely involved in exploiting space systems and capabilities in the future. To support this requirement, the ARSST sought to evolve into a space analysis-focused organization, capable not only of translating space capabilities into tools for the supported commander but also of understanding the threat from neutral and adversary space systems, fully exploiting the capabilities of U.S. and commercial space assets, anticipating space environmental impacts, proactively identifying and addressing U.S. vulnerabilities and opportunities, and developing a "space estimate" for incorporation into the warfighter's planning process.

Looking at the long-term trends in the military space environment and the Army's requirements for space support, personnel assigned to the ARSST described three future organizational constructs for the teams. Under the first concept, the ARSST would continue to deploy as a task-organized team of space personnel, but would have self-contained and integrated equipment, mounted in a tactical vehicle. Under the second concept, technology would evolve to the point where a single soldier would be capable of providing the full spectrum of space support through a small laptop computer. Under a third vision of long term ARSST evolution, the successful implementation of space education throughout the Army coupled with the assignment of space operations officers on Corps and Division staffs would render the ARSST unnecessary. In other words, space analysis would be part of every Division and Corps Headquarters' integral capabilities.

Each of the visions for future evolution of the ARSST was dependent upon a number of variables—the future threat, the evolution of space technology, the development of Functional Area 40 and the introduction of a space operations officer to the field, and the level of resources allocated to space support and space operations by the Army. No matter how the military space environment evolves in the future or how the Army organizes the ARSST to address it, however, one fact remained unchanged: The Army Space Support Team experience established a firm foundation for the application of space on behalf of the warfighter. For years to come, this experience will guide how the Army addresses space at the tactical and operational levels of war.

CHAPTER ONE:

SPACE COMES TO THE WARFIGHTER

"While the ultimate weapon of war is still the soldier with a trench-knife, those soldiers are precious and few. Space helps to preserve them, make them more lethal, get them to where they are needed on time, get them resupplied with enough and on time, and convince potential adversaries that these are soldiers who would make better friends than enemies."

-Ed Kiker, Army Space Institute, 1992[1]

In October 1994 General Joseph Ashy, Commander-in-Chief of U.S. Space Command (USSPACECOM), directed that a closer relationship be forged between the unified command and its Service components. Shortly thereafter, USSPACECOM and each of its Service components formally activated Space Support Team organizations. This chapter examines early Army efforts to bring space products to the tactical and operational level, focusing upon key structural causes for the Army's interest in activating a Space Support Team capability. Specifically, this chapter assesses:

- The impact of Army Space Institute (ASI) efforts to bring space products to the tactical user, to include the establishment of a successful tactical space demonstration program.

- Key lessons learned during the deployment and use of early space systems, using the Army's experience with the Global Positioning System (GSP) as an illustrative case study.

- Efforts by the U.S. Army to exploit space capabilities in DESERT SHIELD, DESERT STORM, and other subsequent deployments.

- The critical need for trained Army space support personnel who can facilitate the optimal use and exploitation of space-based capabilities for ground commanders.

Introduction

In October 1994, General Joseph Ashy, then serving as the Commander-in-Chief (CinC) of United States Space Command (USSPACECOM), directed that a closer relationship be forged between the unified command and its Service components. Shortly thereafter, USSPACECOM and each of its Service components formally activated Space Support Team organizations, designed to "provide expertise, advice and liaison regarding the application of space systems capabilities for Theater Commanders, Joint Task Forces, and theater component commanders [and] to make space systems' capabilities understandable, and useful for warfare."[2]

While the proximate cause for the activation of the Army Space Support Team (ARSST) lies with General Ashy's directive, the U.S. Army's efforts to exploit space for tactical purposes actually extend much further into the past. Those efforts not only shaped the method in which the ARSST was later activated and the functions the ARSST was subsequently assigned; they also demonstrated the need for a team capable of providing operational space support at short notice and furnished valuable lessons for Army leaders.

This chapter examines early Army efforts to bring space products to the tactical and operational level, focusing upon key structural causes for the Army's interest in activating a Space Support Team capability. It assesses the impact of Army Space Institute (ASI) efforts to bring space products to the tactical user, to include the establishment of a successful tactical space demonstration program. This chapter also highlights lessons learned during the deployment and use of early space systems, using the Army's experience with the Global Positioning System (GPS) as an illustrative case study. It briefly outlines efforts by the U.S. Army to exploit space capabilities in Operation DESERT SHIELD, Operation DESERT STORM, and other subsequent deployments. Finally, the chapter explains how the Army's early experience shaped the attitudes of senior decision makers, who concluded that the Army had a critical need for trained personnel with the skills needed to exploit space-based capabilities for ground commanders.

> **The Four Original Army Space Demonstration Program Efforts:**
>
> 1. Light satellite support for communications at the tactical and operational levels.
>
> 2. WRAASE commercial satellite weather receivers for support at Corps and Division level.
>
> 3. GPS position/navigation capability demonstrations.
>
> 4. GPS vehicle and weapons systems orientations.

Trailblazing Efforts at the Army Space Institute

The Army Space Institute (ASI) was provisionally activated in 1986 and officially activated on 12 January 1988. The Institute was designated as the U.S. Army Training and Doctrine Command (TRADOC) proponent for space and space systems. In this role, ASI assumed responsibility for developing Army space concepts, doctrine, training, and equipment. As TRADOC Commanding General Maxwell Thurman emphasized at the ASI activation ceremony, "the Army must use space smartly — and that's ASI's role."[3]

Early attempts by ASI to bring space products to the tactical user served as a precursor to the subsequent efforts of the Army Space Support Team. ASI aggressively pursued a vision for providing space support at the small unit level, established a demonstration program to educate tactical commanders on the use of space systems, and provided training and support to combat units deploying for Operation DESERT SHIELD. Simply stated, prior to 1990, ASI was the pivotal organization for thinking about and providing space support to the tactical commander.

The ASI approach can best be summed up in one phrase: "tactical focus." When ASI was provisionally

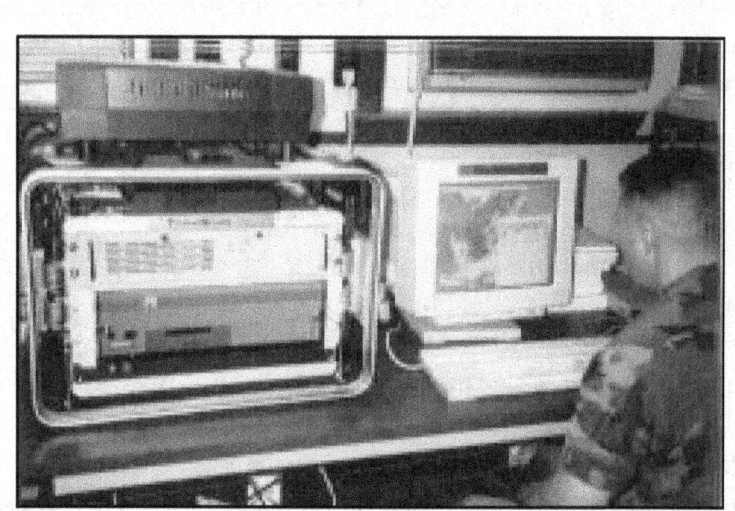

A WRAASE weather terminal, acquired as part of the original Army Space Exploitation Demonstration Program. U.S. Army Europe and U.S. Army Forces Command made the decision to purchase the commercial WRAASE weather receiver in 1989.

activated in 1986, most military space systems were dedicated to supporting the strategic warfighting missions of the U.S. Strategic Command (STRATCOM) and the North American Aerospace Defense Command (NORAD). In a significant departure from previous practices, ASI emphasized the tactical uses of space systems by Army tactical units, down to the level of the infantry squad.[4] Even more remarkable was the aggressive manner in which ASI pursued that objective. At a time when Global Positioning System (GPS) technology had not even been fielded, ASI envisioned a not-so-distant future in which space systems would revolutionize operations at the battalion and company level. For example, in 1987 the Commandant of ASI predicted that advanced positioning systems would soon be able to provide battalion commanders with continuous information on the location and status of their subordinate units; that tactical spaceborne communications would overcome the line-of-sight limitations of ground-based radios, allowing small units to operate cohesively even when spread out over great distances or operating in rough terrain; and that a maneuver battalion's intelligence section would have immediate access to satellite imagery and weather data.[5]

ASI's primary vehicle for experimenting with and demonstrating the tactical applications of space was the Army Space Demonstration Program (ASDP). This program originated from a 19 November 1986 decision by the Vice Chief of Staff of the Army directing the establishment of an Army Space Tactical (ASTAC) Demonstration program. The stated purpose of the program was to "determine how units, down to the squad level, might be supported using existing space technologies."[6] By June 1987, a series of space demonstration concepts had been developed under the program, now officially referred to as the ASDP. The first project involved experiments with light satellites (LIGHTSATs) to evaluate their ability to provide cost-effective support to military tactical/operational commanders. The second project was designed to provide satellite weather support to Corps and Division commanders via commercial weather receiver systems produced by the German company WRAASE. The third project involved demonstrations of the position/ navigation capabilities of the GPS system. A fourth ASDP project involved demonstrations of "the utility of GPS receivers on combat vehicles for orienting vehicles and weapon systems."[7] A fifth ASDP project, which was classified at the time, was the Satellite Early Warning System (SEWS) demonstration. SEWS was an off-line technical demonstration using Defense Satellite Program (DSP) satellites to provide missile early warning data.[8] The Army Staff formally approved the ASDP initiative in August 1987.[9]

By the eve of Operation DESERT SHIELD, significant progress had been made under the demonstration program, referred to after 1988 as the Army Space Exploitation Demonstration Program (ASEDP). Soldiers from ASI and the United States Army Space Command (USARSPACE) provided briefings on the program to Army Major Commands and work was progressing on the four demonstration projects. Under the LIGHTSAT program, two communications satellites were launched which were later used by logistical support units during Operation DESERT STORM. Under the weather support project, ASI provided training on satellite weather systems to the XVIII Airborne Corps, I Corps, Eighth U.S. Army, and a number of TRADOC elements.[10] As a result of these efforts, U.S. Army Forces Command decided to purchase WRAASE weather receivers for every Army unit that had an assigned weather team.[11] ASI also began conducting GPS training and demonstrations in 1989.[12]

In 1990, ASI was deactivated and the TRADOC Program Integration Office for Space (TPIO-SPACE) was established in its place. TPIO-SPACE was placed under the TRADOC Combined Arms Command and staffing levels were reduced from 42 personnel to ten.[13] As part of this reorganization, responsibility for the Army Space Demonstration Program was transferred to USARSPACE.

Background: The Activation of the U.S. Army Space Command

USARSPACE evolved over a period of six years from a 4-man liaison element stationed at Colorado Springs to the Army's operational and planning focal point for space, with a total of 104 assigned personnel. The rapid growth of USARSPACE reflected two structural trends: First, the June 1985 *Army Space Policy* outlined an aggressive approach to exploiting space assets in support of ground operations, with particular emphasis placed on command and control, communications, weather, intelligence, and position/navigation capabilities, and as the Army took steps to implement the vision outlined in the *Army Space Policy*, USARSPACE was assigned a number of new functions, requirements, and responsibilities; The second cause for the rapid expansion of USARSPACE was the decision to assign responsibility for DoD space forces to USSPACECOM, a new Unified Command, in September 1985. As the Army's component to USSPACECOM, U.S. Army Space Command was responsible for integrating Army requirements into the USSPACECOM planning process, for responding to USCINCSPACE-directed taskings, and for performing other joint duties and functions.

USARSPACE can trace its orgins to the Army Staff Field Element, established as the first Army space organization at Colorado Springs in 1984. This four-person element was responsible for performing liaision duties with DoD space organizations. In 1985, planning functions were added to the original Army Staff Field Element and it was renamed the Army Space Planning Group. After USSPACECOM was established, the Army again reorganized its space support structure by activating the Army Space Agency (ASA) in 1986. ASA

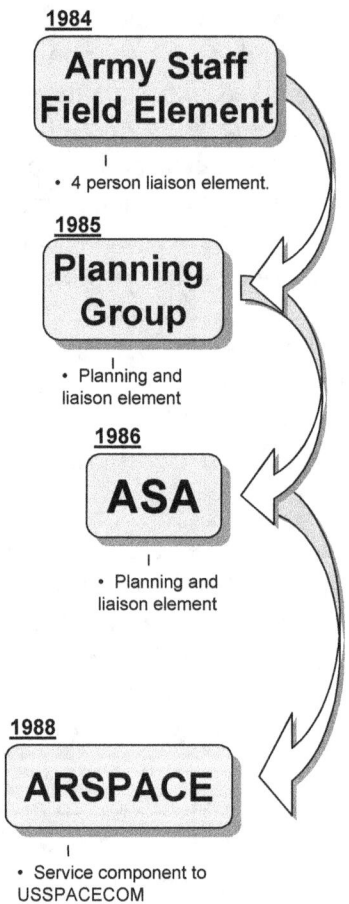

1984

Army Staff Field Element

| • 4 person liaison element.

1985

Planning Group

| • Planning and liaison element

1986

ASA

| • Planning and liaison element

1988

ARSPACE

| • Service component to USSPACECOM

Figure 1: Early Evolution of the Army Space Command.

was designated to "serve as the foundation of the Army's operational capability in space" and was assigned 35 personnel.[14] In 1988, another reorganization took place with the replacement of ASA by the new U.S. Army Space Command. In addition to the planning and coordination functions that were transferred when ASA was deactivated, U.S. Army Space Command assumed responsibility for the Consolidated Space Operations Center Detachment, the U.S. Army NASA-Johnson Space Center Detachment, and three Regional Space Support Centers.[15] The transfer of the space demonstration program from ASI to USARSPACE and the reassignment of the Army Signal Command's Defense Satellite Communication System platform and payload control mission to USARSPACE further extended the operational role of the new Command.[16]

Lessons Learned: The Army Space Institute Experience

Early efforts by ASI to bring space products to the tactical user provided a number of lessons for Army leaders. First, although space systems had traditionally been used to support strategic-level missions, they could also be used at the tactical level. ASI accurately forecasted that space technologies could provide tactical commanders with enhanced position/navigation, weapons targeting, communications, intelligence, and weather support. To realize this objective, ASI conducted a series of experiments with space technologies through the Army Space Demonstration Program (ASDP). Second, the Army discovered that many existing military space systems were not suitable for tactical-level support. As a consequence, ASI began conducting experiments with light satellites to determine if they might provide more cost-effective support at the tactical and operational levels. In addition, ASI conducted experiments with commercial systems (such as WRAASE weather satellites) in areas where existing military systems did not fully satisfy Army requirements.

The Army also learned that commercial, off-the-shelf space products could be leveraged to support tactical units. When the ASDP was initially established, the Vice Chief of Staff of the Army directed that maximum use be made of existing space technologies. By using off-the-shelf products, ASI was often able to fulfill Army space requirements in a low-cost, time-effective manner. Finally, the emerging Army space community determined that one of its key roles would be to support training in the field. As part of the ASDP, ASI and USARSPACE personnel frequently deployed to field units to provide training on space systems and capabilities. This capability would later prove to be invaluable when Army units began deploying for Operation DESERT SHIELD. Units deploying to Southwest Asia requested ASI assistance in exploiting GPS, satellite multi-spectral imagery, and satellite weather products. Personnel from ASI and USARSPACE were quickly dispatched to assist the requesting units. In addition, ASI developed a training program on the use of the GPS system to support XVIII Airborne Corps units.[17] As described in more detail below, the ASI training program for GPS was a major factor helping to rush this developmental system into field use.

From Testing and Demonstration to Tactical Capabilities: The Fielding of GPS and the Gulf War

The use of GPS technology in DESERT STORM is frequently cited as an example of the value that space systems offer to the Army. Often forgotten, however, are the growing pains that accompanied system testing and deployment. Lessons learned during the fielding of GPS were a significant factor in shaping subsequent developments in the Army space community (to include the activation of an Army Space Support Team capability) and provide relevant insights for leaders involved in bringing space capabilities to the field today.

GPS Overview

In the 1960s, two separate space positioning and navigation support programs were established within the Department of Defense. The U.S. Navy sponsored the Timation research program, focused on two-dimensional navigation technology, while the U.S. Air Force studied three-dimensional navigation technologies under a program dubbed 621B. In response to concerns within both the DoD and Congress that these programs were redundant, it was decided in April 1973 to consolidate Timation and 621B into a single, comprehensive system, referred to as the NAVSTAR Global Positioning System. On 1 July 1973, the NAVSTAR GPS Joint Program Office was established, with the U.S. Air Force designated as the executive service. In June 1974, a contract to build nine GPS Block I satellites was awarded to Rockwell International. The first launch of a Block I satellite was conducted in May 1978. In December 1980, a contract to build 28 GPS Block II and Block IIA satellites was awarded to Rockwell International. The first Block II satellite was launched in February 1989, and the GPS system reached Full Operational Capability in April 1995.[18]

GPS currently serves as a satellite-based position/navigation (POS/NAV) tool for support of worldwide military operations. The system employs a constellation of satellites that function as spaceborne beacons. These satellites continuously transmit navigation data that, in turn, can be used by a GPS receiver to determine the operator's location in a process similar to 'triangulation.' GPS is also used for a number of commercial and scientific purposes, ranging from mapping and surveying to international air traffic control.

The GPS system consists of three major segments: the Space Segment, the User Equipment Segment, and the Control Segment. The Space Segment is based upon a constellation of GPS satellites, placed into orbits that allow a GPS receiver to obtain navigational inputs from multiple satellite systems. A GPS receiver can provide location data in two dimensions if it receives input from three satellites; location data in three dimensions can be provided by GPS if input is received from at least four satellites. At the time of DESERT STORM, 16 usable satellites were in operation, providing almost continuous two-dimensional coverage and approximately 19 hours of three-dimensional coverage per day in Southwest Asia.[19]

The GPS User Equipment Segment is composed of a variety of different types of receiver units, as well as related test equipment, antennas, and software. GPS receiver units convert signals from the Space Segment into position, velocity, and time estimate data for the operator. The U.S. Army currently employs a number of hand-carried receiver units, as well as GPS receivers mounted in vehicles and on helicopters. When DESERT STORM began, most of the GPS receivers used by the Army were AN-PSN8 and AN-PSN9 manpack/vehicular (M/V) models and hand-held, commercial, small lightweight global positioning system receiver (SLGR) units.[20]

The GPS Control Segment is composed of a series of tracking systems. GPS monitoring stations are located in Hawaii, Diego Garcia, Ascension Island, the Marshall Islands, and Colorado Springs. These monitoring stations track each GPS satellite, compute orbital and clock corrections, and pass this data to the Master Control Facility at Schriever Air Force Base, CO. The Master Control Facility, in turn, uploads orbital and clock corrections to the satellites.

In many respects, GPS proved to be the ideal position/navigation system for the Army. GPS provides extremely accurate position and velocity data, is available on a continuous basis at any location worldwide, and is not degraded by poor weather or environmental conditions.[21] In fact, GPS met almost every characteristic for the 'perfect' POS/NAV system, defined by the U.S. Army Combined Arms Combat Development Activity in 1986: [1] Ability to provide worldwide coverage; [2] Operation in a "user-passive" mode; [3] Capability to deny use of the system to an enemy; [4] Capability to handle large numbers of users, without a "saturation limit"; [5] Resistance to electronic countermeasures employed by an adversary; [6] Resistance to natural disturbances; [7] Effective, real-time response to users; [8] Availability for combined operations; [9] Lack of difficulties in allocating frequencies; [10] Capability to provide a common grid reference for all users; [11] capability to provide POS/NAV data that is not "degraded by changes in altitude for air and land forces nor by time or year or time of day"; [12] The ability to provide accurate data while the user's vehicle is maneuvering; [13] Ease of equipment maintenance, accomplished by unit-level operators; and [14] the ability for the POS/NAV equipment to be self-contained and mounted in the user's vehicle.[22]

From the Army's perspective, there were only three major disadvantages to the GPS system. First, low power levels are used to transmit GPS signals from space and, thus, it is relatively easy to jam the GPS signal with local or mobile jammers. Second, the GPS receiver needs to be in the line-of-sight of multiple GPS satellites. As a consequence, it does not work as well in rugged or built-up terrain. Finally, the GPS system is dependent on its ground-based control segment, which is susceptible to attacks.[23]

The GPS Testing and Development Process – Army Involvement

The origins of the GPS program extend back to April 1973, when the Deputy Secretary of Defense provided formal authorization for the program to begin. GPS acquisition efforts were managed in three phases: Phase I (Concept Validation), Phase II (Demonstration/Validation), and Phase III (Full Scale Development/ Production).

During Phase I, which lasted from 1973 to 1977, each of the Services conducted initial testing of the GPS concept. Results reported by all Services were satisfactory and the GPS test program proceeded to Phase II.[24]

Phase II (Demonstration/Validation) lasted from 1978 to 1988. As part of Phase II, the Army conducted a series of systems tests, to include the Army Operational Test (OT-II) program of September to December 1983.[25] The initial results were disappointing. It was found that "the overall operational effectiveness of GPS user equipment was marginal except for the UH-60 user equipment." Furthermore, "satisfactory performance often required operator or maintainer work around procedures or corrective actions to compensate for GPS initialization or GPS/host vehicle integration problems."[26] The U.S. Army Test and Evaluation Agency cited 28 problems with the GPS receiver itself, 9 problems with systems maintenance, and 6 problems with training.[27]

In a subsequent report, the U.S. Army Signal School also noted a number of problems with the GPS equipment, to include: [1] Inconsistent system reliability; [2] The need for a new antenna design; [3] A manpack receiver that was too heavy; [4] Problems with the self-test function on the receiver; [5] A display cable that was not durable; [6] Lockups of the receiver, resulting in frozen display units; [7] False "fail" messages; [8] Erratic displays; [9] Batteries running out of power during the course of the tests; [10] "Too many key strokes to enter information"; [11] A technical manual that was "poorly written"; and [12] Failure of the manpack unit during high and low temperature tests.[28]

By 1989, many of the system problems identified during Phase II had been addressed and the GPS program entered into Phase III (Full-Scale Development/Production). Unfortunately, the schedule for GPS to reach Full Operational Capability (FOC) slipped; in May 1988, the Army expected FOC to be achieved by Fiscal Year 1991 (FY91),[29] but Interim Operational Capability (IOC) was not declared until 1993 and FOC was not reached until 1995.[30]

The GPS in Desert Shield and Desert Storm

In 1989, ASI sponsored field demonstrations of the new GPS receivers. The earliest demonstrations were conducted in the fall of 1989, with USARSPACE scheduled to assume responsibility for the program in January 1990.[31] By June 1990, a number of Army units had trained with GPS and the demonstration was judged to be a success.[32] However, Iraq's invasion of Kuwait in August 1990 prompted the Army to rush GPS into immediate service. The GPS Joint Program Office quickly made 900 receivers available to units deploying for Operation DESERT SHIELD. In addition, an emergency purchase of commercial GPS receivers was authorized.[33]

With the exception of a few units that had been exposed to the GPS receivers during the initial ASI demonstration program, most soldiers receiving GPS equipment had no prior training or experience with the system. In August 1990, Major Carlos Velez (ASI) and Sergeant First Class Ball (USARSPACE) traveled to deployment sites at Ft. Bragg, Ft. Stewart, and Ft. Campbell to conduct a "train-the-trainer" program as the GPS receivers were distributed.[34] However, "as more units deployed to the Gulf, the train-the-trainer effort could not be sustained."[35] In September 1990, ASI developed the *Unit and Sustainment Training Support Package for the Small Lightweight Global Positioning System Receiver (SLGR).* This training support package was designed to support a two-hour block of instruction on SLGR operations and contained basic instruction on system capabilities, operations, and maintenance.[36]

The deployment of GPS in Operation DESERT SHIELD and Operation DESERT STORM proved to be of tremendous utility to units deployed in-theater. In an environment with few distinctive terrain features, GPS enabled combat units to navigate quickly to their objectives, helped guide convoy movements in the rear, and supported resupply operations. Iraqi minefields were located and precisely marked using GPS data. Forward observers used GPS when calling in artillery fire and air support, while gun batteries employed GPS as a tool for conducting field artillery surveys on the move. Signal units began to use GPS as a tool for positioning communications equipment. Simply stated, GPS supported a wide number of combat functions in Southwest Asia. This success can be attributed in large part to the deployment of personnel from USARSPACE and the Army Space Institute to conduct GPS systems training. Nevertheless, the rush deployment of the system and the lack of formal training for all units contributed to a series of problems. For example, "some users thought the receivers were more accurate than they really were, and others thought that the receivers worked only in particular parts of the world."[37] Units also reported that the extreme heat of the desert environment was causing system problems, to include operational failures and decreased battery life.[38]

The difficulties that units experienced when employing GPS in DESERT SHIELD and DESERT STORM can only be partly attributed to a lack of formal training for all units. ASI and USARSPACE began conducting "train-the-trainer" sessions in August 1990 and an excellent training package was developed for the field in September 1990. Army units did not begin advancing into Kuwait and Iraq until February 1991. Clearly, sufficient time and resources were available for units to conduct user-level training on the GPS receiver. It would appear that some of the problems experienced by units using GPS reflected a more fundamental dynamic – an overall lack of familiarity with space products. Most of the soldiers who deployed to Southwest Asia in 1990 and 1991 had never previously been exposed to space systems; like the soldier who has never used a personal computer, they did not understand the technology and had not developed an intuitive sense of GPS capabilities and limitations.

Despite the inevitable difficulties that accompanied the rush deployment of GPS on the eve of a war, most users of GPS reported that they were pleased with the system. In fact, the primary complaint voiced about the system during DESERT SHIELD and DESERT STORM was the shortage of available receivers.[39] When the U.S. Army examined its position/navigation requirements in light of the Gulf War experience, numerous requests were made to expand the number of receivers mounted in aircraft[40] and assigned to line units.[41] Concurrently, the Army began to consider requirements for upgraded GPS systems. In August 1991, for example, the Department of the Army conducted a study of the requirement for GPS receivers possessing an accuracy as close as 2 meters[42]

.Although GPS was one of the major success stories of DESERT SHIELD / DESERT STORM, misperceptions regarding the capabilities and use of the system continued to persist for years after the war. For example, in 1997, U.S. Navy Captain George Slaven, a senior naval officer assigned to USSPACECOM, noted "a profound and disturbing lack of knowledge of the system equipment being used by our own forces."[43] Captain Slaven identified a number of areas where warfighting commanders and staffs continued to require help from military space experts, to include data on both friendly and enemy use of GPS, planning for the use of GPS Selective Availability, determination of the optimum launch or execution windows for military operations, the use of local area GPS enhancements, and options for GPS jamming.[44]

Lessons Learned During GPS Fielding and Employment

The U.S. Army's experience in getting GPS to the field provides a number of valuable lessons to leaders today. First, GPS was an extraordinarily powerful position/navigation system. The system proved its worth during DESERT SHIELD

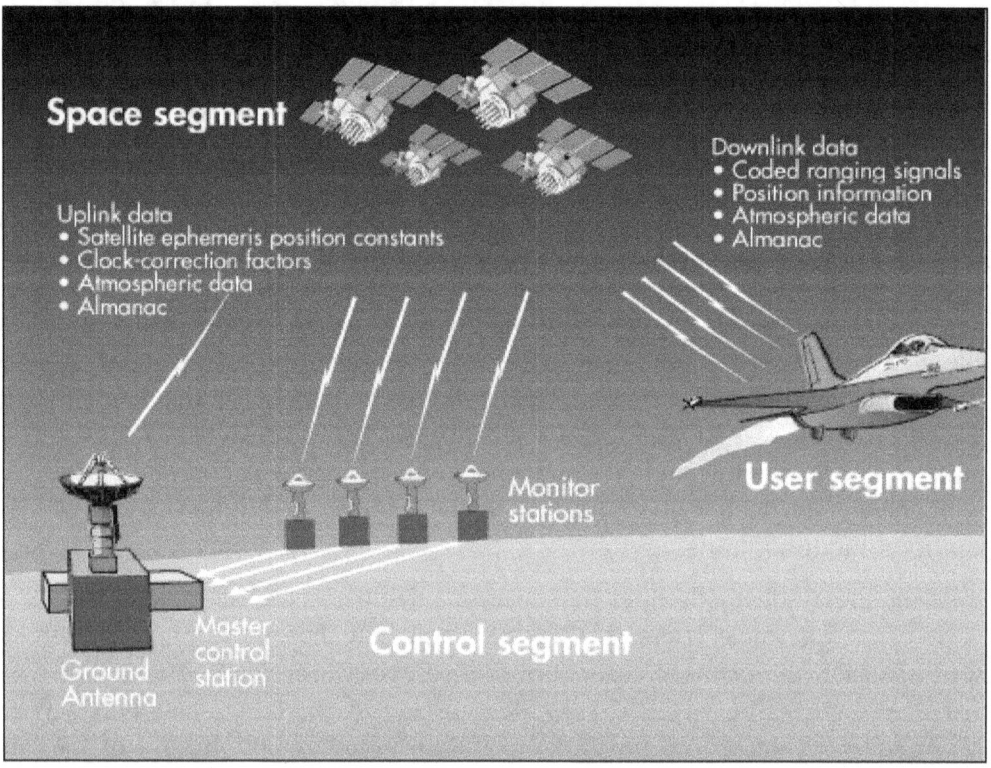

Figure 2: The Three Segments of the Global Positioning System. [SOURCE: GPS Joint Program Office]

/ DESERT STORM. It has been used in every major U.S. military deployment and exercise since 1991. In the future, it will become increasingly valuable as a tool for weapons targeting, situational awareness, and command and control.

Because GPS has been such a success since its operational debut in 1990-1991, it is often forgotten that the process of fielding the system was lengthy, time-consuming, and involved. Although approval to initiate the GPS program was granted in 1973, the system did not achieve Full Operational Capability until 1995. This experience demonstrates the fact that the process of fielding new military space capabilities is typically time consuming and complex.

Importantly, the Army's experience in DESERT SHIELD / DESERT STORM also proved that civilian space systems can have a significant military impact. The use of off-the-shelf commercial GPS receivers provided an excellent example of how civilian systems could be employed by military units. This finding had a large impact on the subsequent decision to activate the Army Space Support Team organization.

DESERT SHIELD / DESERT STORM also highlighted the fact that Army units may not fully recognize the value of space systems and capabilities in a peacetime environment. Prior to DESERT SHIELD, few Army units had been exposed to GPS. After deployment to Southwest Asia, however, GPS was in such high demand that "there were not enough receivers to go to all of the users who wanted them"[45] and units competed for allocations of scarce GPS receivers. In future conflicts, field units may similarly demand access to new and emerging space products. The Army space community should be prepared to respond to such user requirements at short notice by procuring additional space systems and testing and validating their worth by supporting unit and individual-level training.

In addition, the Army's 1990-1991 experience demonstrated the importance of capturing and disseminating lessons learned within the Army space community. In the case of fielding GPS receivers, certain problems noted by soldiers during early testing of the system were experienced again in combat (e.g. operational failures and decreased battery life while operating in high temperatures). It is important that the Army space community capture, analyze, and disseminate lessons learned in order to avoid the repetition of such problems.

Space systems and technology are often perceived by potential users to be technically difficult to use and too complex for field operations. During DESERT SHIELD / DESERT STORM, this factor contributed to misunderstandings regarding GPS system capabilities and limitations. To overcome this problem, familiarization training is needed to 'normalize' the use of space products. When communicating with units in the field, the space community must ensure that soldiers are not inundated with technical data. Users of space products at the tactical level are unlikely to grasp technical nuances. When unnecessary technical information is transmitted to tactical users, misconceptions and false assumptions will almost certainly result. Moreover, the ability to employ space systems successfully is a perishable skill. Even though GPS was successfully used to support combat operations in 1991, misconceptions regarding system capabilities continued to persist for years afterwards. This highlights the need for sustainment training.

The DESERT SHIELD / DESERT STORM experience also demonstrated that Army space experts can provide useful assistance to the field, even when dealing with 'established' space systems like the GPS. For example, more than five years after the end of the Gulf War, space experts reported that most military units did not understand the benefits and risks associated with GPS.[46] Truly understanding and maximizing the potential capabilities of GPS, rather than simply using a receiver to acquire positional data, requires expertise beyond that organic to most units.

In short, the Army's experience in fielding GPS served as a watershed for the space community. GPS was the first space system widely disseminated among tactical units and its performance impressed most field commanders. In effect, GPS introduced the 'rank-and-file' Army to space. However, GPS was only one of many space systems that made its debut in DESERT SHIELD / DESERT STORM. Satellite communications, weather, topographic imagery, and missile warning assets also supported Army units. Like the lessons learned during GPS deployment, the Army's experience with these space systems had a major impact upon the subsequent evolution of the Army space community.

Field Experience and the Operationalization of Space

Space products have been used to support tactical operations by U.S. forces in every major deployment and exercise since 1991. Although GPS garnered much of the attention in DESERT SHIELD and DESERT STORM, critical support was also provided by satellite communications, weather, topographic imagery, and early warning systems. Lessons learned during the deployment of these systems were of particular importance for the Amy's decision to establish the Army Space Support Team organization.

Satellite Communications

Satellite communications systems served as an indispensable component of the command and control network established during DESERT SHIELD and DESERT STORM. During the war, 15 military communications satellites were used to support U.S. operations[47] and more than 1,500 satellite communications receivers were deployed in-theater.[48] It has been observed that "satellite communication was the backbone of long-haul and intra-theater connectivity for the Gulf War."[49]

In the years since the Gulf War, satellite communications systems have continued to play a central role in support of U.S. military operations. For example, satellite systems were used as the primary method of communication during the early stages of Army deployments in Somalia and Zaire, where almost no established communications infrastructure was available. In addition to the increase in the overall reliance of U.S. forces on satellite communications systems, three key trends in the use of satellite communications emerged after 1991. First, satellite communications systems were increasingly used for tactical purposes, particularly in areas with a rudimentary communications infrastructure. During DESERT SHIELD, for example, the Defense Satellite Communications System (DSCS) fulfilled "an important tactical as well as strategic communications role" because the Army had "never operated there before and lacks communications infrastructure in the region." [50] Although DSCS was originally designed to support long-haul strategic communications, units in Saudi Arabia as small as brigades were equipped for DSCS communications in-theater. Another example of

After the 10th Mountain Division (Light) deployed to Haiti, it found that "infantry company missions and tactical convoys out of a brigade sector required use of tactical satellite for command and control." [Lieutenant Colonel David T. Stahl, *10th Mountain Division Operations in Haiti: Planning /Preparation /Execution; August 1994 Thru January 1995.*]

the trend toward the use of satellite systems for tactical communications was provided during the U.S. deployment to Haiti. During this operation, satellite communications were used to control operations down to the company level. The 10th Mountain Division (Light) found that "infantry company missions and tactical convoys out of a brigade sector required use of tactical satellite for command and control."[51]

A second major trend was the use of civilian satellite communications systems to supplement gaps in U.S. military communications capabilities. During DESERT STORM, commercial International Telecommunications Satellite (INTELSAT) terminals carried approximately 25 percent of the satellite communications traffic generated in theater.[52] In Somalia, the International Maritime Satellite (INMARSAT) provided the "primary means of communications during the early stages of the deployment."[53] In Haiti during Operation UPHOLD DEMOCRACY, the Joint Task Force headquarters made extensive use of commercial communications systems, to include a television satellite receiving station.[54] In Zaire, it was observed that the news media possessed "better communications and data processing equipment than the military it covers."[55] U.S. forces in Zaire relied upon INMARSAT and commercial telephone systems for their communications needs.

The third important trend in the use of satellite communications was the rapidly expanding demand for support, which made careful planning for the use of military satellite communications resources imperative. For instance, in DESERT STORM the demand for satellite communications support was so great that it quickly outpaced the capabilities of available military systems.[56] In response, the J-6 "aggressively rationed communications links to assure that units first deploying into the region would not consume all available satellite communication (SATCOM) capabilities."[57] The requirement to ration satellite communications, however, was not a phenomenon limited to DESERT STORM / DESERT SHIELD. U.S. forces in Somalia used more than 10 different data systems (intelligence, personnel, logistics, finance, and other support functions), each of which competed for the scarce satellite communications resources that were available.[58]

Satellite Weather Support

In the midst of Operation DESERT STORM, the worst weather recorded in 14 years swept across the theater of operations.[59] U.S. Army units seeking to operate in this harsh environment became voracious consumers of satellite weather data. This experience helped shape the subsequent development of the ARSST, which was organized with the capability to provide weather and environmental products to a supported unit.

In contrast to GPS, which most units had not been exposed to prior to the beginning of DESERT SHIELD, senior Army commanders clearly recognized the need for responsive weather support prior to deployment to Saudi Arabia. A 1990 TRADOC plan to revamp the existing structure for weather support illustrates this point. In February 1990, six months prior to the beginning of DESERT SHIELD, TRADOC presented a concept for a new Division Standardized Command Post (SCP). One of the objectives of the SCP concept was to eliminate excess vehicles and equipment, thereby making the Division command post both easier to maneuver in the field and lighter for overseas transport. Existing Army doctrine called for the assignment of a nine-person Air Force weather team to each Division headquarters, along with communications and weather equipment mounted in a 5-ton van. Under the SCP concept, the Division weather team would be reduced to two staff officers responsible for disseminating (rather than producing) weather information and the van would be eliminated. Weather products would instead be prepared at Corps level and sent down to each Division headquarters.[60]

Objections to the TRADOC proposal for restructuring weather support were quickly voiced by a number of field units. For example, Headquarters 5th Infantry Division (Mechanized) stated that it required "detailed, accurate, and tailored weather forecasts" and warned that "the current effort to standardize division TOCs has proposed a change that would seriously degrade weather support . . ."[61] Headquarters, 24th Infantry Division (Mechanized) argued that the proposal would "have a negative impact on Division training and operations."[62] The Division G-3 (Operations section) of the 6th Infantry Division (Light) labeled the new weather support concept "stupid, absolutely absurd!"[63] The U.S. Army Intelligence Center and School also registered a number of concerns.

Opposition to the SCP weather concept was noteworthy because it illustrated two essential points. First, field commanders placed a premium on the delivery of high-quality, tailored weather products. Second, units were not satisfied with a system that simply disseminated weather data from a rear area headquarters; they desired the responsiveness inherent in collecting and analyzing weather data themselves. Both aspects were evident during DESERT SHIELD / DESERT STORM, during which additional space weather systems were deployed in theater to provide high-quality, responsive support.

The primary commercial satellite weather imagery system used by the Army in DESERT SHIELD / DESERT STORM was the WRAASE receiver. The WRAASE was selected for use by the Army because it had the capability to provide direct links to all civilian weather satellites flying over a theater of operations. This included the ability to download imagery from the GOES and METEOSAT geostationary satellites (providing weather imagery with a resolution of approximately 10 kilometers) and the TIROS and Meteor polar-orbiting satellites (offering a resolution of 2-4 kilometers).[64]

Prior to DESERT SHIELD, WRAASE receivers had been procured by ASI for demonstration under the ASDP.[65] U.S. Army Europe (USAREUR) and U.S. Army Forces Command (FORSCOM) had also purchased WRAASE receivers in 1989 and most of the weather teams deploying to Southwest Asia had previously been equipped with the system. When DESERT SHIELD began, the XVIII Airborne Corps G-2 (Intelligence section) and the 30th Engineer Battalion (Topographic) requested additional weather support from ASI.[66] Having previously assisted in the deployment of WRAASE weather receivers under the ASDP, ASI took steps to integrate weather imagery with existing terrain analysis systems. Two FORSCOM Automated Intelligence Support System computers were outfitted with a commercial software package, dubbed *Weathertrac*, and networked with WRAASE receivers. ASI subsequently reported:

> "This combination provides the staff weather officer the ability to enhance the visible and infra-red imagery available from the US civilian weather satellites that pass over Saudi Arabia 8-10 times a day. With limited available knowledge of the Saudi weather and no established observation network in the area of operations, this satellite weather information provides the one means of seeing the battlefield."[67]

Training support for the system was provided by Major Royal Koepsell of ASI, who instructed both weather and terrain analysis personnel. The relationship between satellite weather and satellite terrain imagery data was formalized when the 30th Engineer Battalion established a Topographic Technology Exploitation Cell (TTEC). This cell was assigned responsibility for analyzing satellite imagery products, combining terrain and weather data, and producing updated maps.[68]

Efforts to integrate weather and terrain analysis data through the TTEC represent one of the significant trends in satellite weather support that surfaced during DESERT SHIELD / DESERT STORM. The second key trend involved the distribution of weather support systems to units throughout the theater of operations. During the war,

> "US Central Command took steps to procure more receiver terminals to enable the use of weather data at all levels of command. New lightweight prototype desktop receivers were distributed to ensure the Army had access to real-time weather data from a variety of weather satellites."[69]

A third major trend was the demand by analysts outside the staff weather office for access to raw weather imagery data. After the war, the Center for Army Lessons Learned (CALL) recommended that this demand be satisfied by collocating satellite weather receivers with unit intelligence and terrain analysis staffs.[70]

Satellite Topographic Imagery

At the beginning of DESERT SHIELD, many maps of Kuwait and Saudi Arabia were outdated and of limited utility to U.S. forces. To overcome this problem, the Army turned to space.

The XVIII Airborne Corps was the first unit to deploy in DESERT SHIELD. Within hours of their deployment, the supporting 30th Engineer Battalion (Topographic) was providing satellite imagery data to the Corps G-2 (Intelligence section). ASI later reported, "In less than two days the 30th Engineer Battalion was providing LANDSAT imagery for delivery via satellite communications link from Ft Bragg to ground forces in Saudi Arabia."[71] These efforts were followed by the establishment of the Topographic Technology Exploitation Cell with support from Mr. Bob Krieger, a multi-spectral imagery expert assigned to ASI.[72] The TTEC not only served as a central point for integrating weather and topographic data, as previously described; it also employed an ASI multi-spectral imagery workstation to update mapsheets with recent LANDSAT satellite imagery and conducted terrain analysis to determine battlefield trafficability conditions.[73]

The impact of the TTEC upon XVIII Airborne Corps operations was significant. ASI reported:

> "Two thirds of the intelligence preparation of the battlefield can now be combined using as current information as the latest satellite pass allows. One month old LANDSAT imagery combined with weather satellite passes is providing a quantum leap in the ability of the commander to see his battlefield. Intelligence preparation of the battlefield (IPB) can be accomplished on the fly and not remain a pre-deployment or pre-exercise pursuit."[74]

Unfortunately, the slow process for procurement of LANDSAT imagery "effectively left the topographic units without up-to-date imagery until mid-November 1990." [75] Even worse, the Army was unable to obtain the funding needed to obtain access to large quantities of SPOT satellite imagery that could have been made available by the Air Force.[76] Delays in obtaining imagery impeded the work of topographic analysts deployed in theater and, as a result, some Divisions were left "with little or no time to exploit the capabilities available."[77]

Theater Missile Attack Warning

Ballistic missile attack warning is the last key area in which space assets were used to support combat operations in DESERT STORM. During the war, USSPACECOM developed the Tactical Event Reporting System (TERS) to warn units of Iraqi Scud missile launches. Although TERS was unable to provide cueing and vectoring data for U.S. air defense batteries, the system was used to warn U.S. and Allied forces of an impending missile impact with mixed success. During the war, DoD analysts forecasted that the TERS capability "could be pivotal to saving a high percentage of civilians or combatants if the Iraqis launch a chemical/biological attack."[78]

TERS provides an interesting case study in the tactical use of space assets that were originally deployed for a strategic role. The TERS system was based upon the Defense Support Program (DSP), an early warning system employing a satellite constellation equipped with infrared sensors. The DSP network was developed in the 1970s to detect the launch of Soviet intercontinental ballistic missiles (ICBMs) and submarine-launched ballistic missiles (SLBMs), track their burn times, and determine the impact trajectories. DSP data was transmitted to a ground receiver that, in turn, furnished the early warning information to the Missile Warning Center at Cheyenne Mountain, Colorado. The Missile Warning Center would then integrate DSP data with data obtained from other sensors to determine the time and point of impact for the incoming missile. Finally, processed information would be provided to the USSPACECOM Mission Director and the NORAD Command Director.[79]

After the deployment of Patriot air defense units to Saudi Arabia and Israel during DESERT SHIELD, USSPACECOM took steps to connect the theater air and missile defense network to DSP early warning data. The DSP satellites were adjusted to detect Scud launches in the U.S. Central Command (USCENTCOM) theater of operations. After launch warning was received at USSPACECOM, an initial warning would be transmitted to the theater over a voice line. As updates were received, they would also be transmitted by USSPACECOM via this voice line.[80] Unfortunately, the "development of procedures and connectivity were constructed from scratch and took months to setup and finely tune."[81]

The performance of TERS left much to be desired. First, the DSP system had been designed to track strategic missiles possessing much longer flight times and brighter plume signatures than those of an Iraqi Scud missile. As a result, TERS could not provide specific impact prediction data.[82] Second, TERS early warning alert data often proved to be "untimely." [83] When Iraq began launching Scud missiles, TERS often took up to 120 seconds to transmit early warning data to the field.[84] This left relatively little time for U.S. and Coalition forces to respond. Finally, units operating away from Corps air defense units had trouble receiving TERS information.[85]

Despite these problems, the activation of TERS represented an ingenious effort to apply strategic systems to support tactical operations. In the aftermath of DESERT STORM, USSPACECOM took additional steps to develop an improved missile warning system for tactical users. Of particular importance was the development of the Joint Tactical Ground Station (JTAGS), a new missile early warning system operated by the U.S. Army and U.S. Navy that could be quickly deployed into a theater of operations, access and process DSP information, and provide early warning information to support theater missile defense operations.

Key Lessons in Bringing Space to the Warfighter

The Army's early experience in space provided a number of lessons that influenced the subsequent organization of the Army Space Support Team. First, the Army discovered that space could serve as a powerful contributor at the tactical level. Space systems and products were successfully used to support such operations as DESERT STORM and UPHOLD DEMOCRACY. Army units relied on GPS for navigation, convoy control, resupply operations, minefield breaching and marking, and artillery surveying. Satellite weather receivers provided weather data immediately to tactical units. Satellite communications systems were used to allow geographically dispersed tactical units to operate effectively in areas of rough terrain. Satellite topographic imagery was utilized to enhance Army intelligence production, while satellite early warning systems alerted Army units to an incoming ballistic missile attack. After 1990, each of these capabilities significantly enhanced the ability of Army units to accomplish their assigned missions.

Nonetheless, the Army's early operational experience also demonstrated that few commanders knew how to employ space resources effectively. Officers assigned to USARSPACE repeatedly observed that tactical commanders possessed a low level of familiarity with space capabilities. Tactical commanders typically had little understanding of where military space products came from, what the limitations of space capabilities were, or how space could best be integrated into the military planning and decision making processes.

The Army also concluded that, if maximum value

18 January 1991: Patriot launch unit from Battery A, 2nd Battalion, 7th Air Defense Artillery outside Dhahran, Saudi Arabia. (SOURCE: XVIII Airborne Corps photograph DS-F-119-10.)

was to be derived from military space, its use must be 'normalized' in the field through training and application. The Army space community actively sought to provide space products and support to tactical units. Army space experts conducted training in the field and the classroom, sponsored demonstrations of new equipment, and supported units during training exercises and overseas deployments. These early space soldiers learned that the full potential of space-based capabilities would only be realized when space had been "normalized" as an element of tactical operations; in other words, when "the people who ultimately use space systems to maximize combat capabilities — airmen, soldiers and sailors — know what space capabilities are available to them, how to get the data, and how to best exploit it."[86]

Prior to DESERT SHIELD, most Army units had not been exposed to military space systems. USARSPACE and ASI quickly organized training on specific systems (GPS and WRAASE weather receivers) for soldiers in-theater. Given the rush to put new space systems into service on the eve of a major offensive campaign, it is not surprising that training was often conducted in an *ad hoc* fashion and that field commanders were unprepared to exploit the full range of available military space capabilities. Drawing upon these lessons, one military officer emphasized that

> "peacetime training must simulate, as close as possible, wartime conditions to include the deployment and employment of space forces and of equipment required to take advantage of space. Realistic training is the cornerstone of planning for the use of and the continued normalization of space systems into the force structure."[87]

Similarly, the Army discovered that the preplanning of space support to a theater of operations was critical to success. In a post-war assessment of military space operations in DESERT STORM, the Commander-in-Chief of U.S. Space Command "identified preplanning for support from space as his command's number one lesson from the Gulf War."[88] Because space capabilities were never integrated into the joint operations planning process, "too few officers in-theater really understood how and to what extent space supported the theater commander's campaign objectives."[89] In the absence of a pre-established plan of support, a number of space systems were sent to the theater in a disjointed and *ad hoc* fashion. Many problems ensued, ranging from the requirement to procure commercial GPS and satellite communications systems on an emergency basis to the last-minute creation of a theater early warning system that was plagued by problems of inaccuracy and lack of timeliness.

The Army's early experience also highlighted the importance of providing space expertise to field units. Most Army units did not possess an organic capability to utilize space assets fully. Space experts deploying to the field were able to provide such a capability to the commander. For example, space experts may be able to improve communications to a theater of operations by maneuvering certain satellites into better positions. GPS capabilities can be maximized for a commander through a variety of techniques, including the jamming of enemy systems, certain local area enhancements, and the identification of optimum launch or execution windows for operations. Space experts can also assist tactical commanders by developing a tailored process for detecting and disseminating missile attack warning data. Similarly, space experts can help established improved methods of exploiting satellite weather and multispectral imagery capabilities.[90]

The Army discovered that civilian space systems can have a significant military impact. Commercial systems were used to support the entire gamut of military operations in DESERT SHIELD / DESERT STORM, and subsequent military deployments. Military satellite communications capabilities were supplemented by the commercial INTELSAT (carrying approximately 25 percent of all satellite communications traffic) in DESERT STORM[91] and the INMARSAT provided the primary means of communications when U.S. forces first deployed to Somalia.[92] Commercial WRAASE satellite weather receivers were the primary weather imagery systems used by the Army in DESERT SHIELD / DESERT STORM,[93] while the capabilities of topographic units were greatly expanded through commercial equipment and software procured during the war.[94] Few Army units deployed during DESERT SHIELD had access to GPS until the Army sent commercial GPS receivers to the theater.[95]

The trend toward the increased use of civilian satellite systems for military purposes (e.g., weather, imagery, and communications) and military systems for civilian purposes (e.g., GPS) has led some analysts to claim that "the distinction between military and civilian space systems is rapidly disappearing and that structures and doctrines need to be adjusted."[96] While this may in fact prove to be true in the future, the primary lesson learned during DESERT SHIELD / DESERT STORM was that civilian space systems present unique operational considerations for the battlefield commander. For example, during the war the Iraqis were able to receive weather data from three U.S. National Oceanic and Atmospheric Administration (NOAA) satellites. Fearing that the Iraqis could use this data to coordinate air operations or conduct Scud missile attacks, the U.S. Government considered shutting down the weather satellites when they were operating over the Middle East. However, such a course of action would have adversely affected U.S. allies in the region dependent on NOAA weather data, such as Israel, Turkey, and Egypt.[97] In another example, the Air Force offered to provide SPOT imagery data of the theater of operations to the Army. However, the Army was unable to secure enough funding to pay royalties to the SPOT Corporation and, thus, could not access this source of imagery.[98]

In a peacetime environment, Army units may not fully recognize the value of space systems. Army weather support teams were equipped with WRAASE satellite receivers prior to DESERT SHIELD, but it was only after the deployment began that this capability was integrated with satellite terrain imagery data. Similarly, few Army units had been exposed to GPS prior to deployment in DESERT SHIELD. After arriving in-theater, commanders clamored to receive as many GPS units as possible. Provisions for providing early warning data from DSP satellites to Patriot air defense batteries were not established until DESERT SHIELD began. As noted earlier, it should be expected that field units will similarly demand access to new and emerging space products during future deployments. The Army space community should be prepared to respond to such user requirements at short notice, not only by procuring additional space systems but also by supporting unit and individual-level training.

Finally, the Army space community must capture and disseminate lessons learned. The Army defines a lesson learned as "validated knowledge and experience derived from observations and historical study of military training, exercises, and combat operations."[99] Efforts by the Army to capture and disseminate lessons learned are designed to fulfill a number of purposes. First, they serve to institutionalize successful practices and techniques. Second, they indicate areas where the Army needs to change its behavior. Finally, they are used to shape the future evolution of Army systems and concepts. For example, TRADOC's Operational Capability Requirements (OCR) process, which is designed to articulate the capabilities required by the Army to fulfill its role under the National Military Strategy, is "derived within the framework of historical lessons learned from operational experiences as well as the opportunities provided from technology exploitation."[100] While the Army was able to benefit greatly from early lessons that had been learned by organizations such as ASI and USARSPACE, too often these lessons were not received and internalized by soldiers and field commanders.

Summary

The provisional activation of ASI in 1986 marked the beginning of systematic Army efforts to use space systems and technologies in support of tactical operations. ASI took a proactive role in introducing space to units in the field, conducting a series of demonstrations and providing training. These efforts subsequently paid off in DESERT SHIELD and DESERT STORM, when GPS, multi-spectral imagery, weather, and satellite communications systems were used to great effect by U.S. forces.

The Army's early experience in using space systems to support tactical operations was significant for three key reasons: First, these early experiences demonstrated that space capabilities could exert a significant, positive impact on Army operations; Second, space systems and technologies were complex and continued to undergo rapid technological evolution and specialized expertise was required if the Army hoped to exploit the full potential offered by space; Finally, the Army needed to activate a deployable space support organization, capable of providing training and operational support to units deployed in a theater of operations.

The early Army experience in space was also important because it helped establish the parameters under which USARSPACE would later activate the ARSST organization. This experience would help shape the role, functions, and structure of the ARSST, as well as the doctrine used for its employment.

[1] Ed Kiker, Informal Thoughts on the Status of the Army Space Institute. 15 June 1992.

[2] U.S. Army Space Command, Army Space Support Team (ARSST) Concept of Operations (CONOPS) (DRAFT). (Colorado Springs, Colorado: U.S. Army Space Command: 12 December 1994.).

[3] General Maxwell Thurman, Comments at Army Space Institute Activation – Ft Leavenworth, 12 January 1988.

[4] Marquis Shepherd, "Army unit to bring technology of space down to Earth for troops," Kansas City Times, 13 January 1988, p. B-3.

[5] Major Steven C. Siegel, "Army Space Institute," Army Trainer (Summery 1987), pp. 20-21.

[6] Lieutenant Colonel(P) John R. French, Jr., U.S. Army Space Institute Semiannual Historical Report 1 July – 31 December 1986, (Ft. Leavenworth, Kansas: Army Space Institute, 26 January 1987).

[7] Wencis R. Tovar, Combined Arms Center Annual Historical Review: Army Space Institute Input, (Ft. Leavenworth, Kansas: Army Space Institute; 4 August 1989).

[8] The SEWS demonstration was successful and later evolved into prototypical equipment - the Tactical Surveillance Demonstration (Europe) and TSD-Enhanced (Korea). It eventually evolved into what is now known as JTAGS. Editorial comments made by Mr. John Marrs, USARSPACE Technical Advisor, in an e-mail message sent to Dr. James A. Walker on 16 February 1999. For an in-depth history of U.S. Army development of missile early warning systems, see James Hooper, Todd Clark, and James Walker, The Joint Tactical Ground Station: Fielding and Operational Lessons Learned, (Huntsville, Alabama: U.S. Army Space and Missile Defense Command, April 2000).

[9] Public Affairs Brochure, "Army Space Exploitation Demonstration Program," (Colorado Springs, Colorado: U.S. Army Space Command, 6 October 1995).

[10] Briefing, "WRAASE," (Ft. Leavenworth, Kansas: CACDA Library, File ASI-004, 1986).

[11] Public Affairs Summary, "Army Space Exploitation Demonstration Program," (Colorado Springs, Colorado: U.S. Army Space Command, 6 October 1995).

[12] U.S. Army Space Command, USARSPACE Information Paper (Peterson AFB, Colorado: U.S. Army Space Command, 31 July 1989).

[13] Army Space Institute/TPIO Space, Historical Review 1990 (Ft. Leavenworth, Kansas: Army Space Institute, 1990).

[14] Memorandum, Office of the Deputy Chief of Staff for Operations and Plans (DAMO-SWX), Subject: Implementation of Army Space Organization, Undated.

[15] United States Space Command, Directorate of Public Affairs, Fact Sheet: U.S. Army Space Command, 7 April 1988.

[16] Editorial comments made by Mr. Tom Callaghan, USARSPACE, in an e-mail message sent to Dr. James A. Walker, 16 February 1999.

[17] Major Korpsel and Mr. Freeman, Input to LAMP: Space Support for Desert Shield, (Ft. Leavenworth, Kansas: Army Space Institute, September 1990).

[18] U.S. Army Space Command (Forward), Space Support Reference Book, 20 August 1997, p. NAV-5.

[19] Center for Army Lessons Learned, The Ultimate High Ground! Space Support to the Army: Lessons Learned from Operations DESERT SHIELD and STORM. (Ft. Leavenworth, Kansas: Center for Army Lessons Learned Newsletter No. 91-3, Oct 91).

[20] Center for Army Lessons Learned, The Ultimate High Ground! Space Support to the Army: Lessons Learned from Operations DESERT SHIELD and STORM. (Ft. Leavenworth, Kansas: Center for Army Lessons Learned Newsletter No. 91-3, Oct 91).

[21] U.S. Army Space Command (Forward), Space Support Reference Book, 20 August 1997, p. NAV-6.

[22] U.S. Army Combined Arms Combat Development Activity, The Army Position and Navigation Master Plan. (Ft. Leavenworth, Kansas: Combined Arms Combat Development Activity, May 1986), p. II-1.

[23] U.S. Army Space Command (Forward), Space Support Reference Book, 20 August 1997, p. NAV-5.

[24] SD/CWN Headquarters Space Division (AFSC), Los Angeles Air Force Base, Multiservice Test and Evaluation Master Plan for the NAVSTAR Global Positioning System User Equipment. (Los Angeles Air Force Base, California: SD/CWN Headquarters, November 1987), pp. 4-2 to 4-3.

[25] SD/YEA Headquarters Space Division, Los Angeles Air Force Station, NAVSTAR Global Positioning System Coordinated Test Program – II: Test and Evaluation Master Plan Army Annex. (Los Angeles Air Force Station, California: SD/YEA Headquarters, July 1982), p. 4-3.

[26] SD/CWN Headquarters Space Division (AFSC), Los Angeles Air Force Base, Multiservice Test and Evaluation Master Plan for the NAVSTAR Global Positioning System User Equipment. (Los Angeles Air Force Base, California: SD/CWN Headquarters, November 1987), pp. 4-2 to 4-3.

[27] Lieutenant Colonel Francis J. Springer, Independent Operational Assessment of the NAVSTAR Global Positioning System (GPS) Army User Equipment (AUE) Operational Test II, November 1985/January 1986. (Falls Church, Virginia: U.S. Army Test and Evaluation Agency, 3 April 1986), pp. 45-79.

[28] United States Army Signal Center and Fort Gordon, Final Draft: Operational Issues and Criteria for the Operational Test IOTE of the NAVSTAR Global

Positioning System (GPS) Army User Equipment (AUE) Manpack/Vehicular Set (Ft. Gordon, Georgia: 9 August 1987), p. 8.

[29] GENSER Message, "Global Positioning System (GPS); DTG 031800Z MAY 88." (Colorado Springs, Colorado: Army Space Command, 3 May 1988.).

[30] United States Naval Observatory, GPS System Description. 12 June 1998.

[31] U.S. Army Space Command, USARSPACE Information Paper. (Peterson AFB, Colorado: U.S. Army Space Command, 31 July 1989.).

[32] Editorial comments made by Mr. John Marrs, USARSPACE Technical Advisor, in an e-mail message sent to Dr. James A. Walker on 16 February 1999.

[33] "Desert Shield Prompts Acceleration of AMRAAM, SFW Testing," Aerospace Daily (Vol. 155, No. 56, 19 September 1990), p. 457.

[34] Major Korpsel and Mr. Freeman, Input to LAMP: Space Support for Desert Shield. (Ft. Leavenworth, Kansas: Army Space Institute, September 1990.).

[35] Center for Army Lessons Learned, The Ultimate High Ground! Space Support to the Army: Lessons Learned from Operations DESERT SHIELD and STORM. (Ft. Leavenworth, Kansas: Center for Army Lessons Learned Newsletter No. 91-3, Oct 91).

[36] U.S. Army Space Institute, Unit and Sustainment Training Support Package for the Small Lightweight Global Positioning System Receiver (SLGR). (Ft. Leavenworth, KS: U.S. Army Space Institute, 28 September 1990.).

[37] Center for Army Lessons Learned, The Ultimate High Ground! Space Support to the Army: Lessons Learned from Operations DESERT SHIELD and STORM. (Ft. Leavenworth, Kansas: Center for Army Lessons Learned Newsletter No. 91-3, Oct 91).

[38] GENSER Message, "GPS Navigation Availability for 30 Oct 90 (Day 303); DTG 302045Z OCT 90." (Colorado Springs, Colorado: Army Space Command, 30 October 1990.).

[39] Center for Army Lessons Learned, The Ultimate High Ground! Space Support to the Army: Lessons Learned from Operations DESERT SHIELD and STORM. (Ft. Leavenworth, Kansas: Center for Army Lessons Learned Newsletter No. 91-3, Oct 91).

[40] GENSER Message, "Army Aviation Global Positioning System (GPS) Requirements; DTG 251600Z SEP 91." (Ft. Rucker, Alabama: U.S. Army Aviation Center).

[41] GENSER Message, "Global Positioning Systems; DTG 251830Z OCT 91." (Ft. McPherson, Georgia: U.S. Army Forces Command, 25 October 1991.).

[42] GENSER Message, "Improvement of Global Positioning System (GPS) Accuracy; DTG 151300Z AUG 91." (Washington, DC: Headquarters, Department of the Army, DAMO-FDC, 15 August 1991.).

[43] Captain George E. Slaven, <u>What the Warfighter Should Know About Space: A Report on U.S. Space Command Joint Space Support Teams</u>. (Maxwell Air Force Base, Alabama: Air War College Air University, April 1997), p. 26.

[44] Ibid.

[45] Center for Army Lessons Learned, <u>The Ultimate High Ground! Space Support to the Army: Lessons Learned from Operations DESERT SHIELD and STORM</u>. (Ft. Leavenworth, Kansas: Center for Army Lessons Learned Newsletter No. 91-3, Oct 91).

[46] Captain George E. Slaven, <u>What the Warfighter Should Know About Space: A Report on U.S. Space Command Joint Space Support Teams</u>. (Maxwell Air Force Base, Alabama: Air War College Air University, April 1997), pp. 32-33.

[47] Ricky B. Kelly, <u>Centralized Control of Space: The Use of Space Forces by a Joint Force Commander</u>. (Maxwell Air Force Base, Alabama: School of Advanced Airpower Studies, 22 September 1994), p. 26.

[48] Center for Army Lessons Learned, <u>The Ultimate High Ground! Space Support to the Army: Lessons Learned from Operations DESERT SHIELD and STORM</u>. (Ft. Leavenworth, Kansas: Center for Army Lessons Learned Newsletter No. 91-3, Oct 91).

[49] Ricky B. Kelly, <u>Centralized Control of Space: The Use of Space Forces by a Joint Force Commander</u>. (Maxwell Air Force Base, Alabama: School of Advanced Airpower Studies, 22 September 1994), pp. 23-24.

[50] "Army Space Command Demo Efforts Go Operational in Desert Shield," <u>Aerospace Daily</u> (Vol. 156, No. 34, 20 November 1990), p. 305.

[51] Lieutenant Colonel David T. Stahl, <u>10th Mountain Division Operations in Haiti: Planning/Preparation/Execution; August 1994 Thru January 1995</u>, p. 31.

[52] Center for Army Lessons Learned, <u>The Ultimate High Ground! Space Support to the Army: Lessons Learned from Operations DESERT SHIELD and STORM</u>. (Ft. Leavenworth, Kansas: Center for Army Lessons Learned Newsletter No. 91-3, Oct 91).

[53] 10th Mountain Division (Light), US Army Forces, Somalia: After Action Report <u>Summary.</u> (2 January 1993), p. 38.

[54] Lieutenant Colonel David T. Stahl, <u>10th Mountain Division Operations in Haiti: Planning/Preparation/Execution; August 1994 Thru January 1995</u>, p. 29.

[55] Headquarters United States European Command, <u>Operation Support Hope 1994 After Action Report</u> (U.S. Army Peacekeeping Institute: 1994), p. 11-1.

[56] <u>Aviation Week & Space Technology</u>, "Spacecraft Played Vital Role in Gulf War Victory." (Vol. 134, No. 16, 22 April 1991), p. 91.

[57] Ricky B. Kelly, <u>Centralized Control of Space: The Use of Space Forces by a Joint Force Commander</u>. (Maxwell Air Force Base, Alabama: School of Advanced Airpower Studies, 22 September 1994), p. 26.

[58] C. Kenneth Allard, "Lessons Unlearned: Somalia and Joint Doctrine." <u>Joint Forces Quarterly</u> (Autumn 1995), p. 106.

[59] Ricky B. Kelly, <u>Centralized Control of Space: The Use of Space Forces by a Joint Force Commander</u>. (Maxwell Air Force Base, Alabama: School of Advanced Airpower Studies, 22 September 1994), pp. 28-29.

[60] Lieutenant Colonel Arthus C. Kyle and Colonel Nolan W. Schmidt, GENSER Message, "Weather Support to Hvy Div Standardized Command Post; DTG 231930Z FEB 90." (Ft. Leavenworth, Kansas: Combined Arms Center Staff Weather Officer, 23 February 1990.).

[61] GENSER Message, "Weather Support to Hvy Div Standardized Command Post (SCP); DTG 062200Z MAR 90." (Ft. Polk, Louisiana: 5th Infantry Division (M), 6 March 1990.).

[62] GENSER Message, "Proposed Amendment to Standardized Command Post Concept; DTG ??2110Z MAR 90." (Ft. Stewart, Georgia: 24th Infantry Division (M), March 1990.).

[63] GENSER Message, "Support to Hvy Div Standardized Command Post (SCP); DTG 161715Z MAR 90." (Ft. Huachuca, Arizona: U.S. Army Intelligence Center and School, 16 March 1990.).

[64] Center for Army Lessons Learned, <u>The Ultimate High Ground! Space Support to the Army: Lessons Learned from Operations DESERT SHIELD and STORM</u>. (Ft. Leavenworth, Kansas: Center for Army Lessons Learned Newsletter No. 91-3, Oct 91). Briefing, "WRAASE." (Ft. Leavenworth, Kansas: CACDA Library, File ASI-004, 1986.).

[65] Wencis R. Tovar, <u>Combined Arms Center Annual Historical Review: Army Space Institute Input</u>. (Ft. Leavenworth, Kansas: Army Space Institute; ATZL-SI, 4 August 1989.).

[66] Major Korpsel and Mr. Freeman, <u>Input to LAMP: Space Support for Desert Shield</u>. (Ft. Leavenworth, Kansas: Army Space Institute, September 1990.).

[67] Ibid.

[68] Ibid.

[69] Center for Army Lessons Learned, <u>The Ultimate High Ground! Space Support to the Army: Lessons Learned from Operations DESERT SHIELD and STORM</u>. (Ft. Leavenworth, Kansas: Center for Army Lessons Learned Newsletter No. 91-3, Oct 91).

[70] Ibid.

[71] Major Korpsel and Mr. Freeman, Input to LAMP: Space Support for Desert Shield. (Ft. Leavenworth, Kansas: Army Space Institute, September 1990.).

[72] Ibid.

[73] Ibid.

[74] Ibid.

[75] Center for Army Lessons Learned, The Ultimate High Ground! Space Support to the Army: Lessons Learned from Operations DESERT SHIELD and STORM. (Ft. Leavenworth, Kansas: Center for Army Lessons Learned Newsletter No. 91-3, Oct 91).

[76] Ibid.

[77] Ibid.

[78] Craig Covault, "USAF Missile Warning Satellites Providing 90-Sec. Scud Attack Alert" Aviation Week & Space Technology (Vol. 134, No. 3, 21 January 1991), p. 60. For a more complete discussion of theater missile warning in Operations DESERT SHIELD and DESERT STORM, see James Hooper, Todd Clark, and James Walker, The Joint Tactical Ground Station: Fielding and Operational Lessons Learned, (Huntsville, Alabama: U.S. Army Space and Missile Defense Command, April 2000).

[79] Captain George E. Slaven, What the Warfighter Should Know About Space: A Report on U.S. Space Command Joint Space Support Teams. (Maxwell Air Force Base, Alabama: Air War College Air University, April 1997), pp. 22-23. Mr. John Marrs, USARSPACE Technical Adviser, later noted: "TERS warnings disseminated over TRAP went to radios, which for many Army units were provided by the USAF TENCAP and fielded by ASEDP personnel. The TRAP means of disseminating the warning had only gone active in July of 90 and had lots of bugs – mainly in how the TRAP receivers were setup to prioritize incoming messages. ASEDP personnel were instrumental in highlighting problems to CINC Space after the IRAQI test shots in December. Subsequently, getting the high level attention needed to get the problems fixed in time for the shooting war. During the SCUD days it was interesting to sit in the crisis action center – sequence was voice message, then TRAP warning, then sirens over CNN. In theater, the voice warning seldom reached the patriot units before the TRAP warning. (by the way ARSPACE had the only TRAP receiver in Colorado Springs and thus did quality control for US Space.) Keep in mind that TERS would not have existed except that the SEWS demonstration showed that detecting TBM's was feasible and that the Army and Navy were pushing to get permission to build JTAGS. ALERT was built after the Army and Navy had forced the issue after the war." Editorial comments made by Mr. John Marrs, USARSPACE Technical Advisor, in an e-mail message sent to Dr. James A. Walker on 16 February 1999.

[80] Dr. James Walker and James Hooper, "James H. Williamson Oral History Interview, ARSST Historical/Lessons Learned Study," 22 October 1998.

[81] Ricky B. Kelly, <u>Centralized Control of Space: The Use of Space Forces by a Joint Force Commander</u>. (Maxwell Air Force Base, Alabama: School of Advanced Airpower Studies, 22 September 1994), p. 25.

[82] Craig Covault, "USAF Missile Warning Satellites Providing 90-Sec. Scud Attack Alert" <u>Aviation Week & Space Technology</u> (Vol. 134, No. 3, 21 January 1991), p. 60.

[83] Captain George E. Slaven, <u>What the Warfighter Should Know About Space: A Report on U.S. Space Command Joint Space Support Teams</u>. (Maxwell Air Force Base, Alabama: Air War College Air University, April 1997), p. 23.

[84] <u>Aviation Week & Space Technology</u>, "Spacecraft Played Vital Role in Gulf War Victory." (Vol. 134, No. 16, 22 April 1991), p. 91.

[85] Center for Army Lessons Learned, <u>The Ultimate High Ground! Space Support to the Army: Lessons Learned from Operations DESERT SHIELD and STORM</u>. (Ft. Leavenworth, Kansas: Center for Army Lessons Learned Newsletter No. 91-3, Oct 91).

[86] Ricky B. Kelly, <u>Centralized Control of Space: The Use of Space Forces by a Joint Force Commander</u>. (Maxwell Air Force Base, Alabama: School of Advanced Airpower Studies, 22 September 1994), pp. 25-26.

[87] Ibid., p. 30.

[88] Ibid., pp. 23-24.

[89] Ibid., pp. 25-26.

[90] Captain George E. Slaven, <u>What the Warfighter Should Know About Space: A Report on U.S. Space Command Joint Space Support Teams</u>. (Maxwell Air Force Base, Alabama: Air War College Air University, April 1997), pp. 21-22, 25, 32-33, 35-36.

[91] Center for Army Lessons Learned, <u>The Ultimate High Ground! Space Support to the Army: Lessons Learned from Operations DESERT SHIELD and STORM</u>. (Ft. Leavenworth, Kansas: Center for Army Lessons Learned Newsletter No. 91-3, Oct 91).

[92] 10th Mountain Division (Light), <u>US Army Forces, Somalia: After Action Report Summary.</u> (2 January 1993), p. 38.

[93] Center for Army Lessons Learned, <u>The Ultimate High Ground! Space Support to the Army: Lessons Learned from Operations DESERT SHIELD and STORM</u>. (Ft. Leavenworth, Kansas: Center for Army Lessons Learned Newsletter No. 91-3, Oct 91).

[94] Ibid.

[95] Ricky B. Kelly, <u>Centralized Control of Space: The Use of Space Forces by a Joint Force Commander</u>. (Maxwell Air Force Base, Alabama: School of Advanced Airpower Studies, 22 September 1994). pp. 24-25.

[96] Captain George M. Moore, Colonel Vic Budura, and Joan Johnson-Freese, "Joint Space Doctrine: Catapulting into the Future" <u>Joint Forces Quarterly</u> (Summer 1994), p. 76.

[97] <u>Aviation Week & Space Technology</u>, "Iraqis Still Receive Weather Data from U.S. Satellites" (Vol. 134, No. 3, 21 January 1991), p. 26.

[98] Center for Army Lessons Learned, <u>The Ultimate High Ground! Space Support to the Army: Lessons Learned from Operations DESERT SHIELD and STORM</u>. (Ft. Leavenworth, Kansas: Center for Army Lessons Learned Newsletter No. 91-3, Oct 91).

[99] Center for Army Lessons Learned, <u>A Guide to the Services and the Gateway of CALL</u>. (Ft. Leavenworth, Kansas: Center for Army Lessons Learned Handbook No. 97-13), p. 1.

[100] <u>TRADOC Pam 525-66: Operational Capability Requirements</u>. (Ft. Monroe, Virginia: Headquarters, United States Army Training and Doctrine Command, 1 December 1995.).

CHAPTER TWO:

ESTABLISHMENT DECISIONS SHAPING ARSST ACTIVATION AND THE INITIAL CONOPS

"The Army's ARSST capability is a direct evolution from the Army Space Exploitation and Demonstration Program (ASEDP) and a direct outgrowth of the Louisiana Maneuvers (LAM) Task Force."

— Army Space Support Team Concept of Operations (Draft), 12 December 1994.[1]

As the Army began to transform itself to cope with a post-Cold War environment, the Army Chief of Staff established the Louisiana Maneuvers Task Force to experiment with new warfighting techniques and technologies. The Commercial Space Package (CSP) initiative, developed as part of this process, was designed to provide cutting-edge space technologies for both battlefield support and Operations Other Than War.

The CSP initiative was composed of two elements — a Support Package, consisting primarily of equipment designed for integration directly into Corps and Division headquarters, and a Contingency Operations Package, developed as an integrated package that USARSPACE could use to provide rapid space force enhancement to a deploying Army unit. Approval to acquire the CSP Contingency Operations Package was granted by the Army in early 1994 and subsequently formed the basis for establishment of the USARSPACE Contingency Operations (Space) program. In October 1994, this program was renamed the Army Space Support Team in accordance with a USSPACECOM directive.

This chapter provides a detailed examination of the process that led to the creation of the Army Space Support Team, to include:

- An examination of the Louisiana Maneuvers review and decision-making process used to evaluate the Commercial Space Package.

- A consideration of the key decision parameters and issues involved with establishment of the Contingency Operations (Space) program.

- A summary of the early concept of operations developed for the Contingency Operations (Space) program and the Army Space Support Team, and how this concept of operations evolved in 1994.

The Louisiana Maneuvers

With the end of the Cold War, the U.S. Army faced a fundamental transformation in which it would be forced to evolve from a forward-deployed force geared towards high-intensity conflict into a force projection Army based in the Continental United States (CONUS). At the same time the Army grappled with this transformation, it was assigned a series of new responsibilities and dispatched on an ever-increasing number of overseas deployments. For example, in the five-year period between 1991 and 1995, the Army was involved in six major humanitarian assistance missions, four peace enforcement missions, two peacekeeping missions, and one show of force mission, each lasting for more than 12 months. During the entire fifteen year period spanning from 1975 to 1990, the Army had only been involved in a total of six major peacekeeping, show of force, and humanitarian assistance missions.

To energize and guide the Army during this period of restructuring, General Gordon Sullivan (Chief of Staff, U.S. Army, 1991-1995) established the Louisiana Maneuvers (LAM) process. General Sullivan consciously modeled the LAM process upon a series of maneuvers conducted by the U.S. Army prior to World War II in Louisiana and the Carolinas. During those earlier maneuvers, the Army had successfully experimented with new tactics, doctrine, and

General Gordon R. Sullivan, Chief of Staff, U.S. Army, 1991 to 1995.

General Sullivan implemented the Louisiana Maneuvers process to enable the Army to experiment with new tactics, doctrine, and equipment. General Sullivan would later grant final approval to acquire the Louisiana Maneuvers Commercial Space Package, directing the Army Staff on 3 March 1994 to "get on with it."

equipment. General Sullivan hoped that the LAM process would provide a similar opportunity for the Army of the 1990s.

To institutionalize the LAM process, General Sullivan established the Louisiana Maneuvers Task Force (LAM TF). This task force was given responsibility for integrating and synchronizing the LAM process across the Army. The LAM TF would ensure that the Army was able to develop and explore new warfighting concepts, assess progress, provide a framework for decision making by the senior

Army leadership, and facilitate the Army's transformation. In addition, General Sullivan established a LAM General Officer Working Group (GOWG) as a two-star council and a LAM Board of Directors as a four-star executive group. Both groups would later be instrumental in determining the manner in which the Army would activate a formal capability to provide space systems enhancement during contingency operations.

The Commercial Space Package

Background

The Commercial Space Package (CSP) initiative was designed by TRADOC and USARSPACE to provide a limited, near-term space support capability for each Corps and Division headquarters. CSP systems were intended to be low-cost, commercial, off-the-shelf products that had already been proven useful in Army experiments and demonstrations. The initiative was comprised of two basic elements: The first was a Contingency Operations Package, consisting of INMARSAT commercial satellite communications terminals, small weather receivers, Multi-Spectral Imagery Processors (MSIPs) capable of generating special map products, and Mission Planning Rehearsal Systems (MPRSs) designed to provide three-dimensional terrain images and electronic 'fly-throughs' of an area of operations. The Contingency Operations Package was designed to be maintained by USARSPACE for rapid deployment to a Joint Task Force, Corps, or other unit in need of space systems enhancement. The second basic element of the CSP was a Support Package, consisting of systems to be maintained by a field unit. Systems intended for deployment under the CSP Support Package included MSIPs for fielding with Corps, Division, and Separate Brigade headquarters, Tri-Band Terminals for fielding with the 269th Signal Company, and surrogate satellite systems for experimentation at the Battle Command Battle Laboratory (BCBL) at Fort Gordon, GA.[2]

Early Decisions

The original proponent for the development of the CSP was Major General Ellerson. While assigned to the Army Staff (DAMO-SW) in 1993, General Ellerson directed that a study of commercial off-the-shelf space products be conducted to determine what capabilities might be of immediate use at the Corps and Division level.[3] General Ellerson's idea was subsequently briefed to Lieutenant General Lionetti (Commanding General, U.S. Army Space and Strategic Defense Command), Major General Garner (Assistant Deputy Chief of Staff for Operations and Plans, Force Development), Major General Lehowicz, Brigadier General Adams, Brigadier General Franks, and the Army Staff. As a result of this briefing, it was decided to validate the CSP concept through the

TRADOC Louisiana Maneuvers process.[4] After further consultations with the Louisiana Maneuver Office, it was determined that the CSP would be made part of the Command, Control, Communications, Computers, and Intelligence (C4I) LAM issue.[5] In May 1993, TRADOC tasked the Battle Command Battle Laboratory (BCBL) to assume responsibility for the development and validation of the CSP.[6] From May to September 1993, the BCBL worked in close conjunction with USARSPACE to develop and refine the CSP concept. Under the basic CSP concept developed during this timeframe, two separate packages would be developed for the Army. The first space package, consisting primarily of Multi-Spectral Imagery Processors and satellite communications systems, would be fielded directly to Corps and Division units. A second package, designed specifically for contingency operations, would consist of commercial off-the-shelf systems that had already been demonstrated by USARSPACE under the ASEDP. This equipment would include INMARSAT communications terminals, small satellite weather receivers, Multi-Spectral Imagery Processors, and Mission Planning Rehearsal Systems. USARSPACE would maintain this equipment and provide a team capable of deploying with it to support a Joint Task Force or Corps headquarters. USARSPACE took the initiative in developing the contingency operations portion of the CSP. In May 1993, USARSPACE prepared a manning document, estimating that an additional 20 manpower slots would be needed to acquire, field, train and provide CSP contingency operations support to the field.[7] This manning document was submitted to the U.S. Army Force Integration Support Activity (USAFISA), which subsequently validated 11 of the 20 manpower slots requested, consisting of four 2-person contingency teams and three headquarters support positions. In addition, the command assigned a civilian employee to provide configuration management and maintenance support.[8]

Following this initial research, the BCBL hosted a video teleconference with USARSPACE on 3 August 1993 to refine the CSP concept.[9] As a result of this groundwork, the TRADOC Combined Arms Support Command (CASCOM) reported that it supported the CSP initiative, stressing:

> "We need a package that provides assured communications to the combat service support (CSS) community. . . . SATCOM systems in this package that will specifically address CSS operational requirements are High Data Rate Tactical Satellites (HDRTSAT), International Maritime Satellites (INMARSAT), Multi-Spectral Imagery (MSI) processing, and surrogate satellites. . . . METT-T may demand additional data communications above and beyond the proposed LAM package for CSS units in a force projection Army. We would support a 'plus up' in the INMARSAT terminals for CSS commanders."[10]

On 20 August 1993, Lieutenant General Don Lionetti (Commanding General, USASSDC) presented a comprehensive approach for deploying CSP systems, to include a project plan, management approach, project schedule, and resource allocation. Under the plan, USARSPACE would procure four of the systems in the CSP: INMARSAT satellite communications terminals, the MSIP, the Multi-Source Tactical System (MSTS), and the Small Weather System (SWS).

USASSDC based this recommendation on its experience with demonstrating those four systems, noting:

> "The four items selected have been previously demonstrated in the field by USARSPACE as part of the Army Space Exploitation Demonstration Program (ASEDP). The other two capabilities listed in the BCBL CSP (HDRSAT and Surrogate Satellite) cannot be supported by the expertise currently resident within USARSPACE since they have not been field demonstrated."[11]

To accomplish the plan, USASSDC stated a need for an additional 7 civilian and 13 military authorizations.[12]

The Louisiana Maneuvers General Officer Working Group Meeting

The Louisiana Maneuvers General Officer Working Group (GOWG) reviewed the CSP concept on 9 September 1993. Mr. Whelen, (USARSPACE) briefed the GOWG on the space-based capabilities provided by the INMARSAT, the small weather receiver, the MSIP, and the MSTS. Afterwards, Colonel Roundtree (USARSPACE) briefed the GOWG on CSP acquisition and sustainment.[13]

During the briefing to the GOWG, it was explained that four primary objectives had been established for the Commercial Space Package: First, the CSP was intended to provide a limited space-based capability in the near term (defined as six to eight months); Second, the CSP would provide space support for day-to-day Army training; Third, the CSP would serve as a tool for developing confidence throughout the Army in space support systems; Finally, the CSP would provide a contingency support capability for Echelons Above Corps (EAC), special operations units, and Combat Service Support activities.[14]

The members of the GOWG were presented with four different approaches to funding the CSP, each geared to the level of emphasis the Army leadership believed the CSP initiative merited.[15] In addition, the GOWG was presented six options for acquiring and fielding CSP systems. Under the first option briefed, the Army would acquire 71 CSP systems (44 INMARSAT receivers, 11 satellite weather receivers, 7 MSIP, and 9 MSTS with MPRS). All CSP systems would be assigned to USARSPACE and would be deployed to warfighting headquarters as needed. Under the second option briefed, a total of 104 CSP systems would be acquired, of which 64 would be assigned to USARSPACE, 6 would be assigned to Corps headquarters, and 34 would be assigned to Division and Separate Brigade headquarters. Under each of the remaining options briefed, a larger number of total CSP systems would be acquired, with a larger percentage assigned to Corps, Divisions, and Separate Brigades. The option recommended for adoption was Option #6, in which a total of 169 CSP systems would be acquired. Under this option, 41 CSP systems would be assigned to USARSPACE, 43 would be assigned to Corps headquarters, 82 would be assigned to Divisions and Separate Brigades, 1 would be assigned to the BCBL, and 2 would be assigned to the Engineer School.[16]

The overall reaction of the General Officer Working Group (GOWG) to the CSP initiative was positive. However, the GOWG believed that additional coordination and analysis were required before the CSP initiative could proceed. Brigadier General Anderson, who subsequently summarized the results of the GOWG meeting, noted that four general concerns and comments about the CSP were made by the general officers in attendance:

> "What are the risks and level of expectations if we buy something that is not horizontally integrated and is not currently funded? We run the risk of losing an entire funding line for a program. We need to lay that out up front."

> "We need to determine the status of existing requirements documentation for similar systems and we need to develop an operational concept for the proposed capabilities. The fundamental questions are: When will the objective systems be fielded? What can we do in the interim? What can we do to graft interim capability onto the objective system?"

> "We have had requirements for objective systems and have been working them for years. Yet every time a unit gets ready to deploy, they go to ARSPACE for support. We can put these CSP capabilities into soldier's hands next year. The Army needs to have these capabilities, somewhere. Then, if the need arises, we can go back to the manufacturers and get more."

> "We can't afford to resource duplicate capabilities. We need to have the right amount of the right capability." [17]

The Louisiana Maneuvers GOWG made two key decisions during the 9 September 1993 meeting. First, additional analysis of the CSP initiative would be conducted prior to submission of the CSP Issue Decision Package (IDP) in October to the LAM Board of Directors. Second, responsibility for each of the CSP systems would be assigned to a general officer.

The GOWG tasking for additional CSP analyses reflected the key areas of concern that had been expressed during the briefing. In response to concerns that the CSP equipment was not horizontally integrated, the GOWG directed that a cross-walk of each proposed CSP system be conducted to: [1] Determine whether the CSP system, by itself, would provide sufficient capability to meet the requirements driving an existing or planned objective system; [2] Describe in operational terms the capabilities of the CSP systems in comparison to planned or existing systems; [3] If the analysis revealed that the CSP and the planned objective system were redundant, to describe the duplication and explain why it is needed; and [4] To describe how CSP system capability might be horizontally integrated or otherwise applied to existing or planned equipment. In response to concerns regarding documentation of equipment requirements, the GOWG directed that a statement of the requirement for the CSP system be developed, as well as a statement of the operational concept. Finally, to address funding issues associated with CSP procurement, the GOWG directed that recommendations be developed for the quantities and timing of acquisition, the acquisition agent, the fielding plan and agent, the sustainment plan and agent, and the training plan and agent. Furthermore, the GOWG directed that funding levels required to implement the CSP recommendation be summarized by fiscal year and procurement account.[18]

The second key decision made at the 9 September 1993 GOWG meeting was to assign each of the CSP systems to a flag-level officer. Major General Bob Gray (Signal Center) accepted the lead on the INMARSAT initiative. The general consensus expressed about the INMARSAT was that the current Army inventory needed to be upgraded and that the value-added by the INMARSAT over current and planned single-channel tactical communications satellite terminals needed to be identified. The GOWG also asked about the restrictions placed upon the use of INMARSAT for supporting military operations.

For the Small Weather System and the Multi-Source Tactical System, Major General John Stewart (Intelligence Center) assumed responsibility. The general consensus at the GOWG was that the Small Weather System was

General Frederick Franks, Commanding General, U.S. Army Training and Doctrine Command, 1991 to 1995.

After commanding VII Corps during the Gulf War, General Franks was selected to be the TRADOC Commanding General. On 12 January 1994, General Franks presented the TRADOC position on CSP procurement to the Army Chief of Staff, recommending that a contingency support capability be developed. General Franks' recommendation was adopted by the Army, leading to subsequent activation of the Contingency Operations (Space) team at USARSPACE (Forward).

required at the Corps and Theater levels but would be too bulky for use at the Division level. Concerns were expressed about the value-added of the Small Weather System when compared to the existing weather terminal (WRAASE) or the planned weather system (IMETS). For the MSTS, the general consensus was that the six systems should be acquired to ensure that each Corps headquarters could be equipped with the system and that enough equipment would be available for experimentation at the battle laboratory. A series of issues and concerns were raised regarding the MSTS, to include the amount of training time required to use the capability, the operational concept and impacts of using MSTS with the Success R Radio or Commander's Tactical Terminal-Hybrid (CTT-H), whether MSTS software might simply be rehosted onto an existing system, and the capabilities of MSTS in comparison to other systems (such as the Aviation Mission Planning System or Battlefield Visualization Software).[19]

Responsibility for the Multi-Spectral Imagery Processor, the fourth CSP system, was assumed by Colonel Flowers (Engineer Center). The general consensus was that the MSIP should be fielded to each Division and Corps headquarters, as well as the Engineer Center. The primary issue raised during discussions at the meeting was whether or not the MSIP capability might later be grafted onto the objective system (DTSS).[20]

Major General Jay Garner, Assistant Deputy Chief of Staff for Operations and Plans, Force Development, 1993-1994.

General Garner attended the meeting in which the Commercial Space Package concept was originally proposed by Major General Ellerson (DAMO-SW). On 9 May 1994, Major General Garner took action to validate the Army's requirement for the Commercial Space Package. As a Lieutenant General, Garner would later command USASSDC.

Senior-Level Review and Refinement of the CSP Initiative

On 4 October 1993, the CSP initiative was briefed to General Frederick Franks, TRADOC Commanding General. Three deployment options for the CSP were presented: Under the first option, enough equipment would be acquired to allow USARSPACE to support warfighting headquarters during contingency missions; Under the second option, enough CSP equipment would be acquired to provide a USARSPACE contingency capability and to outfit the units scheduled for earliest deployment; The last option would permit CSP equipment to be provided both for a USARSPACE contingency capability and to outfit all Corps and Division headquarters. Each of the options was evaluated in terms of the impacts on doctrine, training, leader development, operations, and materiel.[21]

The recommendation made to General Franks was that the second option be selected and that the CSP be funded in FY94 to provide an immediate warfighting capability. General Anderson expected that the second option would,

> "improve the Army's ability to conduct military operations; help close the gap between technology and modernization; will create demand pull for space based technology; give operators the opportunity to help define future requirements; and may show the way how to rapidly insert commercially available technology into the force."[22]

On 20 October 1993 the CSP was presented to the Louisiana Maneuvers Board of Directors (BOD). During this briefing, it was decided that the CSP initiative still needed to be matured. The Board of Directors directed that the CSP proposal be reviewed by Joint Task Force Somalia, that near-term CSP acquisition and deployment options be developed for FY94 and FY95, and that another CSP review be conducted with the Army Chief of Staff, the Vice Chief of Staff, and the Deputy Chief of Staff for Operations.[23]

The TRADOC Combined Arms Center responded to the first Louisiana Maneuvers Board of Directors tasking on 1 November 1993 by requesting input from JTF Somalia on the CSP initiative. The JTF Commander was asked to review a CSP package designed to support a Division-sized land joint task force with INMARSAT, small weather satellite receivers, Multi-Spectral Imagery Processors, Mission Planning Rehearsal Systems, and the surrogate satellite concept.[24] On 18 November, the JTF Commander supported the CSP outlined by TRADOC. The JTF supported the quantities and types of systems suggested by TRADOC and provided examples of the use of such capabilities during operations in Somalia.[25]

On 23 November 1993, General Anderson coordinated the response to the second element of the Louisiana Maneuvers Board of Directors tasking. General Anderson recommended an FY94 CSP package designed for Joint Task Force contingency support. This package would consist of 12 INMARSAT terminals, 2 small weather systems, 2 MSIPs (with an additional 17 MSIPs for Corps/Division terrain teams), 5 MPRS, and 2 surrogate satellite systems. For a CSP program

Brigadier General Edward Anderson III, Deputy Commanding General, US Army Combined Arms Command and Ft. Leavenworth, 1993-1994.

General Anderson took a leading role in developing, refining, and staffing the Louisiana Maneuvers Commercial Space Package initiative. As a Lieutenant General, Anderson would later be appointed Commanding General, U.S. Army Space and Strategic Defense Command.

follow-on in FY95, General Anderson prepared two alternatives. Under the first option, General Anderson recommended procurement of 28 INMARSAT terminals, 6 MPRS, 6 Tri-Band SHF terminals, and 4 surrogate satellite systems. Under the second option, General Anderson proposed that 76 INMARSAT terminals, 10 small weather systems, 17 MPRS, 6 Tri-Band SHF terminal, and 6 surrogate satellite systems be acquired.[26]

Implementation: Procurement Actions For The CSP

General Franks presented the TRADOC recommendation on CSP procurement to General Sullivan, Chief of Staff of the U.S. Army, on 12 January 1994. General Franks recommended that enough CSP systems be procured in FY94 to support one Army deployment in support of a Joint Task Force. This CSP contingency support package would consist of 12 INMARSAT terminals, 2 small weather systems, 2 MSIPs, and 5 MPRS. In addition, General Franks recommended that the Army "buy 6 Tri-Band SHF Terminals to support the PowerPAC III Company, 2 surrogate satellites for Battle Laboratory experimentation and contingency support, and 17 Multi-Spectral Imagery Processors for Corps and Division terrain analysis teams." The estimated FY94 cost for the contingency support package was estimated to be $1.9 million, with an additional $15.3 million for procurement of the Corps and Division MSIP systems, $316,000 for the surrogate satellite systems, and $10,000 for the Tri-Band SHF Terminal systems. General Franks recommended to the Chief of Staff that the CSP initiative be extended into FY95, with a recommended purchase of CSP systems to be provided directly to those Army units slated for the earliest deployment. The total recommended FY95 procurement consisted of 28 INMARSAT terminals, 6 MPRS, and 4 surrogate satellite systems, with an estimated total cost of $3.5 million. General Franks also recommended, however, that "Lieutenant General Don Lionetti, Major General Bob Gray, and Major General John Stewart validate the FY95 buy recommendation as part of Don's LAM Space Issue. In this manner, we get some equipment on the ground this year, plan to buy more, but continue to revisit to keep our options open."[27]

On 3 March 1994, General Sullivan responded positively to the TRADOC recommendations for the CSP initiative. In a letter to General Franks, the Chief of Staff wrote: "Appreciate the work your people have done to reaffirm the need for the JTF package and in refining the entire CSP. . . . The guidance I have given the staff is 'to get on with it.'"[28]

With the approval of the Chief of Staff, the CSP initiative was rapidly executed. On 18 March 1994, General Anderson submitted an Operational Needs Statement (ONS) for the CSP to the Assistant Deputy Chief of Staff for Operations and Plans, Force Development (DAMO-FD).[29] In the meantime, the Funds Mid-Year Review allocated funding for the CSP initiative[30] and, on 30 March 1994, the Army staff released funding for procurement of CSP systems. Funding was provided to the Program Executive Office, Command and Control Systems (PEO-CCS) for immediate acquisition of the small weather system, 2 MSIPs, and 5 MPRS systems.[31]

Headquarters, Department of the Army formally approved the CSP concept plan on 1 April 1994 and authorized the immediate requisition and fill of manpower spaces requested by USARSPACE to support contingency operations. Twelve personnel positions were approved for addition to the USARSPACE Table of Distribution and Allowances (TDA).[32] On 9 May 1994, Major General Jay Garner (Assistant Deputy Chief of Staff for Operations and Plans, Force Development) validated the Operational Needs Statement submitted by General Anderson on 18 March. The validation memorandum sent by General Garner summarized four key decisions made in reference to the CSP initiative: First, authorization was provided for the acquisition of a single CSP package tailored for contingency operations support, as outlined in General Anderson's ONS; Second, the CSP would be used only for contingency purposes and Operations Other Than War; Third, no additional personnel or manpower were authorized beyond the level set for USARSPACE by the Army Staff on 1 April 1994; Finally, $1.93 million in funding would be reprogrammed for the CSP Contingency Operations Package during the mid-year review. Of this amount, $1.77 million would be provided in FY94 OPA (Other Procurement, Army) funding and $0.16 million in FY94 OMA (Operations and Maintenance, Army) funding.[33]

With senior Army leadership approval of the CSP secured, USARSPACE next focused its efforts on standing up a contingency deployment capability for the Army. This capability, dubbed the Contingency Operations (Space) team, or COPS, was scheduled for activation on 1 January 1995.[34]

COPS: THE CONTINGENCY OPERATIONS (SPACE) TEAM

The CSP initiative established the key parameters for activation of a contingency deployment support capability by USARSPACE. When Major Mike Jensen was appointed to lead the Contingency Operations (Space) team, its mission, equipment, and personnel had already been established as a result of the CSP process. Nevertheless, a number of additional operational factors shaped the manner in which the contingency deployment capability was established, to include the USSPACECOM directive that resulted in the renaming of COPS as the Army Space Support Team (ARSST).

The Army Audit Agency Review Of 1994

The Army Audit Agency was conducting an analysis of space support operations at the same time that the senior Army leadership was assessing the merits of the CSP Contingency Operations Package. A draft report, issued by the Army Audit Agency on 8 June 1994, validated the need for an organization dedicated to providing warfighting commanders and staffs with space support. In this report, the Army Audit Agency noted that USARSPACE had successfully supported the Army during a number of contingency missions, specifically citing three cases. First, INMARSAT communications support had been provided for humanitarian relief efforts after Hurricanes Iniki in Hawaii and Andrew in Florida. Second, commercial space systems had been used to provide mapping, communications, weather, and GPS support to the 10th Mountain Division during Operation RESTORE HOPE in Somalia. Finally, commercial space capabilities had supported mapping and communications requirements during Operation PROVIDE PROMISE in Bosnia.[35]

The Army Audit Agency observed that support to field units had been provided as part of the existing USARSPACE space demonstration program. However, they emphasized,

> "the mission of the program is to demonstrate space technologies to field soldiers in an attempt to identify operational needs, help shape operational requirements, and provide data for the materiel developer – not to actively support contingency missions with various assets from the program. Providing operational support for field commanders isn't part of the Army Space Command mission."[36]

Because USARSPACE had neither been assigned a contingency operations mission nor the resources required to perform such a mission, the Command had been unable to provide sustained, operational support to field units. The result was that "commanders must go to many different organizations to obtain needed space technology support and communications."[37]

Based upon the USARSPACE experience in supporting field units during deployments and the space systems expertise resident within the organization, the Army Audit Agency recommended that the Army assign a contingency support mission to the Command. The auditors defined three components of this mission: [1] To support battle zone operations or other missions; [2] To bring the latest space technology to the field; and [3] To train soldiers to use the technology.[38]

Standing Up the COPS Capability

After the Army granted formal authorization to procure the CSP Contingency Operations Package and provided USARSPACE with the requisite personnel and funding, the Command took active steps to develop the Contingency Operations (Space) capability. Major Mike Jensen, who was assigned responsibility within the Command for activating COPS, envisioned that staffing for the COPS teams and procurement of the CSP systems would take place from May to November 1994. In December 1994, the COPS teams would train-up and prepare to support deployments. By 1 January 1995, COPS would be operational.

Although Major Jensen had a great deal of flexibility in establishing the concept of operations for COPS, three key parameters constrained his approach. First, the Army Chief of Staff had already defined the COPS mission. As Major Jensen noted in an early information paper, "General Sullivan directed that the mission of COPS will be to provide world-wide space operations support to contingency

---

COPS Activation: Issues of Concern.

- **Uncertainty in COPS funding.**
- **COPS equipment configuration management and equipment sustainment.**
- **Officer requisition lead times.**
- **COPS relationship with USSPACECOM.**
- **Continuance of the CSP initiative in FY95.**
- **Need for a COPS team to be prepared for an immediate contingency.**

---

missions and operations other than war like floods, earthquakes, or humanitarian support."[39] Second, COPS manning levels had already been established during the Louisiana Maneuvers process. The Contingency Operations (Space) program was assigned 12 personnel, who were scheduled for assignment to ARSPACE by October 1994.[40] Third, each of the major items of equipment assigned to the COPS teams had already been selected during the Louisiana Maneuvers decision-making process.

After being assigned the mission to activate the COPS capability, Major Jensen identified several areas of concern. First, funding levels for COPS in both FY94 and FY95 were viewed as uncertain. During the USARSPACE Program Budget Advisory Committee (PBAC) conducted on 11 April 1994, no funding requirement had been identified.[41] At the 21 June 1994 PBAC, a new requirement for $261,000 in funding was established for COPS; however, only $175,000 was funded, leaving an unfunded requirement of $86,000.[42] USARSPACE funded the O&M costs ($175,000) of the COPS program, to include money for civilian pay, travel, training, and planning support.[43] In the meantime, FY94 HQDA funding for COPS remained uncertain and the FY95 COPS program was unprogrammed. Second, there was no established equipment configuration management process or equipment sustainment program.   Third, officer requisition lead times were estimated at 9 to 10 months, requiring realignment of personnel within the USARSPACE. Fourth, the COPS relationship to USSPACECOM was undefined. Fifth, it was unknown if the CSP program would continue in FY95 and, if so, what the USARSPACE role would be. Sixth, Major Jensen noted that a contingency mission could happen at any time and, thus, the COPS teams would have to be prepared to respond quickly.[44]

Developing The COPS Concept Of Operations

Under Major Jensen's initial concept of operations for the Contingency Operations (Space) program, two five-person teams would be prepared to deploy worldwide to support Army operations.[45] Deployment taskings for the COPS teams would be made by Headquarters Department of the Army (HQDA), with units requesting support through the HQDA Emergency Operations Center. During a deployment, the COPS team would be placed under the operational control (OPCON) of the supported unit.[46]

With only 11 personnel available to the COPS program, USARSPACE decided to acquire contractor support to refine the COPS concept of operations. A Task Order was prepared by USARSPACE for assistance to the COPS program in developing, staffing, and finalizing a COPS Concept of Operations (CONOPS), COPS Standard Operating Procedures (SOP), a training plan, a series of generic operations plans, and an exercise support plan.[47]

A first draft of the COPS Standard Operating Procedures was submitted on 16 August 1994. This SOP assumed that a four-phased deployment process would be used when a COPS team deployed on a contingency mission. Phase I, as outlined in the SOP, consisted of pre-deployment actions and alert notification. Phase II consisted of COPS team deployment actions and employment in the field. Phase III of the SOP outlined redeployment actions for the COPS team while Phase IV summarized recovery actions.[48] In addition, the SOP outlined the major responsibilities of key USARSPACE staff officers, the COPS Division Chief, COPS team leaders, and all deployable personnel.

Operating under the assumption that COPS teams must be prepared to deploy at a moment's notice, the SOP also established three cycles for deployment readiness. The highest COPS deployment readiness posture was classified as the Blue Cycle (Deployment Standby), in which team personnel and equipment would be prepared for rapid movement overseas. Within the Blue Cycle, two separate levels of standby readiness were established. Under Blue High, a 2-hour recall requirement was placed into effect. Blue Normal entailed a 6-hour recall requirement. The second priority for COPS deployment was classified as the Green Cycle (Unit Planning). When a COPS team was placed on the Green Cycle, personnel would coordinate with supported units to help update operations plans, orders, and accompanying documentation. In addition, the COPS team would conduct systems demonstrations and training with supported units. The final COPS readiness posture was classified as the Red Cycle (Exercises and Training). A

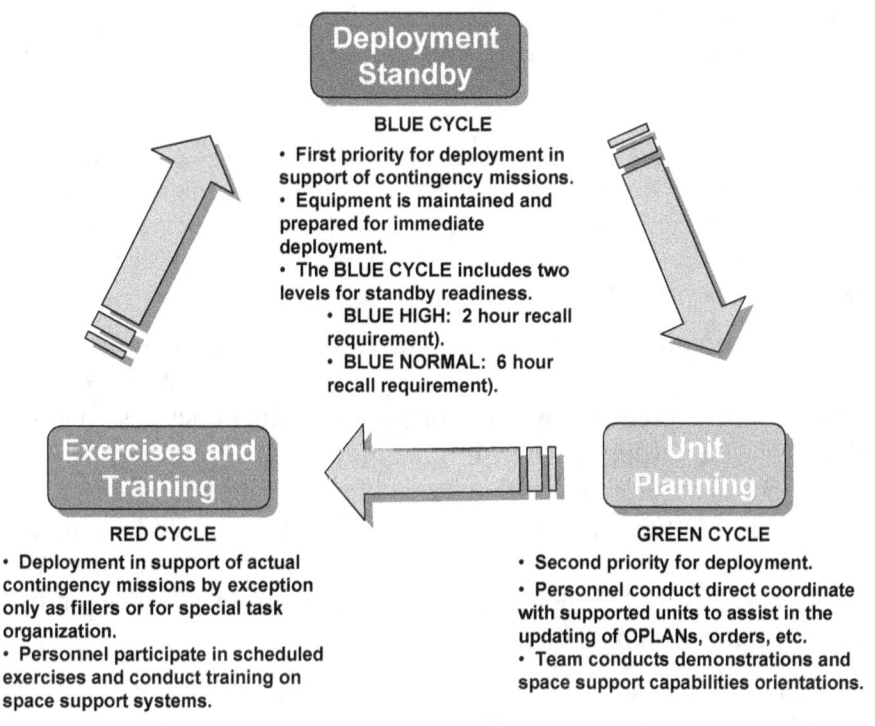

Figure 3: Original COPS Team Deployment Readiness Cycle Concept.

COPS team on the Red Cycle would deploy in support of an actual contingency mission only as individual fillers for another team or as part of a special task organization. COPS personnel on the Red Cycle would continue to participate in unit exercises and training.[49]

The first draft of the COPS SOP contained procedures for only the pre-deployment and alert actions of a COPS deployment; it did not speak to the full process of COPS deployment planning, deployment actions, employment in-theater, or redeployment/recovery. When Colonel E. Paul Semmons (USARSPACE Commander) reviewed the document, he directed a series of revisions to the SOP. First, he directed that the SOP be printed as a pocket-sized document (rather than the 8 ½ by 11 inch paper on which the draft had been printed). Second, he wanted the SOP to be written as a checklist-oriented document. Finally, Colonel Semmons wrote that the "operational concept is off track" and sketched a revamped concept on the back of the document.[50]

The original draft of the COPS Concept of Operations was also presented to USARSPACE in August 1994. The draft CONOPS elaborated on many of the themes that had been introduced in the COPS SOP, to include the level of units supported by the COPS teams, the deployment process, the command and control of the COPS teams, and the employment of COPS teams in the field, as described below.

Units Supported by the COPS Teams. The draft CONOPS envisioned that the focal point for COPS team support would be at the Corps headquarters level. However, the concept of operations also stressed that the COPS teams had to be prepared to support a variety of other units. Examples cited in the draft CONOPS included,

> "CONUS based non-contingency Corps assets, National Guard units, FORSCOM Army Reserve units, and other government agencies (Federal Emergency Management Agency, Bureau of Land Management, Drug Enforcement Agency, State and Federal Law Enforcement Agencies, State Adjutants General, etc.)."[51]

The COPS Deployment Process. The draft COPS Concept of Operations established a phased deployment process, much like that outlined in the draft SOP. The first phase of this process consisted of pre-deployment actions. During this phase, USARSPACE would establish communications with the unit to be supported and begin developing mission planning and support requirements. An Army Space Liaison Officer (ASPLO) from USARSPACE would lead an advance party to the supported unit to refine mission planning and support requirements. In the meantime, USARSPACE would tailor a COPS mission team, load equipment, and prepare to deploy within 48 hours.

During the second phase of the COPS deployment process, USARSPACE would conduct mobility planning for the COPS team and its equipment. For movement within the Continental United States (CONUS), USARSPACE would arrange transportation via the Defense Transportation System, scheduled commercial airline flight, or ground movement. Movement outside of CONUS would be conducted "in accordance with supported unit approved OPLANS, the Time Phased Force Deployment List (TPFDL) and air flow plans."[52] As an alternate method for overseas movement, USARSPACE would schedule a commercial flight for the COPS Team.

Once a COPS team was deployed to support a unit, the Army Space Liaison Officer would serve as both the COPS team leader and the "Space Capabilities Advisor" to the supported unit. The draft CONOPS envisioned the ASPLO role as "advising and recommending COPS employment based on the OPLAN and the operational situation, [providing] user assistance and interface between the unit and HQ USARSPACE, and [facilitating] logistics support for the equipment."[53] In the meantime, COPS team members would prepare hard copy products for use by the support unit and provide equipment training to supported unit personnel.

After completion of the COPS mission, the team would initiate redeployment actions. During this phase of a COPS team deployment, the draft CONOPS envisioned that "the supported unit will arrange necessary transportation for movement of COPS assets to USARSPACE home station or other HQDA DCSOPS designated destination."[54]

The final phase of a COPS team deployment in the draft CONOPS was the recovery phase. Upon return to home station, the COPS team would be debriefed on lessons learned and a mission performance assessment would be conducted. The COPS team would then undergo "an intensive recovery program" to allow the team to redeploy again within two weeks.[55]

COPS Command and Control Relationships. Under the draft COPS CONOPS, approval and tasking for all support missions were the responsibility of Headquarters, Department of the Army. Upon deployment, the COPS team was directly attached to the supported Army organization for "operational control, rations, quarters, logistics, and UCMJ [judicial responsibility]." USARSPACE retained command and technical control of the COPS team during the deployment and was assigned responsibility for "providing administration and logistics support."[56]

USSPACECOM and the Renaming Of COPS

At the same time that Major Mike Jensen was activating the Contingency Operations (Space) program, decisions by U.S. Space Command affected the direction of Army efforts. For commonality and standardization, USSPACECOM directed in October 1994 that each of the contingency space capabilities of Services be referred to as Space Support Teams.[57] In accordance with this directive, the Army Contingency Operations (Space) program was officially renamed the Army Space Support Team (ARSST).

USSPACECOM's interest in establishing a space support team capability to support theater commanders stemmed from two key factors. First, under the 1993-1995 Joint Strategic Capabilities Plan (JSCP) USSPACECOM was formally assigned responsibility for supporting the Combatant Commands. The JSCP is a key planning document which fulfills three primary functions: [1] To provide guidance to the Joint Chiefs of Staff, the Services, and the Combatant Commands for the accomplishment of assigned tasks and missions; [2] To apportion resources among the Combatant Commands; [3] To serve as the principal vehicle for tasking of the Combatant Commands to develop Operations Plans, Concept Plans, and Functional Plans. The 1993-1995 JSCP assigned responsibility to USSPACECOM for providing "assured mission support from space systems throughout the spectrum of conflict to the National Command Authority (NCA), Chairman Joint Chiefs of Staff (CJCS), combatant commands and other agencies." [58] To respond to the JSCP requirement to support the Combatant Commands, USSPACECOM developed the Support to Theater Operations Management Plan (STOMP). STOMP, in turn, established an early blueprint for providing space support for theater operations.

The second major factor driving USSPACECOM's effort to develop a space support team structure was the command emphasis exerted by General Chuck Horner, then serving as Commander-in-Chief at U.S. Space Command. While serving in Saudi Arabia during DESERT STORM, General Horner had been disappointed by the lack of support provided to U.S. Central Command by USSPACECOM. While USSPACECOM took few proactive steps to support the USCENTCOM commander and staff, each of the Services responded individually to the requirements of their own units in-theater. For example, USSPACECOM's theater missile early warning system had to be cobbled together just prior to the initiation of hostilities. Simply stated, USSPACECOM had exerted minimalinfluence on combat operations during DESERT STORM. When General Horner assumed command of USSPACECOM, he took deliberate steps to ensure that a similar situation was not repeated in the future.[59]

By September 1994 USSPACECOM and Air Force Space Command (AFSPACECOM) were involved in several initiatives to provide space support to theater commanders. One such initiative was the development of teams designed to provide space planning support, which were then referred to as "Annex N" teams.[60] A second initiative was the activation of Forward Space Support in Theater (FSST) teams, which were intended to normalize the process of providing space support at the theater level. In addition, USSPACECOM and AFSPACECOM began to participate in and develop military space exercises.[61] These efforts, however, exerted little influence on either COPS or the Army Space Support Team. No direct line of control was established between USSPACECOM and the ARSST. No formal coordination mechanisms for joint operations were incorporated into the ARSST Concept of Operations, Standard Operating Procedures, or training programs. Tasking for an ARSST operation, like that for COPS team deployment, continued to be the responsibility of HQDA. If USSPACECOM sought to task an ARSST to provide support, it would have to forward this request "to HQDA DCSOPS by USARSPACE for concurrence and Army mission guidance."[62]

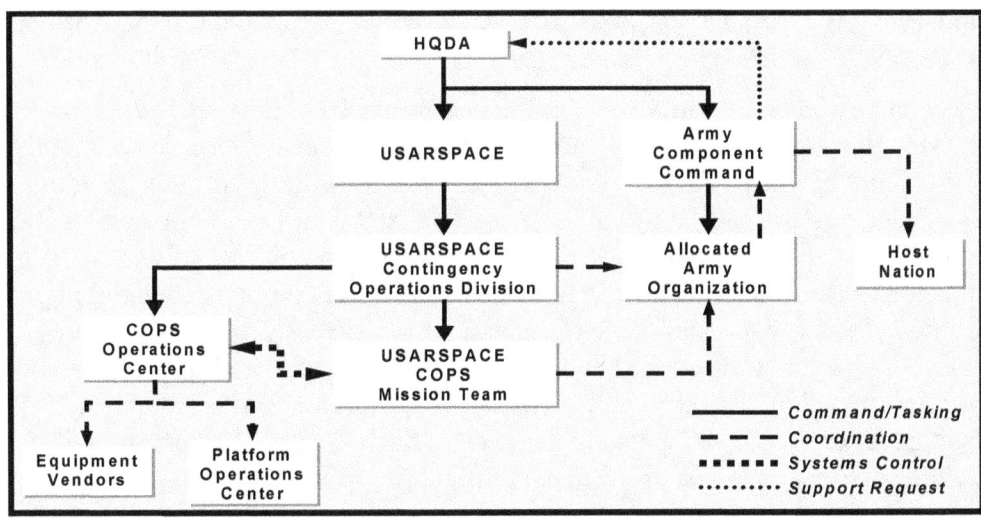

Figure 4: COPS Planning and Coordination Relationships, as diagrammed in the original Concept of Operations.

No USSPACECOM oversight or review process was implemented for the Army Space Support Team. In short, USSPACECOM's only major influence on how the Army activated its space support capability was the October 1994 directive that led to the renaming of COPS.

The Transition to Arsst (October To December 1994)

USARSPACE maintained most of the elements of the original COPS concept of operations when the Army Space Support Team was activated. No changes were made to the personnel or equipment assigned to the ARSST. In addition, the basic mission assigned to the teams remained unchanged.

Similarly, there were few changes in organization made when the ARSST was activated. The December 1994 version of the ARSST CONOPS established a headquarters section, composed of the ARSST chief and a civilian analyst, and three deployable ARSST teams of 3 personnel each. As with the COPS capability, the ARSST teams would be maintained on a three-tiered readiness cycle. Each of the teams would be prepared for global deployment. The ARSST team on the highest readiness cycle would be prepared to deploy within 48 hours. In another carry-over from the original COPS concept of operations, the leaders of each of the ARSST teams were referred to as Army Space Planning Liaison Officers.

The December 1994 draft of the ARSST Concept of Operations did introduce two new elements. First, not only would HQDA provide deployment taskings to the ARSST; it would also "review, validate and prioritize requests" and "resolve conflicts for ARSST support."[63] If USSPACECOM wanted to task the ARSST for a contingency support mission, it would have to forward a request to HQDA for consideration. HQDA would then task USARSPACE to provide ARSST team support based on the most recent readiness status reports and USARSPACE recommendations.

The second new element introduced in the December 1994 draft CONOPS was an extensive reporting process for the ARSST. Under this reporting process, monthly reports would be provided to both USASSDC and HQDA on "the operational status of each system, availability of each system, status of personnel, and location and posture of deployed systems and personnel. The monthly report will include a Commander's Assessment of the ARSST capability readiness and availability."[64] In addition, within two hours of mission completion USARSPACE would provide a "HOTWASH" report to USASSDC and HQDA, to be followed by a formal after action report within 30 days. A system of spot reports was established for "impacting events such as personnel or equipment losses, equipment failures, impacting personnel actions, or mission conflicts."[65]

Summary

As the Army experimented with new tactics, doctrine, and equipment under the Louisiana Maneuvers process, space was identified as a significant combat multiplier. Past operational experience in the field, coupled with ongoing space demonstration efforts, convinced the Army that space systems could be used to

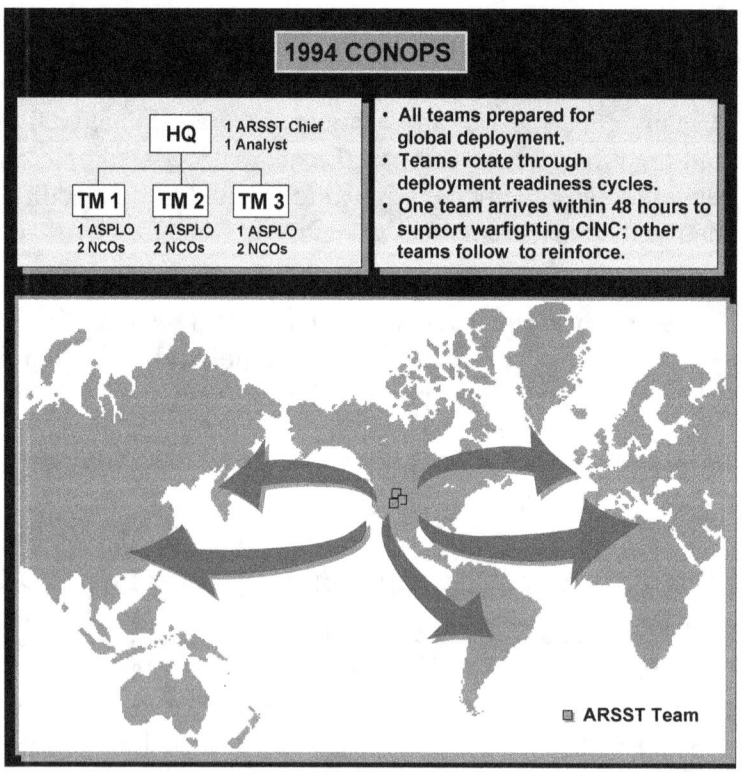

Figure 5: The ARSST Concept of Operations, December 1994.

assist warfighters at relatively low cost and risk. Better yet, the Army could purchase commercial space systems, many of which had already been demonstrated under the Army Space Exploitation and Demonstration Program, to achieve an immediate operational impact.

In the meantime, the Army had repeatedly requested deployment support from USARSPACE for contingency missions in Somalia, Haiti, and the Continental United States. The Army Space Exploitation Demonstration Program had been used by USARSPACE as the vehicle for providing contingency space support but, due to competing missions and a lack of resources, ASEDP had been unable to provide sustained operational support in the field. As a result, Army units were forced to "go to many different organizations to obtain needed space technology support and communications."[66]

To address this problem, the Army decided in 1994 to purchase a suite of equipment under the Commercial Space Package to support contingency operations. This equipment would be manned by personnel at USARSPACE under the Contingency Operations (Space) program. The program, commonly referred to as COPS, established a prototype space support organization prepared to deploy within 48 hours to support a Joint Task Force or Army headquarters. This marked a significant departure from earlier Army space initiatives. Unlike the previous demonstration efforts conducted by U.S. Army Space Command, COPS would receive the staffing, equipment, and training needed for deployment and integration into a field unit. Although the COPS teams would be prepared to conduct education and training, the primary focus of the team would be to use space systems to support a unit's operational planning and execution.

[1] U.S. Army Space Command, Army Space Support Team (ARSST) Concept of Operations (CONOPS) (DRAFT). (Colorado Springs, Colorado: U.S. Army Space Command: 12 December 1994.).

[2] Ibid.

[3] Facsimile Transmission, Daryll Nottingham, USARSPACE, to Richard Koval, PEO CCS, Subject: Commercial Space Package Background. 23 June 1994.

[4] Battle Command Battle Laboratory Briefing, "Louisiana Maneuver General Officer Working Group," 9 September 1993.

[5] Facsimile Transmission, Daryll Nottingham, USARSPACE, to Richard Koval, PEO CCS, Subject: Commercial Space Package Background. 23 June 1994.

[6] Ibid.

[7] Major Minnon (U.S. Army Space Command, MOSC-SR-F), Information Paper – Manpower Requirements for Contingency Space Capabilities and Commercial Space Package. 18 February 94.

[8] Ibid. Editorial comments made by Mr. Tom Callaghan, USARSPACE, in an e-mail message sent to Dr. James A. Walker on 16 February 1999.

[9] U.S. Army Space Command Briefing, "Contingency Operations Space," Undated.

[10] Memorandum, Colonel Ben E. Wedding, Director of Training, U.S. Army Combined Arms Support Command and Fort Lee, to Commander, U.S. Army Combined Arms Command and Fort Leavenworth, Subject: Louisiana Maneuvers (LAM) FY93 C4I Implied Task: Commercial Space Package. 11 August 1993.

[11] Memorandum, Lieutenant General Donald M. Lionetti, U.S. Army Space and Strategic Defense Command, to Director, Battle Combat Battle Lab (BCBL), Fort Leavenworth, Kansas, Subject: Acquiring and Placement of Commercial Space Package (CSP). 20 August 1993.

[12] Ibid.

[13] Battle Command Battle Laboratory Briefing, "Louisiana Maneuver General Officer Working Group," 9 September 1993. Colonel Roundtree was later promoted to Brigadier General.

[14] Ibid.

[15] Ibid.

[16] Ibid.

[17] Memorandum, Brigadier General Edward G. Anderson III, Deputy Commanding General, US Army Combined Arms Command and Ft. Leavenworth, to Deputy Chief of Staff for Combat Development, Subject: FY93 LAM Commercial Space Package. 2 October 1993.

[18] Memorandum, Brigadier General Edward G. Anderson III, Deputy Commanding General, US Army Combined Arms Command and Ft. Leavenworth, to BCBL LAM GOWG Participants, Subject: FY93 LAM Commercial Space Package (CSP), 14 September 1993.

[19] Ibid.

[20] Ibid.

[21] Ibid.

[22] Ibid.

[23] Memorandum, Brigadier General Edward G. Anderson III, Deputy Commanding General, US Army Combined Arms Command and Ft. Leavenworth, to Deputy Chief of Staff for Combat Development, TRADOC, Subject: FY93 LAM Commercial Space Package (CSP). 23 November 1993.

[24] Ibid.

[25] Ibid.

[26] Ibid.

[27] Memorandum, General Frederick M. Franks, Jr., U.S. Army Training and Doctrine Command, to General Gordon R. Sullivan, Chief of Staff, United States Army, Subject: FY93 LAM Commercial Space Package (CSP). 12 January 1994.

[28] Memorandum, General Gordon R. Sullivan, to Commander, Training and Doctrine Command, Subject: FY93 Commercial Space Package (CSP). 3 March 1994.

[29] Memorandum, Brigadier General Edward G. Anderson III, U.S. Army Training and Doctrine Command, to Deputy Chief of Staff, Operations, ATTN: DAMO-FD, Subject: Operational Needs Statement (ONS) for the Commercial Space Package (CSP). 18 March 1994.

[30] U.S. Army Space Command Briefing, "Contingency Operations Space," Undated.

[31] Headquarters, Department of the Army, "HQDA Program Release Worksheet for Input into the Program Budget Accounting System to SAFM-BUI-I from SARD-RR." 30 March 1994. Acquisition responsibilities were divided between four project managers, with PEO-CCS serving as the Milestone Decision Authority. Under this acquisition approach, the Project Manager Satellite Communications acquired the INMARSAT Terminals, the Project Manager CTIS acquired the MSIPs, the Program Manager IMETS was responsible for acquisition of the (2) weather receivers and worked the acquisition through the ARSPACE contracting office, and the Project Manager ASAS was responsible for the acquisition of the 5 MPRSs and worked the acquisition through the ARSPACE contracting office. Editorial comments made by Mrs. Daryll Nottingham, USARSPACE, in an e-mail message sent to Dr. James A. Walker on 16 February 1999.

[32] Editorial comments made by Mr. Tom Callaghan, USARSPACE, in an e-mail message sent to Dr. James A. Walker on 16 February 1999. The number of authorized personnel was listed as eleven in original source documentation. Femme Comp Incorporated, Satellite Communications Group, Draft Contingency Operations (Space) Concept of Operations (September 1994 Draft). Electronic copy of document on floppy diskette. Diskette found in ARSST Division files.

[33] Memorandum, Major General Jay M. Garner, Headquarters, Department of the Army (Office of the Deputy Chief of Staff for Operations and Plans), to Assistant Secretary for Plans and Programs, Office of the Assistant Secretary of the Army (Research, Development and Acquisition), Subject: Urgent Operational Requirement for a Commercial Space Package (CSP) Contingency Set. 9 May 1994.

[34] U.S. Army Space Command Briefing, "Contingency Operations Space," Undated.

[35] Ibid.

[36] Ibid.

[37] Ibid.

[38] Ibid.

[39] Major Jensen, Call the COPS. (Colorado Springs, Colorado: U.S. Army Space Command, undated.).

[40] Editorial comments made by Mr. Tom Callaghan, USARSPACE, in an e-mail message sent to Dr. James A. Walker on 16 February 1999. The number of authorized personnel was listed as eleven in original source documentation. Major Jensen, Call the COPS. (Colorado Springs, Colorado: U.S. Army Space Command, undated.).

[41] PBAC is a committee comprised of the principal staff officers of a command, agency, or installation headquarters, and established for the purpose of coordinating program and budget actions within the command.

[42] U.S. Army Space Command Briefing, "4th Qtr PBAC," 21 June 1994.

[43] Editorial comments made by Mr. Tom Callaghan, USARSPACE, in an e-mail message sent to Dr. James A. Walker on 16 February 1999.

[44] U.S. Army Space Command Briefing, "COPS IPR," Undated.

[45] Major Jensen, Call the COPS. (Colorado Springs, Colorado: U.S. Army Space Command, undated.).

[46] U.S. Army Space Command Briefing, "Contingency Operations Space," Undated.

[47] Femme Comp Incorporated, Satellite Communications Group, Task Order Plan 95-08: Contingency Operations (Space) / COPS Documentation Development. 26 September 1994.

[48] Femme Comp Incorporated, Satellite Communications Group, Contingency Operations – Space (COPS) Standard Operating Procedures (SOPS) Initial Draft. 16 August 1994.

[49] Ibid.

[50] Ibid.

[51] Femme Comp Incorporated, Satellite Communications Group, Draft Contingency Operations (Space) Concept of Operations (September 1994 Draft). Electronic copy of document on floppy diskette. Diskette found in ARSST Division files.

[52] Ibid.

[53] Ibid.

[54] Ibid.

[55] Ibid.

[56] Femme Comp Incorporated, Satellite Communications Group, <u>Task Order Plan 95-08: Contingency Operations (Space) / COPS Documentation Development</u>. 26 September 1994.

[57] U.S. Army Space Command, <u>Army Space Support Team (ARSST) Concept of Operations (CONOPS) (DRAFT)</u>. (Colorado Springs, Colorado: U.S. Army Space Command: 12 December 1994.).

[58] U.S. Space Command, <u>USSPACECOM Regulation 11-5: USSPACECOM Support to Theater Operations Management Program</u>. (Peterson Air Force Base, Colorado: Headquarters United States Space Command, 14 April 1993), pp. 2-3.

[59] Dr. James Walker and James Hooper, "James H. Williamson Oral History Interview, ARSST Historical/Lessons Learned Study," 22 October 1998.

[60] In joint operational plans (OPLANs), Annex N was reserved to address space support.

[61] Ricky B. Kelly, <u>Centralized Control of Space: The Use of Space Forces by a Joint Force Commander</u>. (Maxwell Air Force Base, Alabama: School of Advanced Airpower Studies, 22 September 1994), p. 32.

[62] U.S. Army Space Command, <u>Army Space Support Team (ARSST) Concept of Operations (CONOPS) (DRAFT)</u>. (Colorado Springs, Colorado: U.S. Army Space Command: 12 December 1994.).

[63] Ibid.

[64] Ibid.

[65] Ibid.

[66] Memorandum, L.D. Pawlak, Army Audit Agency, to Commander, U.S. Army Space and Strategic Defense Command, Subject: Draft Report on the Audit of Mission Contingency Stock, U.S. Army Space Command. 8 June 1994.

CHAPTER THREE:

EVOLUTION OF ARSST OPERATIONS (1995 TO 1998)

"Space is the highest hill around, but since it does not have dirt on it too many in the Army are not prepared to deal with it."

--Ed Kiker, Army Space Institute, 1992.

This chapter provides an historical summary of ARSST operations from 1995 to 1998, tracing ARSST team deployments as well as the evolution of concepts for field space support. The chapter has been divided into four subsections, each corresponding to a particular year of ARSST operations. The subsections nclude an overview of the concept of operations, a synopsis of deployments, a consideration of the major issues, and a summary of key space support lessons learned.

1995: On 1 January 1995, the ARSST was officially activated and teams began deploying to the field to provide space support enhancement. At the beginning of the year, the ARSST was divided into three teams, each aligned with a Combatant Command (EUCOM, PACOM, and CENTCOM). Over the course of the year, the ARSST took steps to respond to the heavy demands for support placed on the team by the XVIII Airborne Corps and Army special operations forces, negotiating an agreement under which an ARSST team would be forward-deployed at Ft. Bragg.

1996: The ARSST CONOPS and organizational structure underwent significant changes in 1996. In January 1996, the ARSST formally reviewed lessons learned in 1995 and examined options for restructuring the teams to provide enhanced support to warfighting units.

1997: ARSST operations in 1997 were conducted under a new organizational construct, with 5 teams prepared to support each of the Corps Headquarters and U.S. Army Special Operations Command. The ARSST continued to explore ways to improve the level of space support, however, to include the forward deployment of ARSST teams and liaison personnel, the rotational deployment of teams, and the establishment of a self-sustainment capability.

1998: During this year, the Army Space Support Cell concept was implemented and exercised. In another development, the only forward-deployed ARSST team was reassigned from Ft. Bragg to Colorado Springs.

Arsst Operations and Evolution, 1995

On 1 January 1995, the ARSST teams officially began deploying in support of field units. During the course of the year, ARSST personnel would gain valuable insights into supported unit requirements, develop and refine processes for integrating the ARSST into field operations, and reorganize to provide more responsive support to the heaviest consumers of ARSST products (XVIII Airborne Corps and U.S. Army Special Operations Command).

1995 Concept Of Operations

On 20 April 1995, the draft ARSST Concept of Operations was formally approved by the Commander, USARSPACE (Forward).[1] In its essential elements, few changes had been made from the CONOPS that had been drafted and revised over the August-December 1994 timeframe. The April 1995 CONOPS still envisioned that the ARSST would be divided into three teams, each led by an Army Space

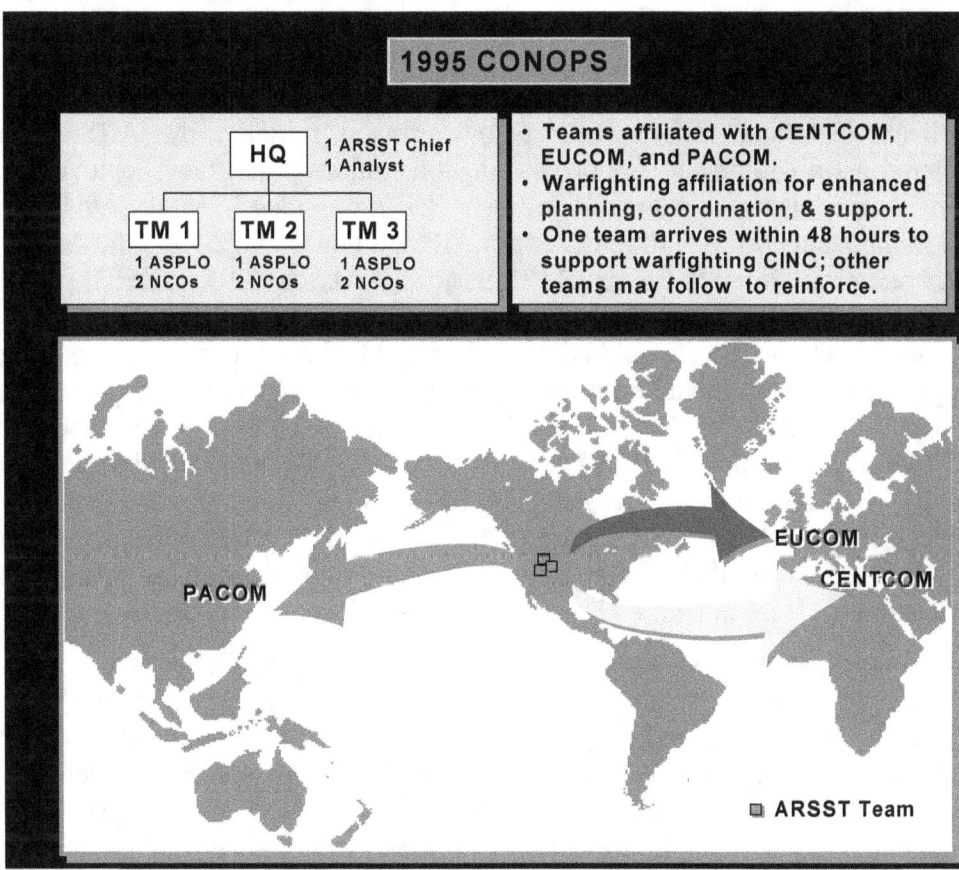

Figure 6: The ARSST Concept of Operations, 1995.

Liaison Officer and staffed with two non-commissioned officers who would be responsible for manning equipment and training supported units. As with previous versions of the CONOPS, an ARSST team was to be prepared to deploy within 48 hours of an alert notification. The major difference between the April 1995 CONOPS and previous versions was in the concept of deployment readiness cycles and ARSST team affiliation. The April 1995 CONOPS no longer included a three-tiered deployment readiness structure, with a Blue Cycle, a Green Cycle, and a Red Cycle. Instead, each of the three ARSST teams was aligned with a specific Combatant Command headquarters. The Combatant Command headquarters designated for support were U.S. European Command (USEUCOM), U.S. Pacific Command (USPACOM), and U.S. Central Command (USCENTCOM).

ARSST Field Deployments

At the beginning of the year, the ARSST focused on training operators on employment of the satellite weather receiver and the Mission Planning Rehearsal System.[2] Once this training was completed in February 1995, the ARSST started deploying teams on an aggressive schedule of field exercises and system demonstrations. By the end of the year, the ARSST had supported six Corps and Joint Task Force-level exercises, three Division-level exercises, and three special operations exercises. In addition, the ARSST conducted an estimated 13 equipment demonstrations and sent personnel to support three Force Projection Tactical Operations Center (FP TOC) exercises. Initially, the ARSST teams centered upon equipment support and demonstrations when they deployed to the field. From January to March 1995, the ARSST provided INMARSAT terminals and training support to both the 1st Marine Expeditionary Force and the Army's 7th Transportation Group.[3] From 26 February to 3 March 1995, ARSST personnel supported FP TOC demonstrations conducted at the Army War College and the Pentagon.[4] The ARSST would continue to provide demonstrations and equipment support to the field, including a training support mission to the U.S. Air Force 5th Weather Squadron in Korea that lasted from 30 May to 15 June 1995[5]; INMARSAT training for the 4th Infantry Division (Mechanized) during exercise INTRINSIC ACTION in Kuwait; MPRS training for the III Corps terrain detachment; and INMARSAT support for an 82nd Airborne Division exercise in the Ukraine.[6] Nevertheless, the focus of ARSST support began to shift in spring 1995 as teams were integrated into Corps- and Division-level exercises

On 10 April 1995, ARSST Team 1 deployed to ROVING SANDS 95. After providing air and theater missile defense support in conjunction with the Force Projection Tactical Operations Center, the ARSST team redeployed to Colorado Springs on 28 May 1995.[7] In the meantime, ARSST personnel had deployed in support of the 82nd Airborne Division's exercise BIG DROP II. The ARSST supported BIG DROP II from 2 to 9 May 1995 by providing equipment demonstrations and field training.[8]

In 1995, the ARSST also supported the annual COBRA GOLD exercise in the Pacific theater of operations. ARSST team members participated in the planning of the exercise and supported a 1st Special Forces Group (SFG) Command Post Exercise (CPX) designed to prepare for COBRA GOLD that was conducted from 20 to 31 March 1995. ARSST Team 3 subsequently deployed from 24 April to 31 May 1995 in support of COBRA GOLD 95.[9]

The 82nd Airborne Division was supported again by an ARSST when Team 1 deployed to GIANT STEP XX. Team 1 personnel participated in this Division exercise from 30 June to 20 July 1995.[10] The ARSST also supported XVIII Airborne Corps during the annual FUERTAS DEFENSAS exercise. During FUERTAS DEFENSAS 95, ARSST Team 2 deployed to Panama from 14 August to 18 September 1995 to support the Corps headquarters.[11]

While ARSST Team 2 was deployed in Panama, ARSST Team 3 was providing support in Korea during ULCHI FOCUS LENS 95. ARSST team members participated in the ULCHI FOCUS LENS planning process from February to July 1995, to include deployment to a 1st Special Force Group CPX from 10 to 20 July 1995. During ULCHI FOCUS LENS, the ARSST provided support to both the Eighth U.S. Army staff and the 1st Special Forces Group.[12]

The ARSST also supported U.S. Army operations in Europe. The ARSST supported the 1st Armored Division during a Warfighting Exercise (WFX) from 13 to 19 November 1995. ARSST personnel developed imagery maps and 3-dimensional fly-throughs of Macedonia for the 1st Armored Division. In addition, the ARSST supported V Corps during exercises MOUNTAIN SHIELD I and II.[13]

ARSST Team 1 supported BRIGHT STAR 95 in Egypt from 28 October to 15 November 1995, deploying in support of the 24th Infantry Division (Mechanized).[14] During this exercise, the ARSST also supported the FP TOC with MPRS.[15]

One of the heaviest consumers of ARSST products in 1995 was the special operations community. During 1995, every one of the active-duty Special Forces Groups received support from an ARSST. The 1st Special Forces Group received equipment support in January 1995 and exercise support during COBRA GOLD 95, ULCHI FOCUS LENS 95, and an internal CPX. The 3rd Special Forces Group received INMARSAT training during a deployment to Tunisia. The 5th Special Forces Group was supported with imagery products during ROVING SANDS 95. The 7th Special Forces Group was loaned ARSST equipment from 18 February to 25 March 1995. During JRTC Rotation 95-6, the 7th Special Forces Group was provided INMARSAT, imagery, and training support. Also, the ARSST provided imagery support to the 7th Special Forces Group during a border dispute between Peru and Ecuador. Finally, the ARSST supported the 10th Special Forces Group during a Command Post Exercise from 4 to 8 October 1995. ARSST Team 2 later deployed to support the 10th SFG during the WARRIOR FOCUS Army Warfighting Experiment (AWE) exercise conducted at the Joint Readiness Training Center.[16]

XVIII Airborne Corps Support

The XVIII Airborne Corps was a particularly heavy consumer of ARSST space support products in 1995. Consequently, the Corps headquarters staff and USARSPACE grappled throughout the year with the issue of how the ARSST could best be organized to support XVIII Airborne Corps units. In addition, the

Figure 7: Key ARSST Deployments, 1995.

Support	Quarter	Exercise
I Corps	1st Quarter 1995	
	2nd Quarter 1995	COBRA GOLD 95
	3rd Quarter 1995	
	4th Quarter 1995	
III Corps	1st Quarter 1995	
	2nd Quarter 1995	
	3rd Quarter 1995	
	4th Quarter 1995	
V Corps	1st Quarter 1995	
	2nd Quarter 1995	
	3rd Quarter 1995	
	4th Quarter 1995	V CORPS WARFIGHTER
XVIII Airborne Corps	1st Quarter 1995	
	2nd Quarter 1995	BIG DROP II
		GIANT STEP XX
	3rd Quarter 1995	FUERTAS DEFENSAS 95
	4th Quarter 1995	BRIGHT STAR 95
Echelons Above Corps/Other	1st Quarter 1995	JRTC ROTATION 95-6 (7th SFG)
	2nd Quarter 1995	COBRA GOLD CPX (1st SFG)
		ROVING SANDS 95 (5th SFG)
	3rd Quarter 1995	ULCHI FOCUS LENS 95 (Eighth Army and 1st SFG)
		DYNAMIC MIX (EUCOM)
	4th Quarter 1995	WARRIOR FOCUS AWE JRTC rotation (10th SFG)

U.S. Army Special Operations Command (USASOC), which was also located at Ft. Bragg, North Carolina, reported a high level of demand for ARSST support. These demands led USARSPACE to consider the permanent assignment of space support personnel to Ft. Bragg.

On 24 April 1995, Major Toupin and Mr. Evans of USARSPACE met with the XVIII Airborne Corps G-2 (Colonel Seiter) and Corps G-3 (Colonel Groening) to discuss ARSST support. During this meeting, both Colonel Seiter and Colonel Groening emphasized their desire that an ARSST team be forward-deployed with the Corps Headquarters. The officers emphasized that, "if the ARSST was not part of the day to day business of the Corps, they would not be included in the OPLANS or be of value to the Corps." Colonel Seiter cited the deployment of USARSPACE personnel to support the Corps during Operation UPHOLD DEMOCRACY, noting that they arrived "too late to help influence the decision making cycle. Also, the team was not integrated into the TPFDL or into any G staff section."[17] After this meeting, USARSPACE received a formal request from Brigadier General Akers (XVIII Airborne Corps Chief of Staff) for permanent attachment of an ARSST to the Corps. General Akers argued that the rapid deployment of XVIII Airborne Corps units necessitated that an ARSST team be integrated into the Corps headquarters staff on a daily basis.[18]

In response to the XVIII Airborne Corps request, Colonel E. Paul Semmens (USARSPACE Commander) developed three options for support. Under the first option, an ARSST team would be assigned to provide support to XVIII Airborne Corps, but would remain at Colorado Springs. This option would enable USARSPACE to task-organize an ARSST team for support to the Corps and would allow the ARSST to prepare supporting imagery data using the faster computers available at Colorado Springs. "Disadvantages are that the ARSST chosen to support the contingency will be working behind the power curve. Also there would not be the habitual working relationship and trust that comes from daily face to face interaction."[19] The second option considered by Colonel Semmens was the attachment of an ARSST team to the Corps G-2 (Intelligence) Section. The advantage of this approach would be that the ARSST could interface on a day-to-day basis with both the Corps Headquarters and the U.S. Army Special Operations Command. On the other hand, this option would result in the "loss of immediate control of an ARSST to the commander of USARSPACE (FWD)."[20] The last option considered by Colonel Semmons was to increase the USARSPACE Liaison Officer contingent at Fort Bragg to two personnel, one of whom would support the Corps Headquarters while the other supported USASOC. This would provide increased visibility for USARSPACE and ensure that space support was integrated into the planning cycle. "The disadvantage of this option is that the ARSST is not responsive to contingency as it could be deployed on another mission when a contingency occurs. This situation could call for a long spin up time for the ARSST and thus decrease the value of XVIII Corps/USASOC use of enhanced warfighting capabilities."[21] Of the three options, Colonel Semmens was inclined to adopt the second.

A second analysis of ARSST forward deployment options was conducted on 17 July 1995 by Major(P) Armando R. Macias (ARSPACE Director of Operations). In this analysis, Major Macias included an assessment of the impacts of stationing an ARSST team at Ft. Bragg upon USARSPACE's capability for supporting other Army exercises and contingency missions. Major Macias began his analysis by identifying a series of issues stemming from the proposal to assign an ARSST team permanently at Ft. Bragg. First, the team would have to cope with the issue of keeping imagery files on-hand for its MPRS equipment. Second, it would be more difficult to train ARSST personnel and maintain ARSST equipment if the team was located at Ft. Bragg rather than at the home station in Colorado Springs. Finally, support relationships with XVIII Airborne Corps and USASOC would have to be delineated. After identifying these key factors, Major Macias outlined three options for supporting XVIII Airborne Corps.

OPTION 1: Attach a four-man ARSST team to XVIII Airborne Corps Headquarters with a standard suite of ARSST equipment (1 satellite weather terminal, 1 MSIP 1 MPRS, 4 INMARSAT terminals). Major Macias notes that this approach would reduce the timeline for deployment of an ARSST during an actual contingency mission and would "allow involvement in all XVIII ABC activities." However, training and maintenance support for the team would be degraded. Furthermore, since the ARSST only had a total of 2 MSIPs and 2 weather receivers assigned at the time, this would leave "only one complete suite of equipment ... to support the rest of the Army for both exercises and contingencies."[22]

OPTION 2: Attach a four-man ARSST team to the Corps Headquarters with a modified suite of equipment (1 MPRS, 2 INMARSAT terminals). Send additional ARSST equipment from Colorado Springs as required. Major Macias believed that this approach would yield the same advantages of Option 1 (reduced timelines for ARSST deployment and involvement in all ARSST activities) and would suffer from similar disadvantages (training and equipment maintenance difficulties). However, this option would not degrade the ability of the ARSST to provide support to the rest of the Army.

OPTION 3: Attach an officer to XVIII Airborne Corps to perform daily coordination and planning. Personnel from USARSPACE would deploy from Colorado Springs on temporary duty to support the Corps and USASOC as needed. ARSST equipment forward-deployed at Ft. Bragg would include 1 MPRS and 2 INMARSAT terminals. Major Macias cited a number of advantages stemming from this option. First, it would allow daily coordination between the ARSST and the Corps Headquarters. Second, ARSST personnel could be trained to standard at their home station in Colorado Springs. Third, there would be less degradation of technical and maintenance support. Fourth, USARSPACE would have maximum flexibility in the deployment of ARSST personnel and equipment to support other Army exercises and contingencies. Major Macias cited no disadvantages stemming from the adoption of Option 3. Given existing ARSST equipment and personnel resource constraints, Major Macias recommended that the Command adopt the third option.[23]

Lieutenant General Jay Garner, then serving as Commanding General, U.S. Army Space and Strategic Defense Command, intervened on 26 July 1995 and made the decision to assign an ARSST team to the XVIII Airborne Corps Headquarters at Ft. Bragg. Three reasons were cited for this decision. First, this would allow XVIII Airborne Corps and its subordinate units to make routine use of ARSST equipment and capabilities. Second, a habitual relationship would be established between the ARSST team and the supported units, allowing the ARSST to be integrated into all facets of operational planning and deployment. Finally, the forward deployment of an ARSST team would be in accordance with the Army's "train-as-you-fight" principle.[24]

In accordance with Lieutenant General Garner's guidance, Major Toupin was reassigned to Ft. Bragg on 1 August 1995 and directed to establish the forward-deployed ARSST team. Major Toupin requested that his ARSST team be provided the following equipment: 2 MPRS/MSTS, 2 MSIP, 1 High Resolution Weather Satellite Receiver (HRWSR), and 2 INMARSAT terminals.[25] Five days later, the XVIII Airborne Corps requested that all personnel assigned to the ARSST team at Ft. Bragg be airborne qualified.[26] These decisions would be incorporated into a Memorandum of Agreement between the XVIII Airborne Corps, the U.S. Army Special Operations Command, and U.S. Army Space Command (Forward), which was signed in March 1996.

Figure 8: Options for ARSST forward deployment (COLONEL Semmens).

Option	Advantages	Disadvantages
Designate an ARSST team at Colorado Springs to support XVIII Airborne Corps.	Task-organize the ARSST for specific missions. Utilize the better equipment at Colorado Springs.	ARSST not integrated into planning at early stage. Lack of daily interaction with supported units.
Attach an ARSST team to the Corps G-2.	Daily interface with Corps and USASOC staff.	Difficult for USARSPACE to control and support the ARSST team.
Increase the size of the usarspace liaison at ft. Bragg.	Daily LNO coordination with the Corps and USASOC staffs. Space support integrated into planning cycle.	ARSST team support not be available during early stages of contingency planning and execution.

Figure 9: Options for ARSST forward deployment (Major Armando Macias).		
Option	Advantages	Disadvantages
Attach a four-man ARSST team to XVIII Airborne Corps Headquarters with a full suite of equipment.	Reduced timeline for deployment. Would allow frequent interaction with the Corps staff.	Training and maintenance difficulties. Would leave only one complete suite of equipmer for rest of the Army.
Attach a four-man ARSST team to the Corps with a modified suite of equipment.	Reduced timeline for deployment. Would allow frequent interaction with the Corps staff.	Training and maintenance difficulties.
LNO stationed at Fort Bragg. Some ARSST equipment forward- deployed. Arsst personnel deploy as needed.	Interaction with Corps and USASOC staff. Train ARSST at home station. Better equipment support. Maximum USARSPACE flexibility to support other Army exercises and contingencies.	None identified.

1995 ARSST Lessons Learned

By the end of 1995, the ARSST had participated in a number of exercises and deployments. During a review of ARSST operations conducted on 11 January 1996, a number of key lessons learned were identified and discussed. First, the ARSST must be able to provide all types of space support, rather than simply operating specific items of space support equipment. The existing commercial space package (CSP) equipment was insufficient to meet all requirements in Army field units and headquarters. Second, the ARSST teams needed a limited self-sustainment capability. A number of supported units had reported that the requirement to provide sustainment support to ARSST personnel placed heavy demands and burdens on their own operations. Third, the ARSST must obtain the capability to receive large data files in remote locations. This would enable the teams to access space products and capabilities generated by U.S. Army Space Command and U.S. Space Command in Colorado Springs, Colorado. Fourth, the operational process for the warfighter to obtain space support must be streamlined. Fifth, the existing force structure was insufficient to provide space support to more than one major regional conflict (MRC). Six, ARSST support had been largely focused at the corps and division headquarter level. ARSST personnel desired to extend space information, capabilities, and products down to brigade commanders and staffs, where the demand for space support seemed to be quite high.

The ARRST teams also reported that they had little ability to communicate and interface with the deployed space support teams from other Services. Related to this issue was a need for communications security (COMSEC) equipment that met military standards. ARSST personnel also reported problems with existing maintenance procedures. Much of the equipment employed by the ARSST consisted of commercial, off-the-shelf systems. The ARSST teams identified the need to streamline and tailor maintenance procedures to account for military requirements. Finally, the ARSST teams emphasized the need for additional training and experience to incorporate space capabilities into the tactical decision-making process of field units. This issue would require further experimentation, exercises, and development by the Army.[27]

The collection, analysis, discussion, and dissemination of these lessons learned during the first year marked an important step in the evolution of the ARSST. Major Jensen would use these lessons as the basis for his efforts to upgrade the Army Space Support Team capability in 1996.

Arsst Operations and Evolution, 1996

During 1996, the ARSST attempted to digest the lessons learned during the previous year and restructure its operations to provide enhanced support to warfighting units. Major Jensen urged that the ARSST be upgraded to support two major regional conflicts, that new systems and technologies be provided to the ARSST, and that the ARSST focus on space advisory and liaison functions. Throughout the year, the ARSST would pursue a number of initiatives intended to achieve this vision.

1996 Concept of Operations

When 1996 began, the only change to the ARSST Concept of Operations was the alignment of the ARSST teams with the Combatant Commands. Under the 1995 ARSST concept of operations, the teams were affiliated with USCENTCOM, USEUCOM, and USPACOM. In January 1996, USSPACECOM reported an extended ARSST team alignment structure, with one team affiliated with both USCENTCOM and U.S. Atlantic Command (USACOM), one team affiliated with both USEUCOM and U.S. Southern Command (USSOUTHCOM), and the last team affiliated with USPACOM.[28]

The ARSST organizational structure would undergo further revisions over the course of the year. In March 1996, a Memorandum of Agreement between XVIII Airborne Corps, U.S. Army Special Operations Command, and USARSPACE (Forward) was signed under which an ARSST team would be forwarded-deployed at Ft. Bragg. The ARSST was reorganized to reflect this change. As of July 1996, the ARSST was authorized a headquarters section (3 personnel), a USCENTCOM team (2 personnel), a USEUCOM team and a USPACOM team (both with 4 personnel), and a XVIII Corps team (3 personnel).[29] By 1997, the focus of ARSST support had changed again. Rather than aligning the ARSST teams with Combatant Commands, the teams were aligned with each of the four Corps headquarters (I Corps, III Corps, V Corps, and XVIII Airborne Corps). In addition, based upon the repeated requests for ARSST support made by the special operations community, a fifth ARSST team was activated specifically to support special operations units.

ARSST Planning, January 1996

On 11 January 1996, the ARSST Division conducted another formal review of operations and lessons learned in 1995, with the goal of providing enhanced support to warfighting units in the coming year. A number of concerns were expressed by ARSST team members at this review session. From an operational standpoint, ARSST team members noted that they did not have the personnel or equipment to provide simultaneous support for more than one major Army deployment. Current resource levels also precluded the ARSST from providing support at the maneuver brigade level, where it was felt that space information and products would significantly enhance operations. In addition, ARSST team members expressed concerns about the logistical and administrative burdens imposed upon a supported unit by a deploying ARSST team. Furthermore, it was noted that the ARSST teams had had little interface with other deployed space support teams during exercises in 1995. This was viewed as another area of weakness.

From an equipment standpoint, concerns were expressed in a number of areas. Foremost was the perception that the ARSST teams were simply manning the four systems acquired as part of the Commercial Space Package. It was asserted that the "ARSST must be able to provide all types of space support – not just four pieces of equipment." ARSST team members also noted the need for a communications capability that would allow them to acquire large data files in remote locations, access the full spectrum of USARSPACE (Forward) capabilities while deployed in the field, and interface with other space support elements operating in theater. Finally, concerns were expressed regarding the maintenance of equipment; ARSST team members saw a need for the streamlining of the support process.[30]

 More fundamental than the concerns about weak areas of ARSST organization and employment, however, were fears that the ARSST was not truly providing a value-added to the supported unit. For example, during one briefing on Army

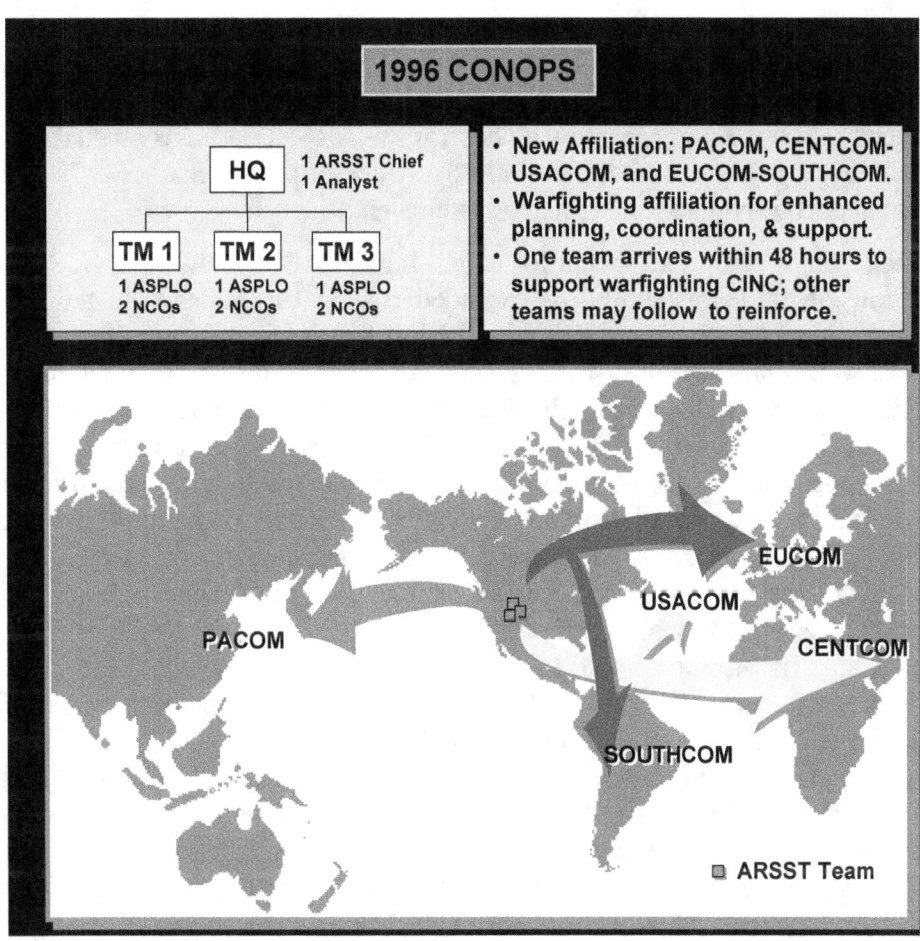

Figure 10: The ARSST Concept of Operations, 1996.

space support it was claimed: "The Army views our capabilities with interest but has not really wanted them in T[ask] F[orce] XXI or Bosnia and, as a result, doesn't have the best that is currently available. That means ASEDP, demos, ARSST have limited success."[31]

Given these identified areas of concern, Major Jensen proposed three major efforts to upgrade the ARSST. First, he recommended that the ARSST Division be provided with additional personnel, equipment, and resources. This would allow the ARSST to support two simultaneous major regional conflicts, which Major Jensen viewed as a DoD requirement he was currently unable to meet. The *National Security Strategy of the United States* called for DoD to maintain the capability to fight two MRCs at once. Major Jensen may also have been influenced by the USARSPACE experience in Haiti, where "Both 10th Mtn Division and XVIII Airborne Corps perceived that they were slighted by the Space Support Team structure, which was designed for one division, but was split across two Joint Task Forces. In October [1994], when forces were alerted for deployment to Kuwait, little space support equipment was on hand to augment divisions slated for movement at that time."[32]

Second, Major Jensen recommended that an aggressive strategy of equipment acquisition and upgrades be pursued. This would include close coordination with the Army Space Exploitation and Demonstration Program process to ensure that new technologies and systems were fed to the ARSST teams, as well as continued upgrades to existing equipment to remain on the technological cutting-edge. Most importantly, Major Jensen foresaw a need for the ARSST to focus on space advice and analysis. He emphasized, "Instead of just operating systems ARSST must be able to support warfighter on all space systems and issues."[33]

Central to Major Jensen's concept for upgrading the ARSSTs was his view that the future role of the teams should be extended past that established in the existing ARSST concept of operations. Under Major Jensen's vision of the future, the ARSSTs would provide multi-faceted space support to the Army, extending from operational support and space analysis to force development and education. On an operational level, the ARSSTs would continue to provide a rapidly deployable space support capability and would be responsible for helping supported units develop and execute operations plans. ARSST personnel and equipment would be available to augment Army units during exercises as needed. The ARSSTs would also serve as the space liaison to the supported unit, providing a "'home' for all steady state capabilities assigned to ARSPACE." ARSSTs would support the entire Army, providing "direct space support liaison to selected Brigades, all Divisions and Corps." The ARSST would also participate in Army force development efforts. As the Army restructured itself to take advantage of new technologies under the Louisiana Maneuvers process, the ARSSTs would "test and evaluate Force Development employment and organizational concepts." Furthermore, the ARSST would play a leading role in the space education of the Army by providing technology demonstrations and equipment training. However, this role would be extended through a "'Green Suit' education program to TRADOC schools."[34]

Space Demonstration Program Planning, January 1996

Major Jensen's emphasis on acquiring new technologies and capabilities was shared by personnel involved with the ASEDP process. On 8 January 1996, ASEDP conducted the first in a series of reviews of the program. During the first meeting, the need for close cooperation between ARSST and the demonstration program was stressed. A three-pronged ARSST approach was envisioned, under which the "ARSST must be prepared to assist demo personnel train, deploy with limited assets when requested, [and] assist Division Commanders buy more capability quantity when that is possible."[35]

On 12 January 1996, a second meeting on the ASEDP process was conducted. During this meeting, the need to provide new systems and capabilities to the ARSST was established as a key priority. One week later, a third ASEDP meeting was conducted. During this meeting, a series of impediments to the ASEDP process were discussed, to include problems in identifying exercise opportunities, a declining level of participation by both field units and industry, and management difficulties arising from the diffusion of ASEDP funding sources and approval authority.[36]

During the 19 January 1996 ASEDP meeting, participants also discussed a long-range vision for the future. The ASEDP vision consisted of five primary elements. First, ASEDP would demonstrate new technologies and identify systems for possible further development. Second, ASEDP would educate tactical commanders on the use of space-based assets. Third, ASEDP would be responsible for identifying and defining space system requirements for materiel development. Fourth, ASEDP would be involved in the design and development of future space systems. Finally, the ASEDP would provide a rapid prototyping capability to support Army contingency operations.[37] Clearly, some overlap existed between the ASEDP and ARSST visions of their future roles and missions. Most important, however, was the fact that general agreement existed between the two programs on the need to supply the ARSST with the latest systems and technologies. ASEDP understood this requirement and continued to discuss possible solutions in 1996.

ARSST Field Deployments, 1996

The most significant ARSST deployment in 1996 was the deployment to Tuzla to support the 1st Infantry Division in Bosnia. This deployment marked the first time that an ARSST deployed in support of an actual contingency mission rather than a training exercise.

The Bosnia deployment began in October 1996 with the deployment of an ARSST team led by Captain Cuthbertson. The team traveled to Vicenza, Italy where an Air Force Space Support Team was supporting air operations in the region.[38] Here, the ARSST team received software upgrades for some of its equipment and trained its personnel on the new capabilities. The ARSST team then deployed to Tuzla on 22 October 1996 and began testing its equipment.[39]

After deployment in-theater, the ARSST provided imagery, weather and Mission Planning Rehearsal System (MPRS) support to the 1st Infantry Division, with primary focus on the 11th Aviation Regiment. Hardware and software difficulties were experienced with the Space Support Platform and High Resolution Weather Satellite Receiver (HRSWR), detracting from the level of support the ARSST was able to provide. The ARSST continued to work those issues, while "experimenting with imagery merge combinations of Landsat TM, SPOT, IFSARE, and national imagery in order to provide new products which may be of higher value to the Division." The ARSST also provided training to 1st Infantry Division soldiers on weather systems and the Mission Planning Rehearsal System (which was retained in theater).[40] On 8 December 1996, the ARSST was redeployed to Colorado Springs, with a mission to provide continued support to the 1st Infantry Division and OPERATION JOINT ENDEAVOR as required.

A number of key lessons were learned during the deployment to Bosnia. First, when the ARSST concept of operations was developed in 1995, it had been assumed that deployment taskings would originate from HQDA. During the Bosnia deployment, the tasking order was issued instead by the Joint Staff. Due to confusion regarding tasking responsibility during an actual contingency mission, Captain Cuthbertson did not receive the tasking order until after he had been deployed in Bosnia for approximately 30 days.[41]

Captain Cuthbertson also found during the Bosnia deployment that the ability of his team to provide support to the 1st Infantry Division was hindered by a lack of involvement in the pre-deployment phase. Captain Cuthbertson would later observe: "I took a mission planning system to an Apache battalion in Bosnia. Unfortunately, by the time we got there they already knew the terrain and they were in a stagnant situation, so they were happy to have it, but it could have been more effective in pre-deployment than after deployment."[42]

During the Bosnia deployment, the Air Force Staff Weather Officer made

> **Lessons Learned — the ARSST deployment to Bosnia.**
>
> - **Tasking for the deployment originated with the Joint Staff rather than HQDA.**
>
> - **The ability of an ARSST to support field units successfully is largely contingent upon the level of preplanning conducted.**
>
> - **The HRWSR was not used to support operations due to an Air Force decision not to cooperate with the deployed ARSST.**
>
> - **INMARSATs were widely used in Bosnia, compensating for the rudimentary communications infrastructure in-theater.**
>
> - **Repeated technical problems with the Space Support Platform were experienced. The ARSST team was never able to overcome all of these problems while deployed.**
>
> - **Captain Cuthbertson returned from Bosnia convinced that a self-sustainment capability needed to be developed for the ARSST teams.**

no use of the High Resolution Weather Satellite Receiver brought by the ARSST. In the view of ARSST personnel deployed to Bosnia, that decision was the result of Air Force objections to the Army's involvement in weather support, which had traditionally been an Air Force mission.[43] Because the ARSSTs did not have the capability to analyze meteorological data on

their own, the HRWSR was of little use in Bosnia. The lack of USARSPACE support to the ARSST team was cited as another area of concern by soldiers deployed to support the Bosnia mission.[44]

Repeated technical difficulties were experienced by the Space Support Platform. The ARSST team was never able to fix all of these problems while deployed in theater. On the other hand, the INMARSAT terminals that the ARSST team brought to Bosnia were widely used. Given the rudimentary communications infrastructure in Bosnia, field units took advantage of INMARSAT to fulfill a number of communications requirements.[45]

In addition to the deployment to Bosnia, ARSST teams supported a broad range of Army exercises in 1996. Perhaps the most significant exercise supported was ULCHI FOCUS LENS 96. ULCHI FOCUS LENS is an annual, theater-wide command post exercise that simulates a North Korean People's Army offensive into South Korea. The Combined Forces Command in Korea uses ULCHI FOCUS LENS as its keystone exercise, enabling commanders and staffs to conduct warfighting training and exercise their operations plans. ARSST support to ULCHI FOCUS LENS 96 was significant for two reasons. First, ULCHI FOCUS LENS simulates combat in the Korean peninsula, where the Army faced an immediate and real-world threat from an enemy force designed and equipped to fight a full-scale conventional war. Few other exercises provided the ARSST with a more significant opportunity to demonstrate the value of space in fighting and winning a major war. Second, high-level emphasis was placed on supporting the annual ULCHI FOCUS LENS exercises by USARSPACE. The Command typically made ULCHI FOCUS LENS one of its highest priorities and experimented with new techniques for providing space support during these exercises.

For ULCHI FOCUS LENS 96, ARSST Team 1 deployed on 6 August 1996 in support of the CJTF Korea staff and the Force Projection Tactical Operations Center. Major Cimino and Staff Sergeant Smith were integrated into the Combined Terrain Analyst Team (CTAT), which supported planning by the Future

Plans Cell and the Future Operations/Deep Operations Coordination Cell. In the meantime, Staff Sergeant Finley was assigned initially to conduct training with soldiers from the 33rd Engineer Detachment. When the exercise began, Staff Sergeant Finley redeployed to support the FP TOC.

After the exercise, a number of lessons learned were reported by the ARSST team. The most significant event of the ARSST deployment occurred when the team's mission planning work prompted a review of OPLAN 5027. Major Cimino later reported:

> "We were able to complete approximately 8 routes that covered almost all of the identified avenues of approach for the NKPA invasion of South Korea. We also worked on two routes that were to be used as a part of OPLAN 5027. This work and some work by the 33rd ENG DET (TOPO) helped the planner identify [that] the timeline in 5027 was somewhat 'optimistic' and caused them to relook the OPLAN. When we left, they were planning to change OPLAN 5027."[46]

Major Cimino believed that his ability to perform space liaison duties was impaired by a lack of personnel and resources deployed during ULCHI FOCUS LENS, coupled with the requirement to provide support to the FP TOC. Major Cimino stated:

> "I spent 11 hours of my twelve hour shift in front of the computer trying to complete a project I knew would be briefed to the CINC and his staff. There was no time for me to coordinate issues with the staff, the rear (ARSPACE) or the JSSTs. I had to make the decision between one or the other." Major Cimino added: "If we are to truly support the warfighter, we need to get more personnel assigned to ARSST/ASEDP and quit pulling operators from ARSST/ASEDP to support the TOC."[47]

Major Cimino also cited problems in getting field units interested in obtaining ARSST support. During ULCHI FOCUS LENS 96, the 33rd Engineer Detachment (TOPO) had been receptive to receiving ARSST support. However, Major Cimino noted that the 2nd Infantry Division had "a Powerscene system from Loral at their location … and probably won't request our support"; the 17th Aviation Brigade had "only a handful of staff members" who had been exposed to ARSST systems; and the 6th Cavalry Brigade refused even to send a representative to receive ARSST training. Major Cimino concluded that a major space education effort needed to be conducted in the Korean theater of operations.[48]

In addition to the support provided by the ARSST during the Army's deployment in Bosnia and the ULCHI FOCUS LENS 96 exercise, teams continued to deploy in support of Corps, Division, and Special Forces Group training throughout the year. ARSST teams were integrated into warfighter exercises conducted by the 1st Cavalry Division, the 1st Infantry Division (Mechanized), the 10th Mountain Division (Light), and the 3rd Infantry Division (Mechanized). A team also supported the Corps-level warfighter exercise conducted by the XVIII Airborne Corps Headquarters. Significant levels of ARSST support were provided throughout the year to each of the four Corps Headquarters and their subordinate units. The ARSST also supported exercises conducted by elements of the 1st, 5th, and 7th Special Forces Groups, experimenting with new techniques to support airborne and ground insertion, long range reconnaissance, and direct action missions.

ARSST Forward Deployment At Ft. Bragg

On 5 March 1996, the Memorandum of Agreement (MOA) between XVIII Airborne Corps, the U.S. Army Special Operations Command, and USARSPACE (Forward) was signed. This MOA formalized lines of coordination for the ARSST team stationed at Ft. Bragg, established administrative and resource support requirements for the team, and outlined procedures for the team's operational deployment.[49]

Mission. The stated mission of the forward-deployed team was to "Provide general support of space based products to Fort Bragg assigned units."[50]

Command and Control. Lines of coordination were established between the XVIII Airborne Corps G-2, USASOC Chief of Staff, USARSPACE (Forward) Commander, and 319th Military Intelligence Battalion Commander. Tasking authority remained a formal responsibility of HQDA. The MOA also established "in the event that both XVIII Airborne Corps and/or USASOC have need for the ARSST in a contingency situation, either or both headquarters must send their request to Headquarters Department of the Army, DCSOPS-ODO. HQDA will set the priority and inform all of the units involved of their decision."[51]

Personnel and Training. Under the MOA the Commander of USARSPACE (Forward) remained responsible for assigning ARSST personnel for duty at Ft. Bragg. USARSPACE (Forward) committed to maintaining at least 3 soldiers at Ft. Bragg, unless total ARSST strength dropped below 80%. The rotation of ARSST personnel at Ft. Bragg was left to the discretion of the USARSPACE (Forward) Commander, but a tour stabilization objective of 24 months was set. Personnel evaluation would remain a USARSPACE (Forward) responsibility, as would training on space systems and space- based support. To meet Army-wide training requirements, ARSST personnel would participate in training programs scheduled by the 319th MI Battalion. USARSPACE (Forward) would ensure that ARSST personnel had attended requisite schools, such as the Primary Leadership Development Course and Airborne School.

Operations. The 319th MI Battalion was assigned responsibility for integrating the ARSST Team into XVIII Airborne Corps operations plans and deployments. This responsibility extended to Time Phased Force Deployment List (TPFDL) and air flow planning, airborne support, and other deployment planning considerations. For USASOC deployments, the Deputy Chief of Staff for Operations was assigned responsibility for handling these functions on behalf of the ARSST team.

Administrative Requirements and Support. USASOC was given responsibility for providing office space, classified materials storage, telephone communications support, and medical/dental support to the ARSST team. The 319th MI Battalion was assigned responsibility for providing barracks space to the ARSST. Other administrative requirements would be satisfied by USARSPACE (Forward), such as personnel evaluations, promotions, awards, finance, unit status reporting, command inspections, and assignment of additional duties.[52]

July-August 1996: ARSST Division Long Range Planning

On 12 July 1996 ARSST operations were assessed again as part of the USARSPACE Program Management Review. During this review, seven key issues of concern were identified by the ARSST Division. First, the ARSST Division again emphasized the need to expand beyond the four systems acquired as part of the Commercial Space Package. Instead of merely manning equipment, the ARSST teams "must be brokers for space force enhancement." Second, the ARSSTs needed a better mechanism for coordination with other space support elements. The ARSST should have the capability to communicate with the Joint Space Support Team, the Air Force Space Support Team, and the Naval Space Support Team. Third, the proper balance between ARSST operational support, exercises, and demonstration support needed to be reached. Fourth, the ARSST might need to expand the levels and types of units supported. Fifth, there were some concerns about the ability of the ARSST to deploy on a contingency mission. Sixth, the ARSST Division saw a pressing need for integration into the contingency plans of supported units. Finally, the ARSST Division expressed some concern about Force Projection Tactical Operations Center operations, the relationship between the FP TOC and the ARSST, and the impact of the need to man the FP TOC upon the ability of the ARSST to accomplish its mission.[53]

Many of the issues identified during the July 1996 Program Management Review reflected concerns identified by Major Jensen in January. The ARSST continued to grapple with the need to expand its role beyond that of manning the CSP systems. The question of which types and levels of units the ARSST should support remained unanswered. Coordination with other space support organizations was still an area of weakness. Concerns lingered regarding ARSST deployment and sustainment capabilities.

Looking into the future, a continued role for the ARSST was anticipated. "The Army probably intends to keep space support teams well into the next century with minimal deviation from their current mission and OPTEMPO. The Army will continue to routinize space-based technologies, however, the SSTs [space support teams] will continue to serve as an operational exploitation/demonstration platform introducing and supporting the warfighter with new technology."[54] Given this long range forecast, the ARSST Division saw a need to meet five interrelated objectives. First, the ARSST should be engaged in the planning and execution of major Corps-level exercises and contingency missions. Second, the ARSST teams should educate Corps staffs on Army space-based force enhancement capabilities. Third, the ARSST teams should be incorporated into the TPFDD listings for imporant Corps missions. Fourth, the ARSST should be integrated into the Corps

Figure 11: Key ARSST Deployments, 1996.

Support	Quarter	Exercise
I Corps	1st Quarter 1996	CASCADE PEAK
		FOAL EAGLE (1st SFG)
	2nd Quarter 1996	PACOM EXERCISE
	3rd Quarter 1996	COBRA GOLD
		COBRA GOLD (1st SFG)
	4th Quarter 1996	ULCHI FOCUS LENS
III Corps	1st Quarter 1996	PHANTOM SABER
		1st CAVALRY DIVISION WARFIGHTER
	2nd Quarter 1996	UNIFIED ENDEAVOR (Phase 1 and 2)
	3rd Quarter 1996	UNIFIED ENDEAVOR (Phase 3 and 4)
	4th Quarter 1996	ULCHI FOCUS LENS
V Corps	1st Quarter 1996	VIGILANT LION (SETAF)
		COMBINED CRUSADE (1st Infantry Division)
	2nd Quarter 1996	1st INFANTRY DIVISION WARFIGHTER
	3rd Quarter 1996	
	4th Quarter 1996	OPERATION JOINT ENDEAVOR
		MOUNTAIN EAGLE
XVIII Airborne Corps	1st Quarter 1996	10th MOUNTAIN DIVISION WARFIGHTER
		JRTC – 7th SFG
	2nd Quarter 1996	3rd INFANTRY DIVSION WARFIGHTER
		JRTC – 7th SFG
	3rd Quarter 1996	CORPS WARFIGHTER
		NTC – 5th SFG
	4th Quarter 1996	UNITED ENDEAVOR
		10th MOUNTAIN DIVISION WARFIGHTER
		JRTC – 7th SFG

battle staff. Finally, the ARSSTs should "integrate current and future ARSPACE space force enhancement capabilities at Corps level and below."[55]

Three key measures of success were established to gauge ARSST progress towards accomplishing these objectives. The first measure of success would be whether or not ARSSTs participated in the planning and execution of major Corps exercises/contingencies. The second measure of success was whether or not the ARSST teams were included in the Time Phased Force Deployment Lists established for major contingency operations. The third measure of success was whether the ARSSTs became the recognized space experts by the Corps headquarters in the field.[56]

ARSST concerns about joint interoperability and the integration of Army space support capabilities with those of USSPACECOM and the other Services were reiterated by Major Wayne Brainerd (new ARSST Division Chief) on 29 July 1996. In response to a Joint Staff inquiry, Major Brainerd wrote: "There is really no relationship between ARSSTs and the other SSTs, including the JSSTs. In past operations the teams normally worked independent of each other, however, in the future we would like to coordinate our operations with the other deployed teams to maximize the overall support we provide to the theater."[57] Major Brainerd also noted, "ARSSTs have provided support to units deployed for DESERT STORM, PROVIDE COMFORT, Zaire NEO, hurricane relief (Iniki and Andrew), Somalia, Bosnia, Macedonia, Rwanda, and Haiti. ARSSTs are deployed approximately 140 days a year supporting unit training exercises."[58]

> **July 1996 USARSPACE Program Management Review: ARSST Objectives.**
>
> - **Participate in the planning and execution of major Corps exercises/contingencies.**
>
> - **Educate the Corps staffs on current and future ARSPACE space force enhancement programs.**
>
> - **Insert teams into selected Corps TPFDDs.**
>
> - **Establish the ARSST as a member of the Corps battle staff.**
>
> - **Integrate current and future ARSPACE space force enhancement capabilities at Corps level and below.**

Technically, many of the operations cited by Major Brainerd in his response had actually been supported by *ad hoc* teams dispatched by the Army Space Institute or USARSPACE, rather than a deployable ARSST team named as such. The significant element of the memorandum, however, was Major Brainerd's reference to an ARSST average of 140 deployment days per year. This reference marks the first time in the historical documentation that this 140-day figure was cited by the ARSST. The idea that the ARSSTs were deploying for 140 days per year would drive a number of subsequent decisions made by USARSPACE.

During the planning process for ARSST FY97 operations, the ARSST Division noted that the USARSPACE Chief of Staff had issued guidance that ARSST personnel should not deploy for more than 140 days per soldier. Given the planned schedule of ARSST support in FY97, which included plans to support twelve Corps exercises, five Division exercises, 2 Army Major Command (MACOM) missions, and 8 other deployments, ARSST personnel would average

201 days on deployment per soldier. The ARSST Division emphasized that the taskings to support the FP TOC would impose additional burdens on ARSST personnel.[59]

To address this problem, the ARSST Division presented four options. First, the ARSST could provide equipment training to operators in supported units, eliminating the need to deploy a full ARSST team to the field. Second, the ARSST could deploy smaller teams when it deployed to the field, resulting in a reduced level of support during each mission. Third, the ARSST could reduce the number of Army exercises and deployments it would support, allowing a full team to support a smaller total number of missions. Finally, a new Table of Distribution and Allowances could be developed to ensure that the ARSST was capable of properly providing the full range of space support to all Army units in need. The ARSST Division recommended that the fourth option be adopted, with the TDA being expanded to activate five teams, each composed of five personnel.[60]

A number of other topics were discussed as the ARSST began planning to support FY97 operations. The ARSST examined a series of changes in the TDA that would give the teams a limited self-sustainment capability. Under one proposal, the ARSST would be provided 5 modular command posts, 2 shelters, 2 M1097 trucks, and 4 cargo trailers. This equipment would provide "a mobile, hard-sided, environmentally controlled, self-powered facility to support one team and hook into supported unit TOCs."[61] The ARSST also stressed the need for a closer relationship with the ASEDP program. Five specific ASEDP items were requested by the ARSST: the Laptop Visualization Device (LVD), Direct PC, Blue Force Tracking devices, Low Earth Orbit Communications (LEOCOMM), and Global Broadcast System (GBS). The ARSST also recommended that classified ("black") and unclassified civilian and commercial ("white") space capabilities be integrated in the future.[62] Each of these issues would be revisited in 1997.

Changes to the ARSST TDA, July 1996

The activation of an ARSST team at Ft. Bragg, coupled with the heavy deployment schedule imposed upon ARSST personnel, prompted USARSPACE to revamp its Table of Distributions and Allowances in July 1996. The previous TDA, effective on 30 May 1995, had established a total ARSST requirement for 11 personnel and had authorized 11 personnel.[63] The new TDA, effective as of 26 July 1996, established a total ARSST requirement for 27 personnel and included an authorization for 16.[64] The primary reason for this change was the activation of a new ARSST team designed to suppport XVIII Airborne Corps, raising the total number of ARSST teams from three to four.

No changes were made in the ARSST headquarters element, under which three personnel were both required and authorized under the two versions of the TDA. However, the strength and organization of each of the ARSST teams was modified under the July 1996 TDA update. The USCENTCOM support team's required personnel level was increased from three to four soldiers under the July 1996 TDA, but the authorized level for the team actually declined from three to two slots. The USEUCOM team, which had both a requirement and an authorization for two personnel in May 1995, was increased to a required strength of eight and an authorized strength of four in July 1996. For the USPACOM team, three personnel had been required and authorized; this number was similarly increased to eight required and four authorized personnel under the new TDA. Although these changes in the ARSST TDA were significant, the change of the greatest significance under the July 1996 TDA was the activation of thee XVIII Airborne Corps support team, with a required strength of four and an authorized strength of three personnel. The assignment of personnel to the XVIII Airborne Corps support team represented a key step in developing a forward deployed capability at Ft. Bragg and paved the way for a reorganization of the way all ARSST teams were aligned with warfighting headquarters. In the future, each of the ARSSTs would be directly aligned with a Corps headquarters, rather than a Combatant Command.

1996 ARSST Lessons Learned

For 1996, no records exist of a formal year-end review of operations and lessons learned, as was conducted after 1995. Few after-action reports from the 1996 timeframe are available. As a result, most of the lessons learned cited below were gathered from oral history interviews conducted in October and November 1998.

First, the ARSST soldiers learned that the mechanism for deploying an ARSST team under the CONOPS was unrealistic. For example, during the deployment to Bosnia it was discovered that the Joint Staff was actually responsible for ARSST taskings. The ARSST needed to develop a systematic mechanism for integration into a contingency operation, to include the integration of the ARSST teams into the TPFDDs of supported units. Second, ARSST operations in 1996 confirmed the earlier 1995 finding that the teams must have a limited self-sustainment capability. Third, the ARSST teams identified a number of lessons involving space support equipment. For example, in Bosnia the INMARSAT had fulfilled an important role due to the rudimentary communications infrastructure. However, technical problems had a major impact upon the level of

Element	REQ	AUTH
ARSST HQ Section	No change	No change
CENTCOM Team	+1	-1
EUCOM Team	+6	+2
PACOM Team	+5	+1
XVIII Airborne Corps Team	+4	+3
TOTAL	+16	+5

Figure 12: Revisions to the ARSST TDA, May 1995 to July 1996.

HRWSR and SSP support provided in Bosnia. The ARSST remained unable to provide interpretative analysis of HRWSR products. During the Bosnia deployment, the Air Force Staff Weather Officer did not employ the HRWSR. In addition, ARSST communication and interface with other deployed support teams remained weak.

The ARSST experience in 1996 highlighted the importance of preplanning of space support prior to a field deployment was necessary if greatest use was to be made of ARSST capabilities. If such advance planning was accomplished, the ARSST could have a major impact upon Army capabilities, even in times of peace. A good example of this was provided during ULCHI FOCUS LENS 96, during which ARSST support prompted a reexamination of OPLAN 5027 timelines. While the ARSST continued to focus upon supporting Corps Headquarters in 1996, increasing emphasis was placed on providing space support to Divisions, Brigades, and Special Forces Groups. This represented a significant expansion of ARSST support.

ARSST soldiers concluded that attempts to balance operational support to field units with demonstrations and training would fail in the absence of concerted USARSPACE emphasis. Some field units did not view ARSST capabilities as value-added and would not send representatives to ARSST training and demonstration sessions. Furthermore, ARSST team members, rightly or wrongly, viewed requirements to support the FP TOC, and the strong emphasis placed upon the FP TOC within USARSPACE, as having a major impact on team operations. Of great importance was the high number of annual deployment days for the ARSST teams (estimated at 140 days per year). By 1996, this level of operational deployment was having a significant impact on the ability of the ARSST to support units in the field.

Throughout 1996, the ARSST teams continued to refine the tactics, techniques, and procedures used to provide space support to field units. Lessons learned during ARSST field exercises and operational deployments would be used as the basis for a number of ARSST reorganization initiatives in 1997.

Arsst Operations and Evolution, 1997

ARSST operations in 1997 were conducted under a new organizational construct, with five teams prepared to support each of the four Army Corps Headquarters and U.S. Army Special Operations Command. The ARSST continued to explore ways to improve the level of space support, however, to include the forward deployment of ARSST teams and liaison personnel, the rotational deployment of teams, and the establishment of a self-sustainment capability. Additionally, USARSPACE experimented with the new Army Space Support Cell concept

1997 Concept of Operations

A series of changes were made to the ARSST organizational structure and concept of operations over the course of 1996. The ARSST Division had been restructured so that one ARSST team was aligned with each of the Army's four Corps headquarters. To ensure that the ARSST teams could provide the full spectrum of space support, a revised Table of Distribution and Allowances had been developed in July 1996. The forward deployment of an ARSST team at Ft. Bragg had been formalized and ARSST personnel were incorporated into the planning cycles of both the XVIII Airborne Corps and USASOC headquarters. In addition, in response to the heavy demands for ARSST space support made by the special operations community, a fifth ARSST team was organized specifically to support USASOC and its subordinate units.

ARSST Field Deployments, 1997

The ARSST maintained a busy schedule of field deployments in 1997. Teams deployed to support each of the five Army Corps Headquarters repeatedly. In

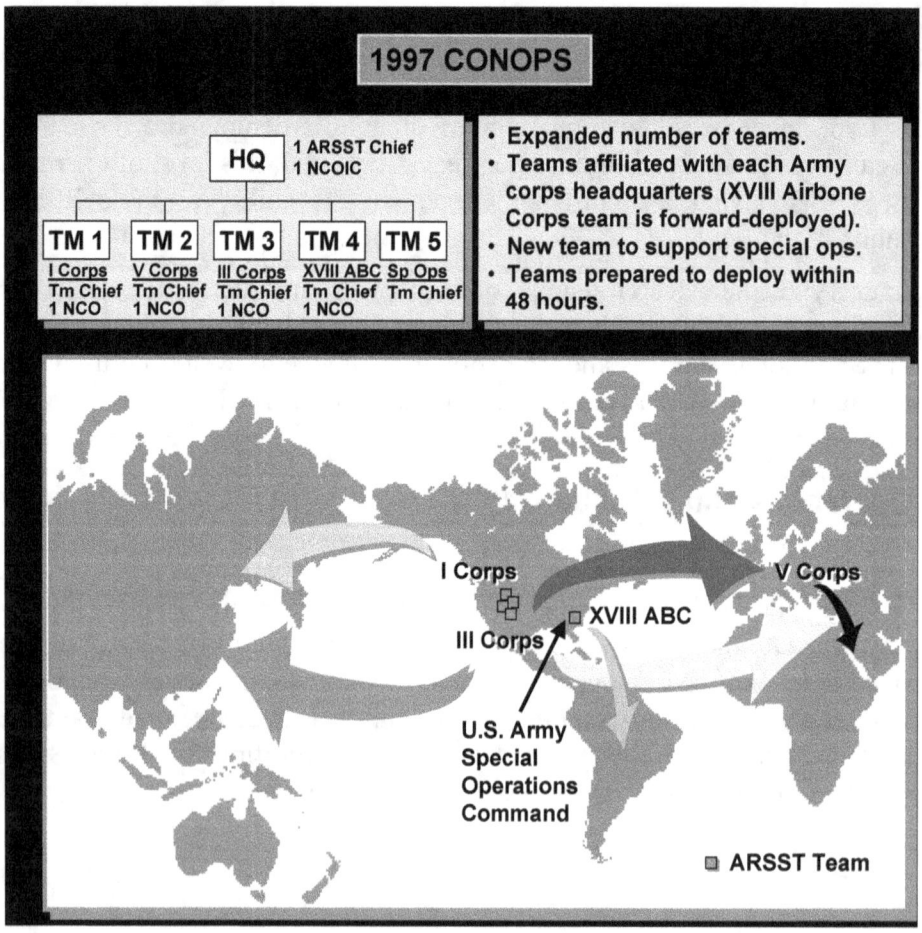

Figure 13: The ARSST Concept of Operations, 1997

addition, a significant level of support was provided to the special operations community, with ARSST teams deploying in support of a number of field exercises.

The first major exercise supported by the ARSST in 1997 was YAMA SAKURA 97. This exercise is conducted annually by the U.S. Army Japan and the Japan Self-Defense Force (JSDF) as a test of their ability to fight together. Captain Gerry Skaw and ARSST Team 1 deployed to YAMA SAKURA 97 to provide continuous support to I Corps. The team provided imagery, satellite weather, and mission planning support to the Corps staff throughout the exercise. In addition, the team provided demonstrations of space system capabilities to a number of U.S. flag officers, including Lieutenant General Crocker (I Corps) and Major General Hicks (US Army Japan). Demonstrations of ARSST capabilities were also provided to senior officers of the Japanese Ground Self-Defense Force, including Chief of Staff General Watanabe and Major General Tomooka (9th Japanese Division). The ARSST redeployed to Colorado Springs on 2 February 1997.

ARSST Team 1 learned a number of valuable lessons during YAMA SAKURA 97. First, advanced planning by the team prior to the exercise paid tremendous dividends after the ARSST deployed. Captain Skaw later reported: "A majority of the planning, for this exercise, had been completed prior to STARTEX. As a result, Team 1 was able to push high quality and timely imagery products into the nightly Deep Attack decision briefings."[65] Second, the ARSST team's ability to provide satellite weather products "became very important due to severe weather encountered during the exercise."[66] Captain Skaw noted that the Staff Weather Officer assigned to I Corps subsequently recommended that real weather be incorporated into future exercises as a result of his experience with the ARSST. Third, Captain Skaw observed that his team had established its credibility with the Corps Commander and Corps staff during YAMA SAKURA 97. He recommended that the ARSST team next take steps to fully integrate itself into I Corps staff operations. Finally, Captain Skaw recommended that a non-deployed space support system be set up at the ARSST home station "to allow all ARSST personnel to train on updated current and future systems, while the deployable systems are recovered, upgraded, and prepared for deployment."[67]

Another key exercise supported by Captain Skaw and the personnel of ARSST Team 1 was the 25th Infantry Division Warfighter. This exercise was significant because the ARSST was able to tie their Space Support Platform into the supported unit's Local Area Network (LAN). This permitted the ARSST to upload imagery files onto the network directly, allowing personnel to select and use relevant imagery to plan operations.[68]

As in 1996, the ARSST provided support to two high-priority Army efforts in 1997: the deployment of troops to Bosnia and the annual ULCHI FOCUS LENS exercise in Korea. For the Bosnia deployment, the ARSST provided pre-deployment training and preparation. For example, ARSST Team 2 traveled to Ft. Bragg to conduct training with the 229th Aviation Regiment (Attack) on the Mission Planning Rehearsal System. While supporting Bosnia operations in 1996, the ARSST had learned that support should be provided to an aviation unit prior to its deployment in a theater of operations, when it would be forced to learn the terrain through flight experience. In April 1997, the 229th Aviation began deploying to Bosnia as part of Operation JOINT GUARD.[69] The ARSST also provided direct support to U.S. elements operating in Bosnia, deploying ARSST Team 2 to Bosnia on 12 May 1997.[70]

For ULCHI FOCUS LENS 97, the ARSST deployed a four-man team, consisting of Major Caesar Jaime, Captain Gerry Skaw, Staff Sergeant Brad Bricker, and Sergeant First Class Howard Smith. During the exercise, Captain Skaw integrated ARSST Team 1 into the Eighth U.S. Army Deep Operation Coordination Cell while Major Jaime (ARSST Team 5) supported the 3rd Marine Air Wing. A variety of ARSST imagery, weather, and space information products were provided to U.S. units during the exercise, including the Eighth Army G-2 and G-3 sections, the U.S. Forces Korea Chief of Staff, the 6th Cavalry Brigade, and the 3rd Marine Air Wing.[71]

After ULCHI FOCUS LENS 97 concluded, the ARSST team members made a series of recommendations for enhancing ARSST support. Captain Skaw and Major Jaime emphasized that warfighting units were requesting imagery with a resolution of 5 meters (or better) that could be downloaded in real-time. This capability was needed for intelligence preparation of the battlefield, operational planning, and battle damage assessment.

The two officers recommended that USARSPACE continue to track the Eagle Vision II and the Lewis and Clark initiatives. They further recommended that the Multi-Source Tactical System (MSTS) be further integrated into the ARSST teams and that the ARSST should develop closer ties with the USARSPACE Deputy Chief of Staff for Intelligence (DCSINT). As part of this relationship, the DCSINT should take the lead in helping the ARSST teams acquire national imagery products. Furthermore, a systematic process should be developed for acquiring national imagery for both actual contingency operations and for exercise play.[72]

Another critical warfighting need identified during ULCHI FOCUS LENS 97 was the integration of ARSST systems and products into the supported unit's command and control network. In addition, the ARSST team emphasized that they needed a secure internet connection to communicate with USARSPACE and other space support organizations. Major Jaime and Captain Skaw noted a continued requirement for ARSST involvement in exercise planning. Other key issues that needed to be addressed by the ARSST included inclusion in the Time Phased Force Deployment List, communications planning, and space support education.[73]

Figure 14: Key ARSST Deployments, 1997

Support	Quarter	Exercise
I Corps	1st Quarter 1997	YAMA SAKURA
	2nd Quarter 1997	
	3rd Quarter 1997	ULCHI FOCUS LENS
	4th Quarter 1997	25th INFANTRY DIVISION WARFIGHTER
III Corps	1st Quarter 1997	1st CAVALRY DIVISION WARFIGHTER
	2nd Quarter 1997	UNITED ENDEAVOR 97-2
		DIVISION XXI, SIMEX I
	3rd Quarter 1997	ULCHI FOCUS LENS
	4th Quarter 1997	
V Corps	1st Quarter 1997	COMBINEDCRUSADE
		JOINT ENDEAVOR
		1st INFANTRY DIVISION CPX
	2nd Quarter 1997	VIGILANT LION
		JOINT ENDEAVOR
		ATLANTIC RESOLVE
	3rd Quarter 1997	1st INFANTRY DIVISION WARFIGHTER
		CENTRAL GUARDIAN
	4th Quarter 1997	
XVIII Airborne Corps	1st Quarter 1997	3rd INFANTRY DIVISION WARFIGHTER
		229th AVIATION REGIMENT
	2nd Quarter 1997	
	3rd Quarter 1997	
	4th Quarter 1997	82nd AIRBORNE DIVISION WARFIGHTER
		CORPS TOCEX
Echelons Above Corps/Other	1st Quarter 1997	5th SFG TF XXI (NTC Rotation 97-06)
	2nd Quarter 1997	1st SFG JRTC (Rotation 97-05)
	3rd Quarter 1997	7th SFG JRTC (Rotation 97-10)
	4th Quarter 1997	FOAL EAGLE 97 (1st SFG)

For the equipment deployed for ULCHI FOCUS 97, Major Jaime and Captain Skaw recommended a series of upgrades. First, all Space Support Platforms should be upgraded with newly available software. Second, all three of the ARSST's MPRS systems should be upgraded to SSPs. Third, more reliable printer equipment was required. Fourth, longer antenna cables were need so that the HRWSR could be used in bunkers. Furthermore, KG-144 encryption devices were needed for the HRWSR as soon as possible.

ARSST Self-Sustainment Capability

Throughout 1997 ARSST team leaders continued to cite the lack of a self-sustainment capability as a key shortcoming in the Army's space support organization. Perhaps the strongest advocate for creating an ARSST self-sustainment capability was Captain Cuthbertson (ARSST Team Chief). Captain Cuthbertson had led the ARSST deployment to Bosnia in 1996 and was convinced that a major overhaul of the ARSST support concept was required.[74]

ARSST Recommendations – ULCHI FOCUS LENS 97 After Action Review.

- Warfighters have a critical need for imagery with 5 meter resolution that can be downloaded in real-time or near real-time.

- The MSTS should be further integrated into the ARSST teams.

- Closer ties should be developed between the ARSST and the USARSPACE DCSINT.

- The DCSINT should take the lead in acquiring national imagery for the ARSST.

- A systematic process should be developed for acquiring national imagery.

- The ARSST must be integrated into the C2 network of supported units.

- The ARSST needs SIPRNET connectivity to communicate with USARSPACE and other space support organizations.

- The ARSST should be involved in planning at an early point to address issues such as the TPFDL, communications needs, and space education.

- The SSP should be upgraded with EDGE software and the latest version of TSOC. All 3 MPRS should be upgraded to SSP.

- Early warning information should be integrated as an ARSST capability.

- ARSST printers crashed repeatedly; more reliable and faster systems were required.

- Longer antenna cables were needed for the HRWSR.

- KG-144 encryption devices were needed as soon as possible for HRWSR operations.

In July 1997, Captain Cuthbertson began coordinating with equipment vendors and collecting cost data for integrating ARSST equipment and systems into a self-contained vehicle. On 28 July 1997, Captain Cuthbertson received a quote from Gichner Shelter Systems on the cost for a shelter system mounted on the back of a tactical vehicle, complete with environmental control, workstations, and a power generator. Gichner Shelter Systems offered to sell such a shelter to the command for $28,000, with an additional $24,400 for the environmental control unit, $8,500 for two workstation units, and $20,000 for a 10 kilowatt power generator.[75] The expense of this equipment, coupled with the difficulties involved with maintaining and deploying a dedicated space support vehicle, prompted the Command to pursue other options for self-sustainment. One approach to this problem that the Command would later experiment with was the Army Space Support Cell.

ARSST Reorganization – The Commanding General's Briefing

The ARSST Division grappled with the problem of structuring the teams to provide the greatest value to supported units throughout 1997. One of the defining moments of this intellectual process was the development of a briefing for the USASSDC Commanding General on a variety of concepts for ARSST reorganization and future operations. This briefing merits special historical consideration because it provided a snapshot of the long-range objectives of the ARSST Division, established six alternatives for organizing the ARSST to meet those goals, and analyzed each option in turn.

In the briefing for the Commanding General, Lieutenant Colonel Rick Brisson of USARSPACE identified eight areas where he believed the ARSST offered value-added to a supported unit. Two of these areas were specifically related to the manning of commercial space systems. First, the ARSST teams offered space-derived information, such as multi-spectral imagery, to a supported headquarters through off-the-shelf technologies and systems. Second, the ARSST was prepared to use these systems to develop tailored products in response to warfighter taskings. The ARSST Division also emphasized the demonstration and materiel development services that it provided to the Army. The ARSST had been

---

ARSST future efforts, as summarized in the briefing to the Commanding General.

- **Increase joint interoperability.**
- **Provide seamless support from the CINC down to the Division.**
- **'One stop shop' with weather, imagery, missile defense, space expertise, and communications.**
- **Integrate GMF planners with ARSST.**
- **Merge state of art technology (ASEDP and material developers).**
- **Continue to enhance black/white space integration.**
- **Space education.**

---

involved in a series of demonstrations and, moreover, had provided operational support with new space systems and initiatives.

TheARSST also played a role in the cultivation of warfighter needs and requirements, which could subsequently be used by the ASEDP to develop new systems. Space expertise analysis was cited as another area where the ARSST added value for the Army. The ARSST, it was explained, offered "rapidly deployable space operational & technical expertise." Finally, two liaison functions were cited as areas where the ARSST provided a value-added. The ARSST could serve as a liaison back to USARSPACE, providing "reach back" support and maintenance to a unit in the field using space systems or requiring analytical support. Moreover, the ARSST was involved in the integration of "black" and "white" space technologies.[76]

Looking to the future, the ARSST saw seven areas where it could increase its current level of support to the Army. First, the ARSST would increase the level of interoperability with the Joint Space Support Team structure. This would enable the ARSST to tap into the resources of the entire space support team structure, thereby offering opportunities to provide enhanced support to Army units. Secondly, the ARSST Division saw a need to provide simultaneous support at a number of levels of command, ranging from the Combatant Command level to the Division headquarters. This idea would later be integrated into the Army Space Support Cell concept and tested during ULCHI FOCUS LENS 98. Third, the ARSST Division saw a need to provide "a 'one stop shop' with weather, imagery, missile defense, space expertise, and communications." Fourth, the ARSST Division wanted to integrate Ground Mobile Force (GMF) planners with the ARSST. Fifth, the ARSST sought to bring the latest technology to the field, whether it was acquired through ASEDP or a materiel developer. Examples of the

The S-788 shelter, also known as the Lightweight, Multipurpose Shelter (LMS) is a lightweight, high strength enclosure designed specifically for use on the HMMWV. The S-788 provides approximately 295 cubic feet of useable interior space and weighs only 608 pounds, allowing it to be transported easily on C-130. The U.S. Army uses the S-788 as its primary electronics platform for wheeled tactical vehicles.

systems sought by the ARSST included Direct PC, LEOCOMM, GBS, Mobile GCCS, BLUFOR Tracking, and LVD. The ARSST also was interested in acquiring systems capable of faster data transfer, direct downlink of imagery, and enhanced communications. Sixth, the ARSST saw a need to continue the process of "black" and "white" space integration. Seventh, the ARSST believed that it could play a key role in the space education of the Army.[77]

To better meet current and future objectives, the ARSST presented a series of concepts for reorganization. Each of those options was evaluated using the following criteria: Space Education and Literacy, Maintain Technical Base and Proficiency, Tailored Support, Planning Response, Execution Response, Command and Control, and OPTEMPO.

Concept One: Maintain the Status Quo. The first concept developed for ARSST organization was a strawman in which the status quo would be maintained. Under this concept, the ARSST would continue to be organized in five teams, with four teams stationed at Colorado Springs and one team stationed at Ft. Bragg. There would be no changes in the level of personnel or equipment authorized for the ARSST. The annual estimated budget for the ARSST Division was estimated at $286,000, with $226,000 earmarked for travel expenses and $60,000 for supplies and equipment. Continued maintenance of the status quo was expected to yield a series of benefits. With most of the ARSST personnel stationed at Colorado Springs, a better space education program could be developed and training would be easier to conduct. It would be easier to maintain the ARSST technical base, to include the acquisition of remotely sensed imagery. Furthermore, the ARSST would continue to concentrate most of its personnel and equipment at Colorado Springs, allowing it to task-organize teams for deployment to the field. The ability to task-organize ARSST teams would enable USARSPACE to manage the number of deployment days for each of the members of the ARSST Division.

Finally, under the status quo organization for the ARSST Division the command and control for each of the teams would remain centralized in Colorado Springs. On the other hand, the planning and execution response times for the ARSST teams was viewed as low due to the stationing of most equipment and personnel in Colorado Springs.

Concept Two: All Teams Forward Deployed. The second concept for ARSST reorganization was based upon the forward deployment of an ARSST team with each of the four supported Corps headquarters as well as U.S. Army Special Operations Command. The ARSST Division would maintain a headquarters element of eight personnel, while 18 personnel would be required for forward deployment with the team elements. To meet this requirement, the ARSST TDA would have to be increased to a total of 27 personnel. Furthermore, new equipment would be required, to include one Space Support Platform, three KG44 encryption devices, one plotter, and one printer. The annual costs under this concept were estimated to be $190,000. An initial $220,000 would be required to procure additional ARSST equipment.

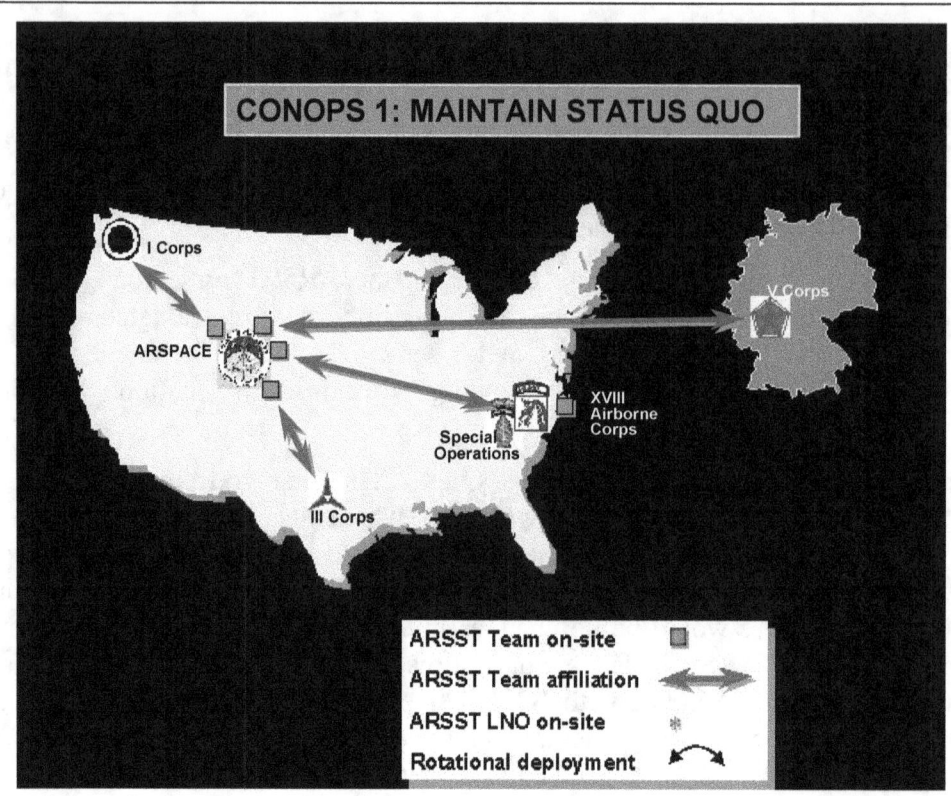

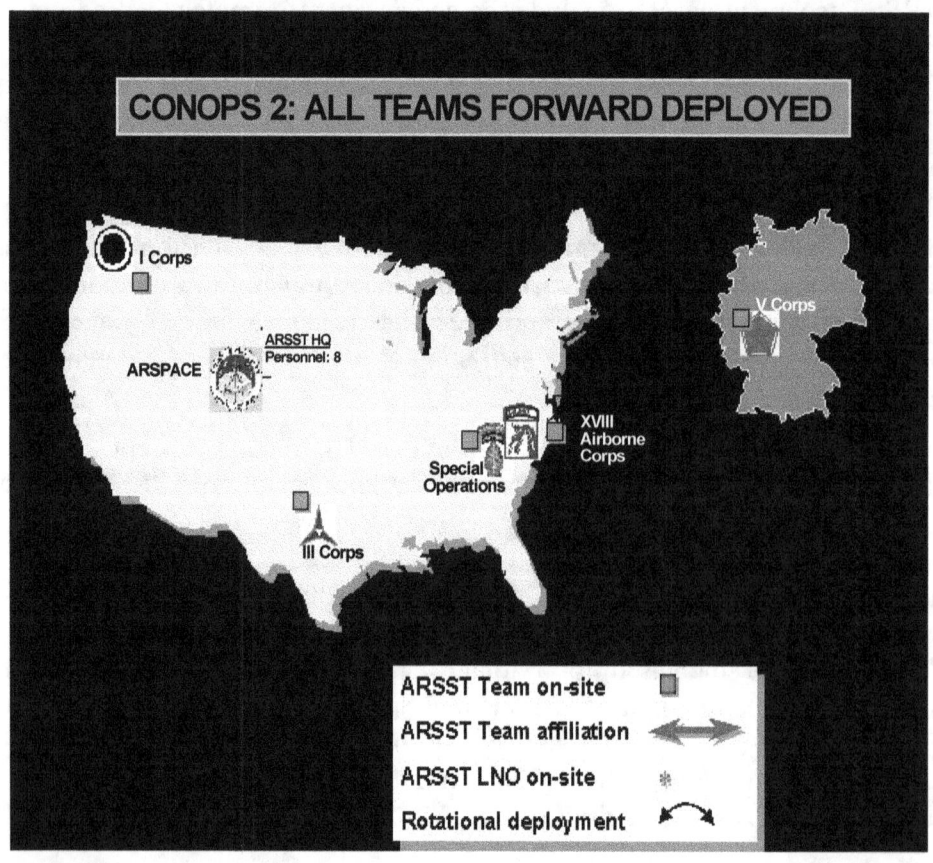

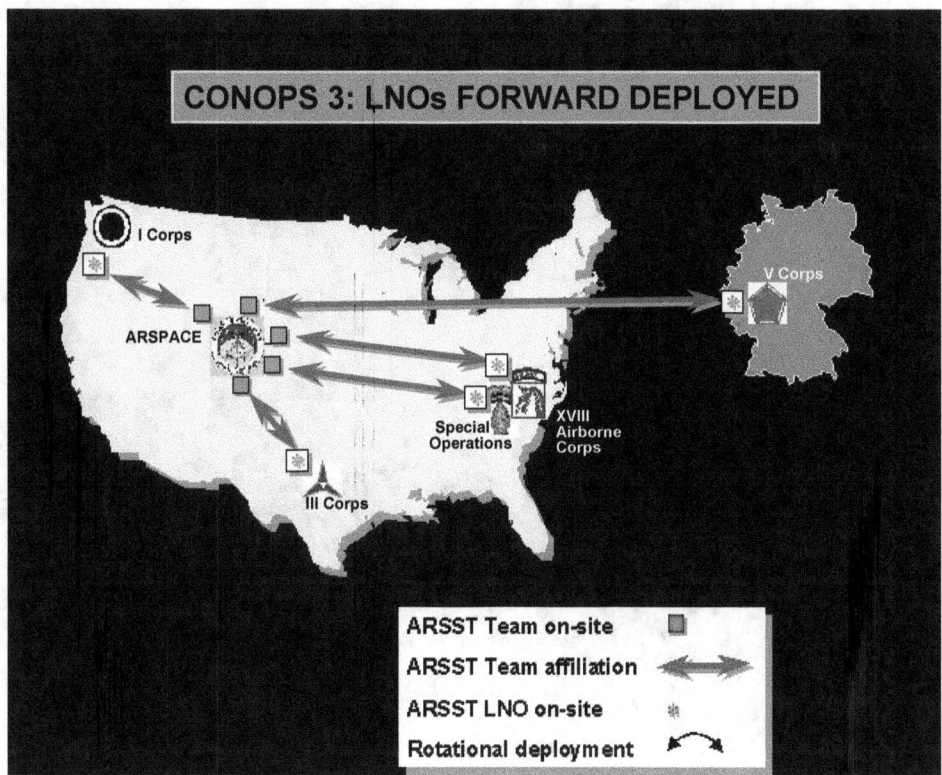

The advantages and disadvantages expected to stem from this concept of reorganization were the diametric opposite of those existing under the existing ARSST organization. Under the status quo, planning and execution response times were low due to the stationing of most personnel and equipment at Colorado Springs. This problem would be solved by the forward deployment of teams with each supported headquarters.

On the other hand, USARSPACE was expected to experience significant problems in providing space education and training, equipment maintenance, and technical support. In addition, USARSPACE would no longer be able to task-organize ARSST teams from Colorado Springs. Command and control of the ARSST teams would be less centralized and the level of OPTEMPO would be highest.

Concept Three: Liaison Officers Forward Deployed. The third concept for ARSST reorganization represented a middle ground between the forward deployment of all ARSST teams and the maintenance of the status quo. Under this concept, ARSST liaison officers would be stationed with each of the four Corps headquarters and the U.S. Special Operations Command. These liaison officers would be responsible for integrating space support into the planning process of their supported units. During a contingency operation or a field exercise, the liaison officer (LNO) could be reinforced by a full ARSST team.

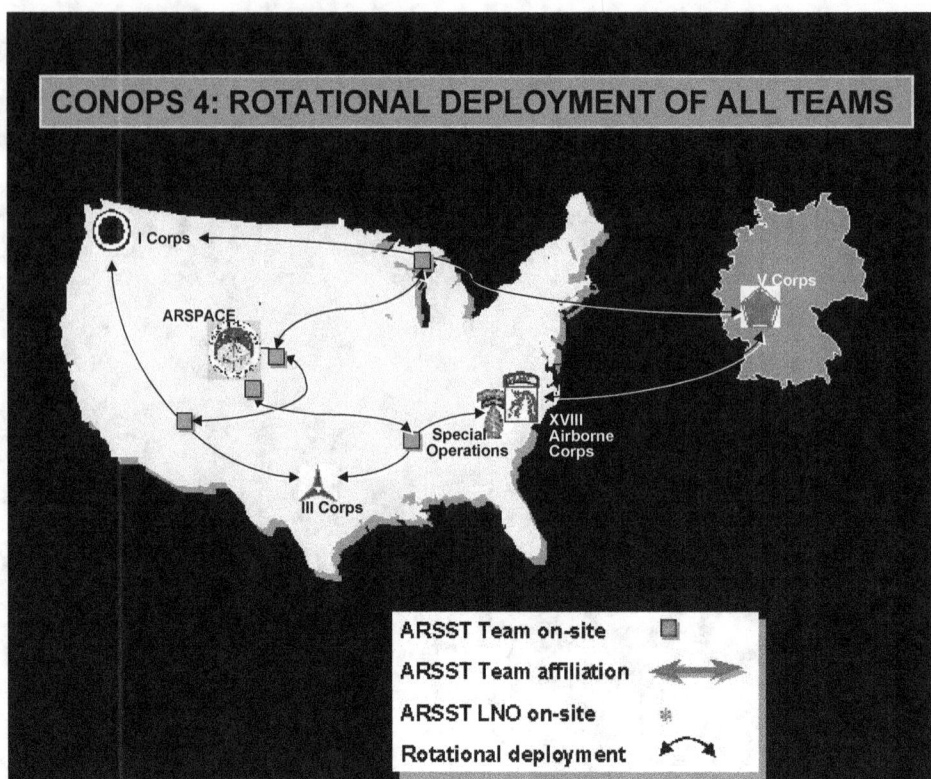

The ARSST Division did not foresee any need for an increase in space support equipment or personnel authorized under the TDA. Of 21 personnel authorized for the ARSST Division, 16 would remain at Colorado Springs while five liaison officers would be forward deployed. An annual budget of $250,000 would be needed, with $190,000 in travel and $60,000 for supplies and equipment.

A number of advantages were expected to result from this concept for ARSST reorganization. With a liaison officer at each supported headquarters, planning response times would be greatly reduced. However, since the majority of the ARSST Division personnel would remain at Colorado Springs, a thorough space education and training program could still be easily conducted.

The maintenance of the ARSST technical base would be simplified. Furthermore, since the ARSST would continue to concentrate most of its personnel and equipment at Colorado Springs it would still be able to task-organize teams for deployment to the field. The command and control for each of the teams would remain centralized in Colorado Springs and OPTEMPO would be manageable. On the other hand, the execution response times for the ARSST teams were still expected to be somewhat slow due to the continued requirement to move equipment and personnel from Colorado Springs.

Concept Four: Rotational Deployment of all Teams. The fourth concept for ARSST reorganization envisioned a rotational deployment for the ARSST teams. A rotational cycle would be established in which each of the ARSST teams would deploy on 90 day rotations. Equipment would remain at Colorado Springs for movement to support a field unit as required. When teams were not on deployment, they would rotate through a USARSPACE space education sustainment program.

The ARSST Division forecasted that it would require significantly higher levels of equipment and funding to implement the concept of a rotational team deployments. A new Space Support Platform, three KG-44 encryption devices, a new plotter, and a new printer would be required, at an estimated cost of $220,000. In addition, the annual travel budget for the ARSST would have to be increased to $420,000.

Although the concept for rotational deployment of the ARSST teams would be more expensive than maintaining the status quo, the ARSST Division expected it would yield a number of advantages. With the rotation of all teams through an ARSST space education and training support program, USARSPACE would easily be able to maintain a high level of proficiency. When not on deployment, most equipment and personnel would remain in Colorado Springs, providing a high degree of flexibility in task-organizing teams for deployment to the field. Command and control would also be enhanced. In the meantime, the rotational deployment of each of the ARSST teams to the field would ensure that responsive planning and execution support was provided to supported headquarters. The only disadvantages anticipated under this concept of ARSST operations stemmed from a higher OPTEMPO level and difficulties in maintaining the technical base.

Concept Five: Forward Deployment of Teams to Support V Corps and XVIII Airborne Corps. The fifth concept for reorganizing the ARSST Division represented a compromise between the existing status quo and the alternative idea that each ARSST team should be forward deployed with its supported warfighting headquarters. Under this concept, the ARSST team deployed at Ft. Bragg would remain while a second ARSST team would be forwarded deployed in Europe. Eleven ARSST personnel would remain at Colorado Springs while ten personnel would be forward deployed.

To implement this concept, the ARSST Division would have to acquire a set of new equipment (one Space Support Platform, two KG-44 encryption devices, one plotter, and one printer). Costs for the new equipment were estimated to be $222,000. Once the new equipment was purchased, annual costs for the ARSST Division would be stabilized at $210,000, with $150,000 earmarked for travel and $60,000 for supplies and equipment.

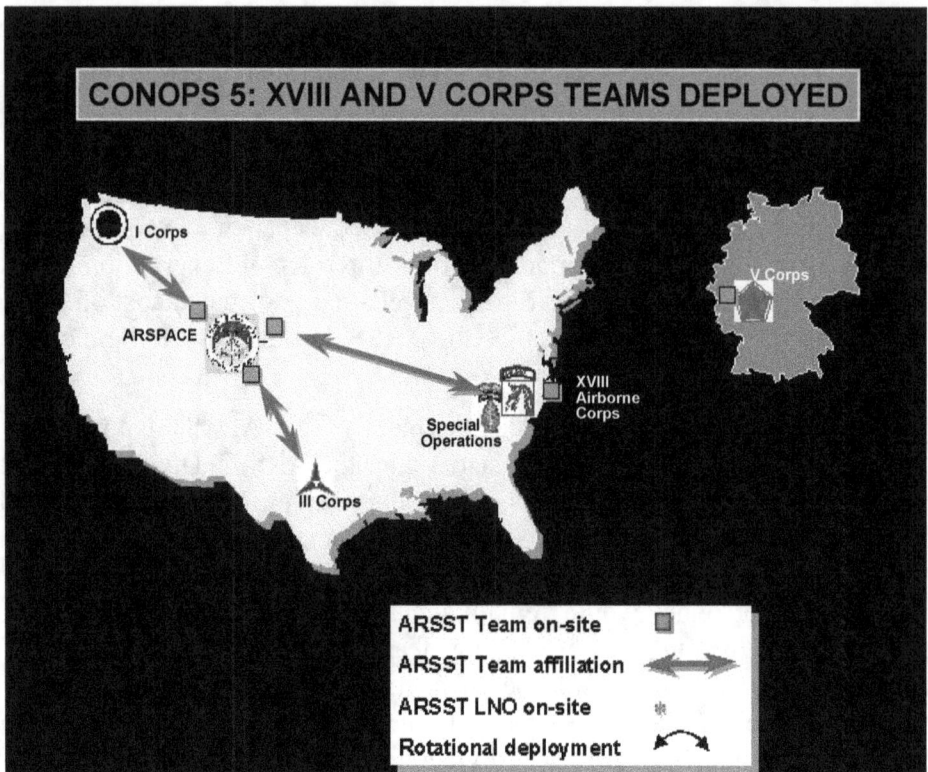

After evaluating this concept of ARSST organization, the ARSST Division concluded that it would improve planning and response support to V Corps and XVIII Airborne Corps while undermining support to the rest of the Army. USARSPACE would have difficulty in maintaining its technical base and the training levels of ARSST personnel, command and control would be decentralized, and the OPTEMPO for the ARSST teams would be high.

Concept Six: Rotational Deployment of Liaison Officers. The last concept for ARSST reorganization envisioned a rotational deployment of liaison officers to supported warfighting headquarters while the remaining ARSST personnel would be prepared to deploy as needed. The ARSST Division anticipated that such an organizational construct would result in a number of advantages. The rotational deployment of liaison officers would ensure that space support planning was integrated into the operations of supported units. Because the majority of ARSST personnel would remain in Colorado Springs and deploy only as required, space education and training could be easily organized. The concentration of personnel in Colorado Springs would ensure that ARSST command and control remained centralized while allowing USARSPACE to task-organize teams. With most of the ARSST equipment also remaining at home station, equipment and technical maintenance would be simplified. The only identified drawback to the concept of rotational LNO deployments was that the execution response times for a full ARSST team would be low.

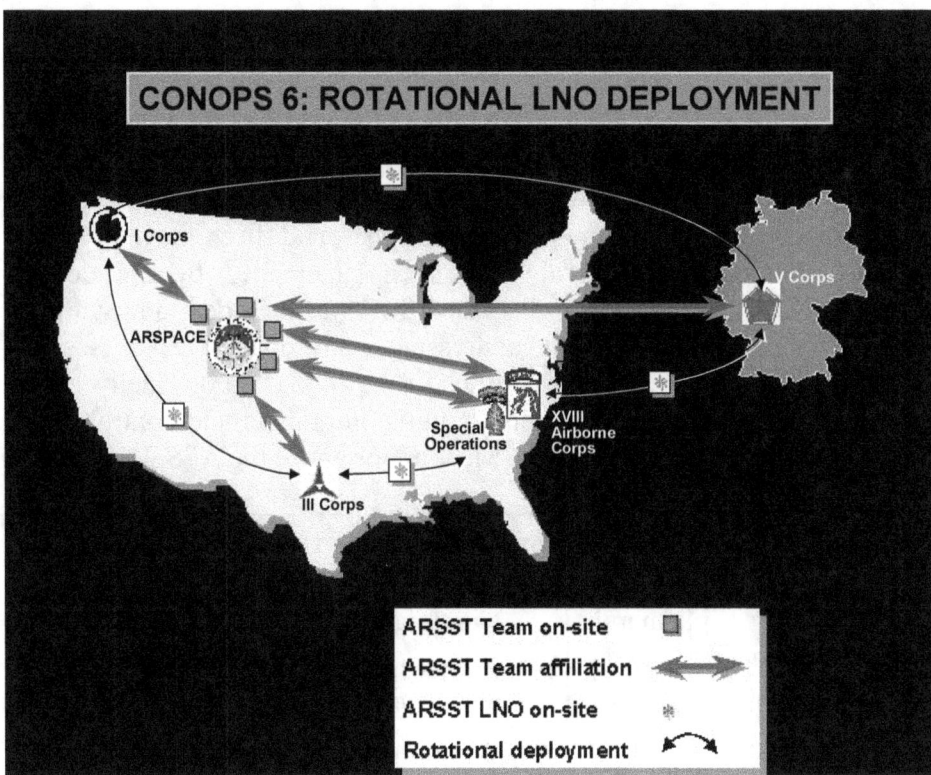

CONOPS 6: ROTATIONAL LNO DEPLOYMENT

ARSST Team on-site
ARSST Team affiliation
ARSST LNO on-site
Rotational deployment

Using the criteria established for assessing ARSST reorganization, Option 3 and Option 6 received the highest overall evaluations. Both options relied on the use of liaison officers to integrate space support into the planning process of warfighting units. Because the majority of the equipment and personnel assigned to the ARSST would remain in Colorado Springs, it was anticipated that space education would be enhanced, equipment and technical maintenance would be simplified, and command and control would remain centralized directly under USARSPACE. The major difference between the two options was the cost to USARSPACE; the rotational deployment of ARSST liaison officers would cost $125,000 more than the permanent assignment of LNOs.

Changes to the MOA with the XVIII Airborne Corps

At the same time the ARSST was evaluating options for reorganization, a revised agreement for support to the XVIII Airborne Corps was developed. Three changes were proposed to the Memorandum of Agreement between XVIII Airborne Corps, USASOC, and USARSPACE (Forward). First, USARSPACE would be committed to the assignment of only two personnel to the ARSST team at Ft. Bragg, rather than the three soldiers agreed upon in the initial MOA. Second, the Commander, USARSPACE (Forward) would be responsible for ensuring that the team was prepared for worldwide deployment. If invited, the ARRST team at Ft. Bragg would participate in unit Soldier Readiness Checks and Emergency Readiness Deployment Exercises. Finally, the funding for ARSST travel was made the responsibility of "the headquarters requesting the support." The new

MOA was approved by Colonel Bowman, then-USARSPACE Chief of Staff, on 15 August 1997.[78]

The Army Space Support Cell (ARSST Plus) Concept

The six options for ARSST reorganization that had been developed for the USASSDC Commanding General were soon superceded by the decision to activate an Army Space Support Cell. The ASSC was intended to provide a broad spectrum of space support services, addressing many of the weaknesses that had been discovered during ARSST operations in the field. As originally conceived, the ASSC would fulfill space analysis, training, command and control, and force development roles for USARSPACE. Most importantly, the ASSC would serve as a "focal point for space support expertise and knowledge."[79]

USARSPACE planners initially developed two approaches for the activation of the ASSC. The first approach was based upon an upgrade of existing USARSPACE capabilities. Under this approach, referred to as the "constrained" option, USARSPACE would activate an Army Space Support Cell of approximately 12 personnel. During a sustained major theater contingency, the ASSC could be expanded to a level of 40-100 personnel. By adopting this approach, USARSPACE would be able to form the ASSC quickly, employing proven technologies and equipment. Furthermore, there would be minimal risk of making "false promises" to the Army.

> **Army Space Support Cell -- Roles:**
> - Focal point for space support expertise and knowledge.
> - Provide training on space capabilities and limitations.
> - Provide linkage and coordination with other space support teams.
> - Provide assistance developing and refining the supporting space annexes and appendices to planning.
> - Provide knowledge of future support capabilities.
> - Provide space force enhancement capabilities to ground forces.
> - Warning of ballistic missile activity.
> - Provide satellite availability and GPS satellite predictions.
> - Provide analytical products, including mission planning and rehearsal.
> - Integrate space-based products.

USARSPACE also discussed a second approach to ASSC activation, under which an objective space support organization would be developed without reference to the existing structure. It was anticipated that this approach, dubbed the "unconstrained" option, would allow more comprehensive space support to be provided to a theater of operations. On the other hand, the unconstrained option would "require [a] greater degree of research and analysis" and would likely "exceed current USARSPACE capabilities."[80] Consequently, USARSPACE instead employed the "constrained" option as the basis for activating the ASSC in the near-term.

As with the ARSSTs, the concept of operations for the ASSC envisioned that USARSPACE would "deploy to a Joint Task Force (JTF), Corps/Division TOC/CP or Warfighting CINC within forty-eight hours" to provide space support in the field.[81] To accomplish this mission, the ASSC would deploy a five person team, consisting of a Team Chief (O-5), Operations Officer (O-4 or O-5), Intelligence Officer (O-3 or O-4), Communications Officer (O-3) and Operations NCO (E-7 or E-8). It was expected that additional intelligence personnel would join the ASSC during a deployment. In addition, it was expected that the ASSC would deploy in conjunction with one or more ARSST teams, which would function as "the production element of the ASSC."[82]

In the draft concept of operations developed for the ASSC, it was explained that USARSPACE would receive a deployment order from either USSPACECOM or the HQDA/Component Commander. Once this deployment order was received by USARSPACE, the ASSC would then begin task-organizing for the mission.

One of the key functions of the ASSC in the field would be to serve as a

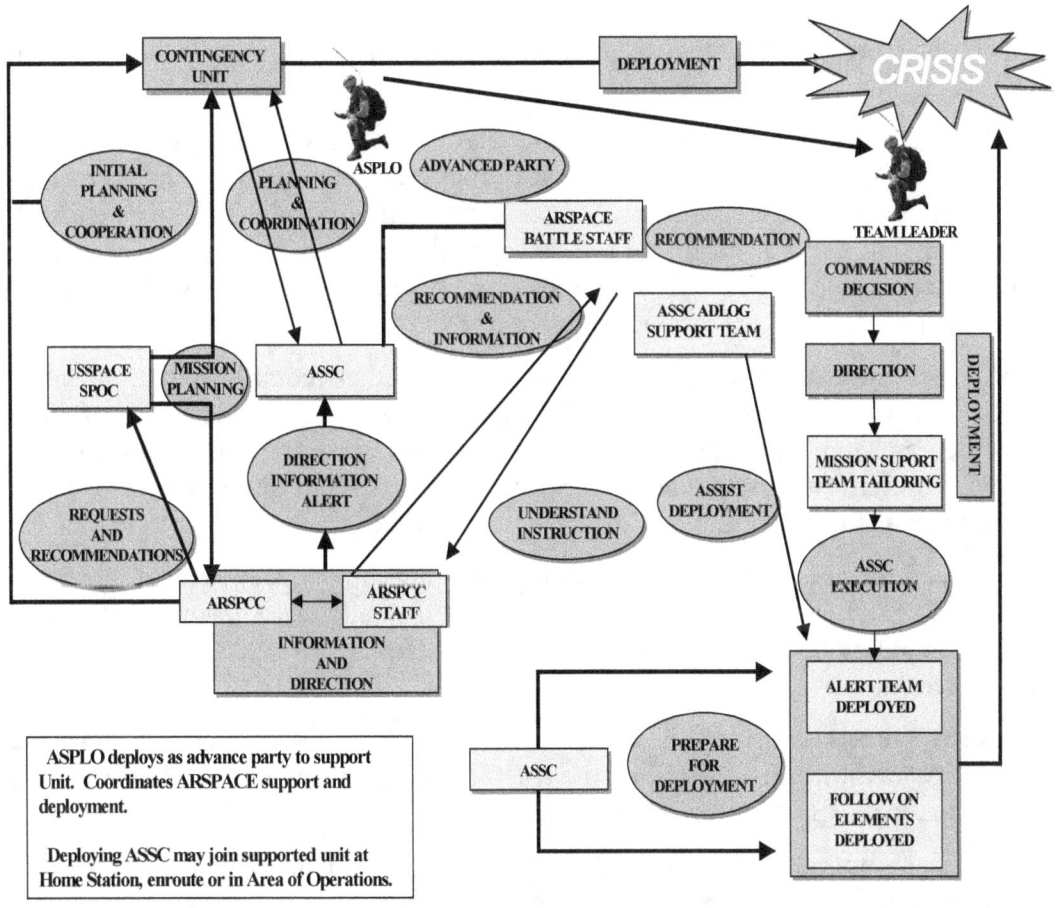

Figure 15: ASSC deployment process (as presented in the draft CONOPS).

centralized node for command and control. The ASSC would provide connectivity for deployed ARSST teams to USARSPACE assets in Colorado Springs, to include arrangements for logistical support. In addition, the ASSC would be responsible for coordinating with the joint and component communities. Unlike the original concept developed for deploying the ARSST teams, in which the tasking for deployment would originate from HQDA, "for Army space support during actual contingencies or crisis response, the ASSC is tasked by JCS through USCINCSPACE."[83]

Two separate types of ASSC support in the field were outlined. Under the first type of support, designed for joint exercises,

> "an ARSST supports each level of command with the ASSC staff and an ARSST collocating with the LCC [Land Component Commander]. In this deployment the ASSC coordinates closely with JSST, other component SSTs and national SSTs in the AOR [area of responsibility] to provide a unified space picture."[84]

Under the second type of support, designed for Corps and Division level exercises, "the ASSC integrates into the Corps or Division staff and provides an ARSST. The ASSC integrates space analysis into the supported decision making process providing value-added products and services."[85]

The draft Army Space Support Cell concept of operations also establshed a seven-phased planning process, as outlined below:

Pre-Crisis. During the first phase (pre-crisis) of the ASSC planning process, the ASSC and ARSST teams train with supported warfighting headquarters, establishing habitual relationships through periodic training sessions and exercises. The ASSC enters the planning process of a supported unit when some specific event occurs, such as an exercise directive, pre-deployment guidance, the issuance of an operations order or warning order, or a tasker.

Analyze Requirements. Once an event occurred that required initiation of the ASSC planning process, the ASSC begins breaking the mission down into specified and implied tasks. These tasks form the basis for the development of ASSC requirements, based upon the Space Force Enhancement missions listed in the Universal Joint Task List (UJTL).

Identify Solution. During this ASSC planning phase, a series of potential solutions to the mission are developed. If the ASSC does not have the ability to provide a solution, assistance is requested from USARSPSACE or another space support team.

Identify Source. During this phase, the ASSC identifies sources that have the capability to fulfill mission requirements. Sources may include an ARSST team in-theater, USARSPACE, or another space support team.

Prioritize Solution Set. After identifying sources capable of performing the required mission, the ASSC schedules and prioritizes the work needed to accomplish the mission. Frequent feedback is obtained from all involved units to improve and modify this process.

Execute. During this phase, the ASSC supervises and/or performs the work required to accomplish the mission.

Deliver Products. The ASSC delivers required support or products to the support unit, employing an undertandable and easy-to-use format.

In 1998, USARSPACE would begin implementing the Army Space Support Cell concept. Training was scheduled for January 1998, to be followed by tests of the concept during the 1st Infantry Division's Battle Command Training Program (BCTP) and ULCHI FOCUS LENS 98.

1997 ARSST Lessons Learned

In 1997, its third year of providing support to units in the field, the ARSST continued to emphasize lessons that had been learned during the early years of ARSST activation while identifying new issues and techniques for space support.

The ARSST teams received a number of requests from field units for enhanced imagery support. They concluded that there was a critical warfighting need for imagery at a resolution of 10 meters, or less, that could be downloaded in real-time or near real-time to support intelligence preparation of the battlefield, tactical planning, and battle damage assessment. Supported units made repeated requests for such imagery. For example, during ULCHI FOCUS LENS, imagery with a resolution of 5 meters was requested. The XVIII Airborne Corps requested live-feed, 1-meter resolution imagery while preparing for JTFEX 98-1 in November 1997. When an ARSST team supported the 5th Special Forces Group Task Force XXI exercise, national imagery was provided by the team. This imagery was well received by the supported unit and provided a potential model for the future use of national imagery products.

The ARSST teams also highlighted the need to be involved in the pre-deployment phase of all major contingency operations and exercises. Such prior coordination allowed the ARSST to take a proactive role in supporting a unit. Furthermore, it provided time for the ARSST to address issues such as incorporation into the supported unit's command and control network, inclusion in the Time Phased Force Deployment List, and time to conduct space training.

The ARSST teams also highlighted a continued need to bring new space systems and technologies to the field. However, they concluded that there was a requirement to expand the level of support provided to include space analytic products to the warfighter, as well as new services such as processed missile early warning data.

The ARSST experience in 1997 demonstrated the importance of being integrated into the command and control network of a supported unit. In addition, the ARSST teams began requesting secure internet connectivity to enhance coordination with other organizations, such as USARSPACE and other space support teams.

Other lessons learned addressed the need for improved coordination measures. For example, ARSST soldiers argued that closer ties should be established between the ARSST and the USARSPACE DCSINT. Furthermore, the USARSPACE DCSINT should take the lead in acquiring national imagery products for the ARSST. The ARSST teams further began work to develop a systematic process so that national imagery products could be used for exercise play and actual contingency missions, as well as a process for quickly sending classified information to an ARSST in the field via electronic means or courier.

The ARSST teams identified a series of areas in which space support equipment could be improved or enhanced. For example, they concluded that the unit's Space Support Platforms and the Mission Planning Rehearsal Systems should be upgraded with new software. The ARSST experienced repeated problems with its printers in 1997. ARSST team members recommended that faster and more reliable printers be purchased by USARSPACE. The HRWSR also provided valuable support during YAMA SAKURA 97. However, its utility in ULCHI FOCUS LENS was impaired because long antenna cables and KG-144 encryption devices were not available. The HRWSR suffered from frequent systems crashes when used on deployments in 1997.

The ARSST experience in 1997 highlighted the need for the teams to continue evolving to support warfighter requirements. A number of steps were taken during the year to upgrade ARSST capabilities, allowing the teams to provide commanders and staffs with full-gamut space analytic support. Those efforts continued in 1998.

Arsst Operations and Evolution, 1998

In 1998, the Army Space Support Cell concept was exercised and tested by U.S. Army Space Command. As part of this process, the Command took steps to develop a more formalized training program for ARSST personnel. In another key development, the only forward-deployed ARSST team was reassigned from Ft. Bragg to Colorado Springs.

1998 Concept of Operations

The ARSST concept of operations underwent significant revision and evolution in 1998 with continued experimentation of the Army Space Support Cell (ARSST Plus) concept. The ASSC was designed, in large part, to provide support to a series of deployed ARSST teams by establishing command, control, and communications networks, conducting liaison with other space support organizations, and fulfilling logistical requirements. During an operational deployment, it was anticipated that the ASSC would deploy within 48 hours in conjunction with one or more ARSST teams. ARSST teams would maintain the capability to deploy independently. When operating in conjunction with an ASSC, however, the primary role of the ARSST teams would be to serve as "production elements" for the Army Space Support Cell.

Two different methods of ASSC employment were experimented with in 1998. In the early part of the year, the ASSC deployed to support a divisional Battle Command Training Program exercise with one ARSST team. During this exercise, the ASSC was integrated into the Division headquarters to provide space support in conjuction with the ARSST. The second concept for ASSC employment, exercised in Korea during ULCHI FOCUS LENS 98, involved the deployment of four ARSST teams to support units at multiple levels.

ARSST Field Deployments, 1998

Even while spending significant amounts of time and intellectual effort in developing and experimenting with the new ASSC concept, the ARSST continued

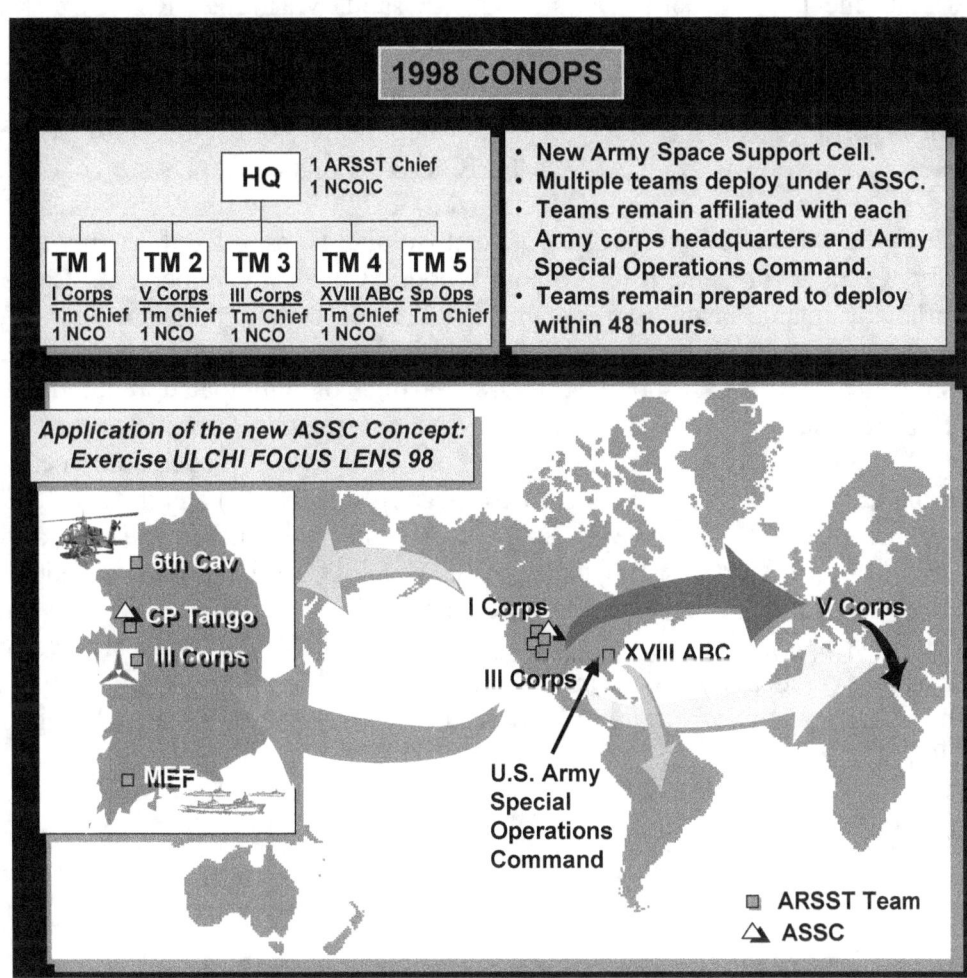

Figure 16: The ARSST Concept of Operations, 1998

to maintain a full schedule of field deployments in 1998. ARSST field support for the year began in January 1998 with a deployment to YAMA SAKURA 98 and continued through the end of the year with the III Corps Warfighter in December 1998.

Throughout the year, ARSST teams continued to deploy independently to the field, providing support to warfighting units without assistance from an ASSC. ARSST Team 1, for instance, deployed to YAMA SAKURA 98 (January-February 1998) with Major Frankie Moore, Staff Sergeant Bricker, Staff Sergeant Stroup, and 1LT Mayfield. The team supported the exercise with the Space Support Platform, Laptop Visualization Device, INMARSAT, and satellite weather terminal. [86] Similarly, ARSST support to XVIII Airborne Corps units was repeatedly provided by an independent ARSST team. For example, during the JTFEX 98-1 (Exercise Purple Dragon), Major Burke and Staff Sergeant Hallam developed the space annex for the operations order and provided imagery and mission planning support to the Corps Headquarters (January-February 1998).[87] Major Burke and Staff Sergeant Hallam, again operating independently, also supported the 82nd Airborne Division Warfighter Ramp-Up (February 1998) and Warfighter exercise (April 1998), and the 101st Airborne Division (Air Assault) Warfighter Ramp-Up (May 1998) and Warfighter exercise (May-June 1998).

While ARSST teams continued to be deployed to the field as independent units, significant effort was placed in 1998 on developing the ability to deploy ARSST teams in conjunction with an ASSC. Early tests of this concept were conducted during the 1st Infantry Division (Mechanized) BCTP exercises from January to March 1998. For these exercises, Lieutenant Colonel Brisson led the Army Space Support Cell, accompanied by Major Woods, Captain Cuthbertson, Captain McFarland, Captain Personius, Sergeant First Class Roberson, Sergeant First Class Smith, and Sergeant Wise.[88] The ASSC/ARSST team was integrated into the Division Headquarters, responding to 48 taskings or anticipated requirements. Most of the support consisted of multi-spectral imagery products, with the ASSC/ARSST team augmenting the capabilities of its own deployed equipment by acquiring imagery files via the Global Broadcast System (GBS) and the SIPRNET. During the exercise, the ASSC/ARSST team integrated its imagery into the Division's planning process, supporting areas where the Division G-2 was not able to devote resources.[89] For example, after the Division suffered heavy losses of helicopters in the initial stages of the exercise, the ASSC/ARSST team used its Multi-Source Tactical System to track the anti-air threat. After this capability was demonstrated to Division planners, no further helicopters were lost during the BCTP.[90]

Figure 17: Key ARSST Deployments, 1998.

Support	Quarter	Exercise
I Corps	1st Quarter 1998	YAMA SAKURA
	2nd Quarter 1998	COBRA GOLD
	3rd Quarter 1998	ULCHI FOCUS LENS
	4th Quarter 1998	
III Corps	1st Quarter 1998	1st CAVALRY DIVISION RAMP-UP
	2nd Quarter 1998	
	3rd Quarter 1998	
	4th Quarter 1998	CORPS WARFIGHTER
V Corps	1st Quarter 1998	1st INFANTRY DIVISION BCTP
		1st INFANTRY DIVISION WARFIGHTER
	2nd Quarte 1998	
	3rd Quarter 1998	
	4th Quarter 1998	
XVIII Airborne Corps	1st Quarter 1998	JTFEX 98-1 (EXERCISE PURPLE DRAGON)
	2nd Quarter 1998	82nd AIRBORNE DIVISION WARFIGHTER
		101st AIRBORNE DIVISION (AIR ASSLT) WARFIGHTER
	3rd Quarter 1998	
	4th Quarter 1998	FUERTAS DEFENSAS
Echelons Above Corps/Other	1st Quarter 1998	
	2nd Quarter 1998	SFOB CPX (7th SFG)
	3rd Quarter 1998	ULCHI FOCUS LENS
	4th Quarter 1998	

A number of lessons were learned during the 1st ID BCTP. First, the ASSC/ARSST team demonstrated the ability to receive products and support from USARSPACE and other military agencies using the GBS and the SIPRNET. Similar experiments had been conducted by the ARSST during ULCHI FOCUS LENS 97. During both exercises, difficulties with the transmission of data were experienced, thus demonstrating a continued requirement for a reliable and easily operated system that would allow space support capabilities anywhere in the world to be leveraged on behalf of a Land Component Commander. Second, the imagery files acquired by the ASSC/ARSST team from the National Ground Intelligence Center (NGIC) Training and Contingency Directorate were well received by the 1st ID staff. Although the archived imagery available for training had some value, the Division staff was far more impressed by the more recent NGIC imagery that had a resolution of one meter. Third, many of the personnel deployed with the

ASSC/ARSST team had not previously served on a division or higher staff and, therefore, had no experience in tactical planning at this level. This lack of experience was seen as a limiting factor in their ability to understand the supported unit's operational flow and provide the right space support products at the right time. Fourth, no space-related events were incorporated into the BCTP and space was not accepted as part of the exercise's free play. As a consequence, no space-specific analytic tasks could exercised by the ASSC/ARSST team and the Division Headquarters. Fifth, the Division Headquarters did not have room for the ASSC/ARSST team to be located in the Main Tactical Operations Center. As a consequence, the ASSC/ARSST team was located approximately two miles away, impairing its integration into the supported staff. In addition, the Division did not provide any facilities to house or provide logistical support. Afterwards, it was again recommended that a self-sustainment capability be developed for the ASSC and ARSST.[91]

The 1st Infantry Division BCTP provided an early opportunity to exercise the ASSC with a collocated ARSST team. During ULCHI FOCUS LENS 98, an even more ambitious test of the Army Space Support Cell concept would be conducted with the deployment of multiple ARSST teams across theater. Four ARSST teams deployed from Colorado Springs for the exercise in August 1998, supporting the Eighth U.S. Army, the 6th Cavalry Brigade, III Corps Headquarters, and the Combined Marine Expeditionary Force. The ASSC was located at Command Post Tango with Eighth U.S. Army, where it provided command and control for the ARSST teams located in–theater.

The annual ULCHI FOCUS LENS exercise had traditionally been used by USARSPACE as a key yardstick for testing ARSST capabilities. Even more emphasis was placed upon ULCHI FOCUS LENS 98 because it served as the first major test of the ASSC concept. When the ASSC and ARSST returned from ULCHI FOCUS LENS 98 in September, a thorough review of operations was conducted, with Captain Gerry Skaw producing a comprehensive evaluation of ARSST operations from pre-deployment training through re-deployment after conclusion of the exercise. Lieutenant Colonel LeRoy Maurer (ARSST Branch Chief) prioritized the top six lessons from Captain Skaw's evaluation and initiated action to address each of them. First, the experience highlighted the need for ARSST teams to undergo a period of formal space education before they can effectively support warfighting units. Lieutenant Colonel Maurer noted that, "personnel are assigned to ARSPACE and within 30 days may be on an exercise deployment without any formal space training."[92] Second, the ARSST teams experienced difficulty in maintaining secure internet connectivity throughout the exercise. The ARSST teams were unable to troubleshoot these technical problems, instead relying on an expert from the J-6. Lieutenant Colonel Maurer recommended that the ARSST teams receive training to allow them to overcome similar problems in the future. Third, ARSST personnel were not integrated into the pre-deployment planning conferences for ULCHI FOCUS LENS 98. As a result, the teams were unfamiliar with the units they supported, hindering operations in the field. To prevent similar problems in the future, Lieutenant Colonel Maurer recommended that both ARSST and ASSC personnel be included in exercise planning conferences. Fourth, coordination problems were experienced in the ASSC-ARSST chain of command during the early portion of the exercise, resulting in conflicting priorities and guidance for the ARSST teams. Lieutenant Colonel Maurer emphasized the need to "have only one clearly defined chain of command."[93] Fifth, the need for an ASSC to deploy in-theater to provide command and control, logistics, and other support was questioned. Lieutenant Colonel Maurer reported:

> "The teams proved in the past and proved during UFL-98 that they can achieve successful mission accomplishment independently and there is no need for a dedicated Command and Control cell for deployed ARSST teams." Therefore, "When a team deploys to support a unit it should be under the tactical control (TACON) of that unit. . . . the ASSC/Battlestaff [should] work from home station with the forward deployed ARSST(s) with perhaps one OIC (Lieutenant Colonel) in country to direct support staff and help resolve issues regarding logistics and life support."[94]

Finally, Lieutenant Colonel Maurer noted that the ARSST teams received new equipment only 12 days before shipment for ULCHI FOCUS LENS, resulting in problems during the exercise. Lieutenant Colonel Maurer recommended that "a cut-off date of 30 days should be set to properly evaluate new equipment and software upgrades."[95]

After digesting lessons learned during ULCHI FOCUS LENS 98, the ARSST teams prepared for another test of the new Army Space Support Cell concept during the III Corps Warfighter exercises. During the ramp-up exercise in November 1998, ARSST teams were co-located with the III Corps Headquarters and the 6th Cavalry Brigade. For the actual III Corps Warfighter exercise in December, the ASSC and one ARSST team were deployed in direct support of III Corps Headquarters, while other ARSST teams deployed to support the 10th Mountain Division (Light), the 6th Cavalry Brigade, and the BCTP White Cell Opposition Force (WCOPFOR).[96] During these exercises, the ARSST again experimented with methods for conducting coordinated operations with multiple teams and an ASSC element.

1998 ARSST Training

In conjunction with the decision in 1997 to exercise the ASSC concept, a formal training plan was established by USARSPACE to provide individual and collective training. This training plan was significant because it marked the first time that a full-fledged space analysis training program had been developed for the ARSST. In the past, the training for ARSST personnel had largely consisted of individual attendance at the Interservice Space Fundamentals Course, the Remotely Sensed Imagery Course at Ft. Belvoir, and hands-on training with ARSST equipment. In fact, some personnel had deployed within 30 days of assignment to USARSPACE without any space education, a problem that had been cited repeatedly in the past.

For the 1998 training program, a three-phased approach was developed. Under this approach, individual training was scheduled for January 1998. Battle staff training, space liaison, and Army-Navy interoperability training was conducted in April. Finally, deployment, systems integration, and joint operations interoperability training was planned for June 1998. ULCHI FOCUS LENS 98 was intended to serve as the capstone exercise for the overall training effort.[97]

The first ASSC/ARSST training session was conducted from 5-9 January 1998. This training began with each ARSST team describing weak areas in their operations. Sergeant First Class Smith, speaking for ARSST Team 1, began by describing problems with the dissemination of information, maintaining secure internet connections, and the movement of large data files. Major Jaime (ARSST Team 5) also described connectivity problems. Captain Cuthbertson (ARSST Team 2) cited weaknesses in the planning process and space education program. Major Kirt Woods (ARSST Team 3) emphasized the absence of space events that influenced exercise and simulation play. Finally, Major Tim Burke (ARSST Team 4) cited a number of issues stemming from his team's forward-deployment at Ft. Bragg, to include problems in obtaining support from USARSPACE and keeping team members trained to standard.

After being asked to summarize weak areas in existing ARSST operations, the ARSST soldiers were released into small groups to conduct training on the MPRS and SSP. This training continued on 6 January 1998 with sessions

> **5 January 1998: Summary of Weak Areas Cited by Team Chiefs during Training.**
>
> - **Connectivity problems.**
> - **SIPRNET hcok up.**
> - **Mission planning process.**
> - **Space education and analysis.**
> - **Absence of space events that influence exercise and simulation play.**
> - **USARSPACE support for forward-deployed team at Ft. Bragg.**

on the MSTS, SSP, and HRWSR and on 7 January with training on TSOC provided by Rhoda Danforth of Decision Source Application.[98] On 8 January, Naval Space Support Team (NAVSST) personnel joined the training session and a comparison of ARSST and NAVSST operations was conducted. Additional training on ARSST equipment was conducted on 9 January. At the conclusion of the training session, Colonel Ferguson (USARSPACE Commander) gathered the participants to describe ongoing USARSPACE Command Group initiatives.[99]

During the April 1998 training session, ASSC and ARSST personnel focused on battle staff training and space liaison functions. Topics covered during the training session included staff organization, the military decision-making process, and mission analysis techniques.[100] The final ASSC/ARSST training session was conducted in June 1998 and was intended to serve as a ramp-up for the ULCHI FOCUS LENS deployment. During the training session, systems checkout and integration tasks were covered and combined operations under OPLAN 5027 were rehearsed.

USARSPACE Long Range Planning

In February 1998, USARSPACE elements were tasked to provide input for the Command's Long Range Plan. Both ARSST and ASSC personnel evaluated space support roles, missions, and capabilities required in the near-, mid-, and long-term and began to develop options to position the Command to address those needs.

Underlying the long range planning response provided by the ARSST were four key assumptions regarding future space capabilities: First, it was assumed that the potential space capabilities of threat forces would continue to increase; Second, the reliance of the U.S. and its potential coalition partners upon space based capabilities would continue to rise, particularly for intelligence, navigation, targeting, munitions guidance, and communications; Third, commercial imagery capabilities would continue to increase and potential adversaries might be able to employ these capabilities to obtain relatively high-resolution imagery products; Finally, commercial satellite communications systems would improve, providing new options for both friendly and adversary forces.

Although the four assumptions regarding future space capabilities were significant, the ARSST anticipated no significant change in mission over either the mid-term (1-5 years in the future) and long-term (5-12 years in the future). It was expected that the ARSST would "continue to maintain the capability to rapidly deploy worldwide to provide space force enhancement to Army units during contingency operations and exercises. ARSST will also be ARSPACE (Fwd) and SMDC's primary link to the warfighters."[101]

While no changes in the ARSST mission were anticipated, it was expected that the evolution of space systems would influence the type of support provided by the ARSST. Specifically, ARSST capabilities were expected to become increasingly focused on space analysis tasks. In the meantime, ARSST equipment would become smaller and easier to integrate into the command and control networks of

> **Long Range Thrusts: ARSSTs.**
>
> • **Integrate ARSST teams into selected BCTP and CTC rotations.**
>
> • **Provide new ARSST equipment and space products to supported units.**
>
> • **Develop and conduct individual and collective initial and sustainment training.**
>
> • **Develop an ARSST Homepage.**
>
> • **Exploit USSPACECOM's and other Space Support Team's capabilities.**
>
> • **Provide feedback to the ARSPACE staff on warfighter operational requirements.**

supported units. Finally, many functions currently performed by the ARSST, such as high quality multi-spectral imagery production, would likely be integrated into supported units as an internal capability.

In May 1998, an in-process review of the USARSPACE Long Range Plan was conducted. During this review, a series of planning thrusts were presented for both the ASSC and the ARSST. For the ASSC, seven key thrusts were identified. First, it was recommended that one ASSC be stationed at Korea, with a second ASSC forward-deployed in Europe. The forward-deployment of the ASSCs was intended to ensure that optimum use of space support resources for warfighters in-theater. The second ASSC thrust was the designation of the ASSC as the focal point for injecting USARSPACE input into the theater planning process. The ASSC would function as a liaison for all space and missile defense support. The third long range planning thrust was integration of the ASSC into the Theater Crisis Action Team, ensuring that space capabilities were integrated into all elements of a warfighter's planning process, both deliberate and *ad hoc*. The fourth recommendation was that the ASSC be assigned the mission of providing logistics support for all SMDC assets in theater. The fifth long range planning thrust was ASSC coordination with in-theater staffs to provide training and ensure that space events and considerations were incorporated into exercises. Sixth, the need for ASSCs to participate in theater exercises was emphasized. Such participation would ensure that space events were properly simulated. Finally, the ASSC recommended that a USARSPACE Battle Staff be established to support military operations. This staff was intended to function as a cohesive planning and coordinating element, with the capability to support all levels of conflict, contingency missions, crises, and exercises.[102]

During the May 1998 review meeting, the ARSST teams also identified a number of key planning thrusts. The first thrust presented was the integration of the ARSST teams into BCTP exercises and combat training center rotations. The objective of this thrust would be to provide full spectrum space support and to introduce space capabilities to Army units. Second, it was recommended that the ARSST teams be used to introduce new equipment and space products to supported units through close coordination with the Space and Missile Defense Battle Laboratory. This would ensure that USARSPACE continued to provide cutting-edge technology to the field. Third, the Army Space Support Team cited a need to develop and conduct additional training for ARSST personnel, to include individual and collective training tasks. Training was needed to educate newly assigned personnel on essential ARSST functions and to maintain the proficiency of experienced personnel. In addition, training programs would need to be updated as new hardware and software were acquired. The fourth long range planning thrust discussed at the review was the development of internet homepage reference material to provide information on ARSST capabilities. The fifth planning thrust presented during the review was the need to exploit the capabilities of USSPACECOM and the other Services. The intent of this thrust was to leverage all of these capabilities on behalf of land forces. The final ARSST long range planning thrust was the use of the ARSST teams to provide feedback on warfighter operational requirements. This data would be integrated by USARSPACE into the Army's formal requirements process.[103]

The Redeployment of ARSST Team 4 to Colorado Springs

One of the numerous changes in the organization of the ARSST in 1998 was the decision to relocate ARSST Team 4 to Colorado Springs. This team had originally been forward-deployed at Ft. Bragg in 1995 in response to a request by the XVIII Airborne Corps. The forward-deployment of this team was significant because it had served as a demonstration of how space support personnel might be integrated into the daily operations of a supported headquarters. Additionally, the forward deployment of this team had been cited as a model for the other teams in a number of ARSST reorganization concepts.

The decision in 1998 to relocate ARSST Team 4 from Ft. Bragg to Colorado Springs was influenced by three major factors: First, the team's OPTEMPO had been extremely high as the result of a requirement to support a Corps Headquarters, four Divisions, and USASOC. Second, it was felt that better maintenance support for the team's equipment could be provided at home station in Colorado Springs. Finally, a stronger basis for space education and institutional knowledge existed at Colorado Springs, enabling better training to be provided to team personnel if they were permanently stationed there.

The proposal to relocate ARSST Team 4 was staffed within USARSPACE by Major Burke (ARSST Team 4), Lieutenant Colonel Brisson (USARSPACE Operations), and Colonel Jackson (USARSPACE DCSOPS). Prior to implementation of the idea, their proposal was briefed to both the XVIII Airborne Corps G-2 and the Corps Chief of Staff, who concurred.[104]

1998 ARSST Lessons Learned

A number of lessons learned were reported by USARSPACE personnel while experimenting with the ASSC concept in 1998. Additionally, ARSST teams operating independently continued to experiment with new tactics and techniques.

Many of the key lessons learned during the course of operations in 1998 reflected long-standing issues. For example, the ARSST teams reported a strong demand by field units for imagery at a resolution of 10 meters (or less) that could be downloaded in real-time or near real-time for IPB, planning, and BDA. During the 1st Infantry Division BCTP, the Division staff was impressed with imagery that had a resolution of 1 meters and was only 1-2 days old.

Additional experience in providing space analytic support in 1998 yielded a number of interesting insights. During ULCHI FOCUS LENS 98, a daily space analysis summary was developed by the Army Space Support Cell, with information on satellite systems, space weather effects, and GPS accuracy. This information was presented to planning staffs to support decision-making and course of action development, with great success.

ULCHI FOCUS LENS 98 reinforced the need, identified in 1997, for the ARSST teams to be involved in the pre-deployment phase of all major contingency operations and exercises. Such prior coordination allowed the ARSST to take a proactive role in supporting a unit. Unfortunately, a recurring theme in 1998 was that very little space play was incorporated into Army or joint exercises. As a consequence, supported units did not have to face the consequences of failing to cope with space events. Furthermore, ARSST and ASSC personnel were unable to exercise space analytic tasks. ARSST soldiers worried that, until space was routinely incorporated into exercises and wargames, supported units would remain focused only on the production of imagery products.

The ARSST teams emphasized the importance of a period of formal space education before they could effectively support warfighting units. For example, after ULCHI FOCUS LENS 98, Lieutenant Colonel Maurer noted that "personnel are assigned to ARSPACE and within 30 days may be on an exercise deployment without any formal space training." USARSPACE further discovered that, when reserve augmentees were incorporated into an ARSST team, this should occur well enough in advance to enable pre-deployment training to be conducted at both the individual and unit level.

The ARSST teams continued to experience problems stemming from insufficient coordination and uncertain command and control procedures. ARSST soldiers emphasized the need to establish a clear ASSC-ARSST chain of command prior to deployment to avoid conflicting priorities and guidance. Similarly, better coordination could be effected with the Joint Space Support Team and the other Service space support organizations.

The ARSST teams highlighted continued need exists for the ARSST to bring new space systems and technologies to the field, particularly technologies such as the direct tasking and downlink of high resolution commercial imagery. They also learned that, by conducting a mission analysis of the supported theater of operations in advance of a deployment, they could prepackage a series of space support products. For example, advance mission analysis prior to ULCHI FOCUS LENS allowed the teams to provide proactive support for analyzing mobility routes and key terrain. With proper use of systems like GBS and secure internet connections, the ASSC and ARSST teams also found that they could leverage space support capabilities anywhere in the world. However, to overcome connectivity problems experienced during the course of exercise support, the ARSST personnel required additional network training.

During ULCHI FOCUS LENS 98, the ARSST teams discovered that a significant amount of classified space information could not be released to South Korean personnel. This posed a problem because the III Corps worked with the 3rd ROK Army during that exercise.[105] Finally, the ARSST experience in 1998 highlighted the need to thoroughly test new hardware systems and software upgrades prior to use on a deployment. The ARSST leadership concluded that team members require at least two weeks of training if they are to be effective in using new technical systems and equipment.

Summary

Since the ARSST began dispatching teams to the field in January 1995, there have been a significant number of changes in Army Space Support Team organization and operations. The number of ARSST teams has been changed and their affiliation with supported headquarters has evolved. A number of modifications have been made to the ARSST TDA. There have been frequent proposals for restructuring the ARSST teams, for using the ARSST to accomplish new missions and responsibilities, and for developing an ARSST self-sustainment capability. The ARSST have grappled with a number of space support issues, such as the deployment of personnel on an average of 140 days per year, the need to provide on-the-job training due to the absence of a structured space education process, and the development of mechanisms to leverage capabilities at USSPACECOM and other military organizations. The ARSST has proposed a number of new space support concepts, to include integration of "black" and "white" space capabilities and experimentation with the Army Space Support Cell concept.

The evolution of the ARSST and the experimentation with the ASSC have revealed one constant – the need for a unit of space experts able to deploy to a theater of operations and translate space capabilities into 'tools' for the ground commander. The form of the team may have evolved over time but the requirement for space expertise and analytic support remains.

---

[1] Memorandum, Major James H. Minnon, U.S. Army Space Command, to Commander, USARSPACE (FWD), Subject: Revised ARSST CONOPS. 12 April 1995.

[2] U.S. Army Space Command, Army Space Support Team Division, "ARSST Deployment Schedule." 10 April 1995.

[3] Ibid. See also, Meeting Notes, Major Foeller, U.S. Army Space Command, "Army Space Support to the Warfighter Review," 11 January 1996.

[4] Ibid.

[5] U.S. Army Space Command, Army Space Support Team Division, "ARSST Deployment Schedule." 10 April 1995.

[6] Major Foeller [Meeting POC], "Army Space Support to the Warfighter Review," 11 January 1996.

[7] U.S. Army Space Command, Army Space Support Team Division, "ARSST Deployment Schedule." 22 May 1995. Meeting Notes, Major Foeller, U.S. Army Space Command, "Army Space Support to the Warfighter Review," 11 January 1996.

[8] U.S. Army Space Command, Army Space Support Team Division, "ARSST Deployment Schedule." 8 May 1995.

[9] U.S. Army Space Command, Army Space Support Team Division, "ARSST Deployment Schedule." 10 April 1995. Meeting Notes, Major Foeller, U.S. Army Space Command, "Army Space Support to the Warfighter Review," 11 January 1996.

[10] U.S. Army Space Command, Army Space Support Team Division, "ARSST Deployment Schedule." 19 June 1995. Meeting Notes, Major Foeller, U.S. Army Space Command, "Army Space Support to the Warfighter Review," 11 January 1996.

[11] U.S. Army Space Command, Army Space Support Team Division, "ARSST Deployment Schedule." 10 April 1995. Meeting Notes, Major Foeller, U.S. Army Space Command, "Army Space Support to the Warfighter Review," 11 January 1996.

[12] Ibid.

[13] U.S. Army Space Command, Army Space Support Team Division, "ARSST Deployment Schedule." 22 May 1995. Meeting Notes, Major Foeller, U.S. Army Space Command, "Army Space Support to the Warfighter Review," 11 January 1996.

[14] U.S. Army Space Command, Army Space Support Team Division, "ARSST Deployment Schedule." 10 April 1995.

[15] Meeting Notes, Major Foeller, U.S. Army Space Command, "Army Space Support to the Warfighter Review," 11 January 1996.

[16] Ibid.

[17] Memorandum, Major Robert E. Toupin, ARSST Team Chief, to Commander, ARSPACE (FORWARD), Subject: Trip Report of Major Toupin. 26 April 1995.

[18] Memorandum, Brigadier General Frank H. Akers, Jr., XVIII Airborne Corps Chief of Staff, to Commander, U.S. Army Space Command (Fwd), Subject: Attachment of an Army Space Support Team (ARSST) to HQ XVIII Airborne Corps. Undated.

[19] Draft Memorandum, Colonel E. Paul Semmens, Commander U.S. Army Space Command, to Commander, XVIII Airborne Corps and Fort Bragg, Subject: Attachment of an Army Space Support Team (ARSST) to the XVIII Airborne Corps G2. Undated.

[20] Ibid.

[21] Ibid.

[22] Memorandum, Major(P) Armando R. Macias, ARSPACE Director, Operations to Commander, ARSPACE (Forward), Subject: ARSST Support for XVIII Airborne Corps. 17 July 1995.

[23] Ibid.

[24] Memorandum, Major Foeller, U.S. Army Space Command to Commander, ARSPACE (Forward), Subject: ARSST Support for XVIII Airborne Corps and Ft. Bragg, NC. 26 July 1995.

[25] Memorandum, Major Robert E. Toupin, ARSST Team Chief, to DIROPS, DIREX, Subject: Coordination of ARSST Equipment for the Fort Bragg Team. 1 August 1995.

[26] Draft Memorandum, Colonel E. Paul Semmens, Commander U.S. Army Space Command, to Commander, XVIII Airborne Corps and Fort Bragg, Subject: Attachment of an Army Space Support Team (ARSST) to the XVIII Airborne Corps G2. Undated.

[27] Meeting Notes, Major Foeller, U.S. Army Space Command, "Army Space Support to the Warfighter Review," 11 January 1996.

[28] USCINCSPACE, UMD38-2: SPACE SUPPORT TEAM OPERATIONS. (Colorado Springs, Colorado: Headquarters, United States Space Command, 2 January 1996.).

[29] Headquarters, Department of the Army, "Approved Document Print (TDA) Table of Distribution and Allowances: DOCNO SCW4XQAA." 26 July 1996.

[30] Meeting Notes, Major Foeller, U.S. Army Space Command, "Army Space Support to the Warfighter Review," 11 January 1996.

[31] U.S. Army Space Command Briefing, "Put Space Capabilities in the Hands of Warfighters Today," 8 January 1996.

[32] Memorandum, Colonel James W. Kulbacki, Deputy Chief of Staff, Operations, U.S. Army Space Command, to HQ USSPACECOM, ATTN: SPJ33Z, Subject: Joint After Action Reporting for Operations Uphold Democracy/Maintain Democracy. Undated.

[33] Electronic Mail Message, Major Mike Jensen, ARSST Division Chief, "Future ARSST Issues." 8 January 1996.

[34] Meeting Notes, Major Foeller, U.S. Army Space Command, "Army Space Support to the Warfighter Review," 11 January 1996.

[35] U.S. Army Space Command Briefing, "Put Space Capabilities in the Hands of Warfighters Today," 8 January 1996.

[36] U.S. Army Space Command Briefing, "Planning Tiger Team: Army Space Exploitation Demonstration Program," 9 January 1996.

[37] Ibid.

[38] James Hooper, "Major Scott Cuthbertson Oral History Interview, ARSST Historical/Lessons Learned Study," 29 October 1998.

[39] Colonel Otis B. Ferguson, Jr., Commander, U.S. Army Space Command, "USARSPACE Weekly Activities Report (7-13 Oct 96)." 16 October 1996. Colonel Otis B. Ferguson, Jr., Commander, U.S. Army Space Command,

"USARSPACE Weekly Activities Report (14-20 Oct 96)." 21 October 1996. Colonel Otis B. Ferguson, Jr., Commander, U.S. Army Space Command, "USARSPACE Weekly Activities Report (21-27 Oct 96)." 29 October 1996.

[40] Colonel Otis B. Ferguson, Jr., Commander, U.S. Army Space Command, "USARSPACE Weekly Activities Report (28 Oct – 3 Nov 96)." 1 November 1996. Colonel Otis B. Ferguson, Jr., Commander, U.S. Army Space Command, "USARSPACE Weekly Activities Report (11-17 Nov 96)." 15 November 1996. Colonel Otis B. Ferguson, Jr., Commander, U.S. Army Space Command, "USARSPACE Weekly Activities Report (2-8 Dec 96)." 6 December 1996.

[41] James Hooper, "Major Scott Cuthbertson Oral History Interview, ARSST Historical/Lessons Learned Study," 29 October 1998.

[42] Ibid.

[43] Dr. James Walker and James Hooper, "Captain David Strombeck and Staff Sergeant William Bates Oral History Interview, ARSST Historical/Lessons Learned Study," 23 October 1998.

[44] James Hooper, "Major Scott Cuthbertson Oral History Interview, ARSST Historical/Lessons Learned Study," 29 October 1998.

[45] Ibid.

[46] Major Cimino, U.S. Army Space Command, After Action Report, Exercise ULCHI FOCUS LENS 96. 11 September 1996.

[47] Ibid.

[48] Ibid.

[49] Memorandum of Agreement between CG, XVIII Airborne Corps and CG, US Army Special Operations Command and Commander, U.S. Army Space Command (Forward). 5 March 1996.

[50] Ibid.

[51] Ibid.

[52] Ibid.

[53] Major Foeller, U.S. Army Space Command, "Army Space Support Team Briefing at the HQ USARSPACE (Forward) Program Management Review." 12 July 1996.

[54] Memorandum, U.S. Army Space Command, MOSC-OO-C, to TSOC PAT, ATTN: Mr. Jim Taylor, SPJTSOC, Subject: ARSPACE ARSST Information. 17 July 1996.

[55] Major Foeller, U.S. Army Space Command, "Army Space Support Team Briefing at the HQ USARSPACE (Forward) Program Management Review." 12 July 1996.

[56] Ibid.

[57] Memorandum, Major Wayne M. Brainerd, U.S. Army Space Command to Directorate for Force Structure, Resources, and Assessment (J-8), Sea, Air, and Space Superiority Division, Subject: Info on Army Space Support Teams. 29 July 1996.

[58] Ibid.

[59] U.S. Army Space Command Briefing, "Army Space Support Division," Undated.

[60] Ibid.

[61] Ibid.

[62] Ibid.

[63] Headquarters, Department of the Army, "Approved Document Print (TDA) Table of Distribution and Allowances: DOCNO SCW4XQAA." 30 May 1995.

[64] Headquarters, Department of the Army, "Approved Document Print (TDA) Table of Distribution and Allowances: DOCNO SCW4XQAA." 26 July 1996.

[65] Captain Gerald R. Skaw, U.S. Army Space Command, After Action Report, YAMA SAKURA XXXI. 25 February 1997.

[66] Ibid.

[67] Ibid.

[68] Editorial comments made by Major Caesar Jaime, USARSPACE, on 11 December 1998.

[69] Major Brainerd, U.S. Army Space Command, Input for U.S. Army Space and Strategic Defense Command Chief of Staff Notes for 28 February 1997, p. 37. U.S. Army Chief of Public Affairs, "U.S. Army Training and Operations Update." 8 April 1997.

[70] Dr. James Walker, U.S. Army Space and Strategic Defense Command, "3QFY97 USASSDC Command Achievements and Initiatives Report," p. 20.

[71] Captain Gerald R. Skaw, U.S. Army Space Command, ULCHI FOCUS LENS 97 After Action Review, 25 September 1997. Ed White, U.S. Army Space and Strategic Defense Command, "Space Support is Current Revolution in How Army Fights and Wins Land Conflicts," The Eagle (Sep/Oct 1997, Vol. 3, No. 5), p. 6. For a brief description of Joint Space Support Team (JSST) activities during this exercise, see General John H. Tilelli, "Ulchi-Focus Lens '97: Putting JV 2010 into Practice." Joint Forces Quarterly (Autumn/Winter 1997-98), pp. 76-80.

[72] Captain Gerald R. Skaw, U.S. Army Space Command, ULCHI FOCUS LENS 97 After Action Review, 25 September 1997.

[73] Ibid.

[74] James Hooper, "Major Scott Cuthbertson Oral History Interview, ARSST Historical/Lessons Learned Study," 29 October 1998.

[75] Facsimile Transmission, Joe Walker, Gichner Shelter Systems to Captain Cuthbertson, U.S. Army Space Command, "Rough Order of Magnitude Cost." 28 July 1997.

[76] U.S. Army Space Command Briefing, "Forward Deployment of ARSST: A One Stop Shop is Our Goal," Undated.

[77] Ibid.

[78] Draft Revised Memorandum of Agreement between CG, XVIII Airborne Corps and CG, US Army Special Operations Command and Commander, U.S. Army Space Command (Forward). Undated.

[79] U.S. Army Space Command Briefing, "ASSC: Army Space Support Cell," January 1998. (NOTE: The development of the Army Space Support Cell concept began in 1997 and carried over into 1998. For simplicity's sake, the concept for ASSC operations is presented in 1997 while ASSC training and exercise support are described in this chapter's subsection on 1998 operations).

[80] Ibid.

[81] Brown International, "Draft Army Space Support Cell Concept of Operations." Undated.

[82] Ibid.

[83] Ibid.

[84] Ibid.

[85] Ibid.

[86] U.S. Army Space Command Briefing, "US Army Space Command." 13 January 1998.

[87] Major Tim Burke, U.S. Army Space Command, "Weekly Activities Report for 10-14 November 1997," Undated.

[88] U.S. Army Space Command Briefing, "US Army Space Command." 13 January 1998.

[89] Jim Williamson and Ken H. Dryden, SY Technologies, "Trip Report: Battle Command Training Program (BCTP), 1st ID Warfighter Exercise," 18 March 1998.

[90] Dr. James Walker and James Hooper, "James Williamson Oral History Interview, ARSST Historical/Lessons Learned Study," 22 October 1998.

[91] Jim Williamson and Ken H. Dryden, SY Technologies, "Trip Report: Battle Command Training Program (BCTP), 1st ID Warfighter Exercise," 18 March 1998.

[92] Lieutenant Colonel LeRoy Maurer III, U.S. Army Space Command, Army Space Support Teams After Action Review (AAR) for UFL 98. 22 September 1998.

[93] Ibid.

[94] Ibid.

[95] Ibid.

[96] Warning Order, U.S. Army Space Command, "III Corps Warfighter Exercise (WFX)," 22October 1998. Warning Order, U.S. Army Space Command, "III Corps Ramp-Up Exercise," 22 October 1998.

[97] U.S. Army Space Command Briefing, "ARSST Training," 16 December 1997.

[98] Ken H. Dryden, SY Technologies, "AAR Notes for Monday 5 January thru Friday 9 January ARSST/ASSC Training." Undated.

[99] Ibid.

[100] U.S. Army Space Command, "Supporting the Supported Commander: ASSC April Training." Undated.

[101] U.S. Army Space Command, "ARSST Long Range Planning Input," February 1998. A copy of this document in electronic format was found on a floppy disk in the ARSST program files at Colorado Springs, Colorado.

[102] U.S. Army Space Command Briefing, "Long Range Plan," May 1998.

[103] Ibid.

[104] James Hooper, "Major Gwynne T. Burke Oral History Interview, ARSST Historical/Lessons Learned Study," 5 November 1998.

[105] The relationship between the U.S. III Corps and the 3rd ROK Army was described in an article published in the *Korea Times*. See Korea Times, "Joint ROK, US Military Exercise Due in Texas," 6 December 1998.

CHAPTER FOUR:

KEY TRENDS AND ISSUES

"ARSSTs are truly a force multiplier and bring a wealth of space systems support."

— I Corps, G-2 Staff Officer

Although the ARSST has only been active since October 1994, the Army now has twelve years of experience in thinking about and addressing the space support requirements of tactical commanders and staffs. This chapter addresses a number of key trends and issues that were identified through an examination of this twelve year historical record, as well as through oral history interviews conducted with current and former ARSST personnel.

This chapter does not represent a comprehensive evaluation of *every* issue of significance over the past four years of ARSST operations. Instead, it addresses certain key issues that have been raised repeatedly in the past and which seem likely to exert a continued influence on the future development of the teams, to include:

- The evolution of the Army space support structure over the past twelve years, to include organizational development and key intellectual trends.

- The impact of resource constraints, which in the past forced the ARSST leadership to make a tradeoff between deployment support functions (such as unit exercise support, demonstrations, space liaison, and operational missions) and institutional development activities (such as space education and training, experimentation with new DTLOMS initiatives, participation in Force XXI initiatives, and involvement in black-white space integration efforts).

- The importance and value of ARSST operations, as perceived by supported units and demonstrated through field survey collection, discussions, and the unit after-action reports maintained by the Army.

- The process for collecting, analyzing, and disseminating space support lessons learned throughout the Army.

- The Army's space education process and the implications for the ARSST.

- The role of the ARSST in providing demonstrations of advanced space systems and technologies to the warfighter.

EVOLUTION OF THE ARMY SPACE SUPPORT STRUCTURE

Organization and Programs

In the twelve-year period spanning from 1986 to 1998, the Army made significant strides in applying space systems and technologies to support tactical commanders. This period was marked by six key milestones: [1] The activation of the Army Space Institute in 1986. As the coordinating body for the development of Army space concepts, doctrine, training, and equipment, ASI served a pivotal role in first introducing the Army to the potential benefits offered by space; [2] The decision in 1987 to implement the Army Space Demonstration Program as a vehicle for bringing new space systems to the field. The demonstration program provided an education to many tactical commanders on methods of using space technologies to support planning and operations.

Although this program was not designed, organized, or funded to provide support to tactical units, the demonstration program also deployed in support of Army operations in Saudi Arabia, Iraq, Haiti, and Bosnia; [3] The growth of USARSPACE from a four-man liaison element at Colorado Springs into the key organization for providing operational space support to the Army. This evolutionary process was capped by the transfer of many ASI functions to USARSPACE in 1990, to include the Army Space Exploitation Demonstration

> **Key Milestones: Applying Space for the Tactical Commander.**
>
> **1986: Activation of the Army Space Institute.**
>
> **1987: Approval granted by the senior Army leadership for the Army Space Demonstration Program.**
>
> **1990: Establishment of USARSPACE as an operational command.**
>
> **1990-1991: Space served as a significant, multi-dimensional force multiplier in DESERT SHIELD and DESERT STORM.**
>
> **1994: The senior Army leadership decided to activate deployable COPS teams.**
>
> **1995-1998: Growth and evolution of the Army Space Support Team.**

Program; [4] The DESERT SHIELD / DESERT STORM experience, where the value of multi-spectral imagery, GPS position/navigation, satellite weather, ballistic missile warning, and satellite communications were clearly demonstrated. This experience also demonstrated the need for the Army to activate a dedicated space support organization, capable of providing training and operational support to units deployed in a theater of operations; [5] The Army's decision in 1994 to equip and man a deployable space support team (COPS) at Colorado Springs. The COPS team was the first Army organization explicitly designed to provide sustained operational support for units in the field; [6] The evolution and growth of the Army Space Support Team from 1994 to 1998. The ARSST represented an extension of the original COPS idea for a deployable space support organization. Equally as important, ARSST support for Army operations worldwide served as a bridge between the USARSPACE and the 'rank-and-file' Army.

Army Space Support: Intellectual Evolution

In the period from 1986 to 1998, the Army grappled with the question of where and how space can best be applied in support of warfighting units. As with the changes made in the Army's organizational structure for providing space support to field units, there were a number of significant shifts in how the Army responded to that question.

In 1986, the Army focused upon developing systems that could directly support tactical operations at the maneuver battalion and company levels. The Army Space Institute experimented with concepts under which spaceborne intelligence and weather data would be integrated into a battalion's planning process, position/navigation systems would be used to control tactical movements, and satellite communications would be employed to support battalion-level command and control.

With the activation of the Army Space Demonstration Program, the Army's approach to space evolved to include support for higher-echelon headquarters involved in campaign planning and other operational-level aspects of warfighting. The LIGHTSAT program and the WRAASE weather satellite receiver demonstrations were both geared to supporting commanders at the operational level. However, the Army continued to experiment with systems, such as the GPS, that could support tactical operations by small units. This dual approach would carry through Operation DESERT SHIELD, where Army space systems played a role at both the tactical and the operational levels of war.

When the Army decided to procure systems under the Commercial Space Package for contingency use under the COPS program, the Corps Headquarters was designated as the focal point for support. Nevertheless, USARSPACE contingency support planning continued to span the operational and tactical levels of war. In addition, USARSPACE grappled with the issue of providing space support across the entire spectrum of military activities. For example, in one early draft of the USARSPACE concept of operations for the COPS program, the Command stated that its teams would be prepared to support a variety of units and agencies:

> "CONUS based non-contingency Corps assets, National Guard units, FORSCOM Army Reserve units, and other government agencies (Federal Emergency Management Agency, Bureau of Land Management, Drug Enforcement Agency, State and Federal Law Enforcement Agencies, State Adjutants General, etc.)."[1]

After 1995, the ARSST grappled with the same intellectual questions. ARSSTs were deployed to support units from the battalion to the Joint Task Force level. Although the Corps Headquarters was traditionally the focal point for ARSST support, two of the most enthusiastic consumers of ARSST support were Aviation brigades and Special Forces battalions. As a consequence, ARSST support from 1995 to 1997 was characterized by support to higher-level headquarters, including

Corps and Echelons Above Corps, as well as tactical support for units at the brigade level and below.

The Army Space Support Cell concept introduced a new element, in which multiple ARSST teams were deployed to provide simultaneous support to units from brigade to theater level. During ULCHI FOCUS LENS 98, which served as the first key test of the ASSC concept of split-level support, four ARSST teams deployed from Colorado Springs to support Eighth U.S. Army, the 6th Cavalry Brigade, III Corps Headquarters, and the Combined Marine Expeditionary Force. In the meantime, an ASSC was located at Command Post Tango with Eighth U.S. Army, where it provided command and control for the ARSST teams located in-theater. The ASSC concept represented a new approach to the recurring question of where the Army should focus its contingency space support efforts; rather than selecting a single echelon to support or making a trade-off between operational and tactical warfighting, multiple ARSST teams would now be prepared to deploy simultaneously to support all types of operations, conducted by Army units at a number of echelons.

The Bottom Line: The Army Has a Demonstrated Need for a Deployable Space Support Organization

One constant requirement emerged from the Army's early experience in bringing space to tactical commander, the use of space systems and technologies in DESERT STORM and subsequent operations, and the activation and subsequent evolution of the ARSST – the need for a unit of space experts able to deploy to a theater of operations and translate space capabilities into 'tools' for the ground commander. The form of the ARSST evolved over time but the requirement for sustained space expertise and analytic support, integrated seamlessly into a supported unit in-theater, remained constant.

Arsst Resource Constraints and Tradeoffs

Resources available for ARSST operations were tightly constrained in the five years since the organization was activated. The result was a situation in which the deployment support functions of the ARSST were often conducted at the expense of longer-term ARSST institutional development.

The ARSST historically faced a zero-sum tradeoff between the need to conduct deployment support activities (such as unit exercise support, equipment demonstrations, space liaison, and operational mission support) and the need to support continued institutional growth and development (through activities such as internal space education and training programs, experimentation with new DTLOMS initiatives, participation in the Army's Force XXI and Army After Next process, involvement in "black" and "white" space integration initiatives, etc.). Both elements were essential to the long-term success of the ARSST. Field units have an immediate need for space support, which could only be satisfied by the

ARSST teams. ARSST teams served as the primary link between USARSPACE and the warfighter. On the other hand, space technologies and capabilities continued to evolve rapidly, the Army was engaged in a process of conceptual and organizational experimentation under the Force XXI process, and Army materiel developers were introducing new space-related systems to the field. If the ARSST failed to adapt and grow, its members feared they would eventually be overwhelmed by those larger trends and ARSST teams would provide a capability to the field that was either redundant or obsolete.

From 1995-1997, USARSPACE made a deliberate decision to emphasize ARSST deployment support to field units, even if institutional development activities were curtailed as a result. ARSST personnel were conscious of the importance of introducing the warfighter to space and ARSST teams were deployed to support exercises and unit training as often as possible. Due to the limited personnel and budget resources available to the ARSST, however, institutional development activities had to be conducted in an *ad hoc* fashion, whenever the pace of field deployments slackened. As a consequence, ARSST personnel could only sporadically support institutional development activities such as attending TRADOC Force XXI planning sessions, developing coordinating mechanisms for operating in a joint environment, exploring new systems and technologies that might be of use for an ARSST, sharing lessons learned with personnel from the Joint Space Support Teams, developing a self-sustainment capability for the ARSST teams, and engaging in self-guided space education. Although the ARSST leadership recognized the need to invest in the future, the highest priority remained introducing space and providing operational support to units in the field. With an average of 140 deployment days per man per year, the ARSST found the sustained pursuit of any institutional development initiative to be extremely difficult.

The *ad hoc* approach to ARSST institutional development from 1995-1997 did not stem from a lack of interest by USARSPACE or the ARSST leadership. To the contrary, ARSST personnel emphasized the need for continued institutional growth even before the teams were officially activated. USARSPACE personnel began reporting that they were providing a redundant capability to supported units as early as August 1994, when the Contingency Operations – Space (COPS) program was being implemented. After a deployment to support Joint Task Force Support Hope in Rwanda, Major Cafaro reported:

> "[W]e must remember that there is no present ARSPACE augmentation capability which does not exist elsewhere. INMARSAT is widely used by all services and many Army Agencies, as well as the Diplomatic Corps. The capability to provide satellite weather images exists in the Air Force, and they also have the forecasters, which we do not. Image maps are available through TEC and unit terrain teams, and for this operation the Air Force was quicker to obtain raw data than we were. . . . Also, our mission planning and rehearsal system is dependent on digital terrain elevation data, which we do not produce and was not available for the area of this operation. There are other mission planning systems besides ours as well."[2]

Given the redundancy of the systems deployed by USARSPACE, Major Cafaro concluded that the COPS teams would have to "concentrate on applying them better to truly make a difference in supporting Army units."[3]

By 1996, officers assigned to the ARSST were stressing the need for the team to evolve into an organization that focused on space analysis. For example, the first lesson learned reported at the year-end review of ARSST operations for 1995 was that the "ARSST must be able to provide all types of space support – not just four pieces of equipment."[4] On 8 January 1996 Major Mike Jensen (ARSST Division Chief) stressed that it was necessary to "concentrate on expanding [the] ARSST role as a space advisory/liaison capability. Instead of just operating systems ARSST must be able to support [the] warfighter on all space systems and issues."[5] At the HQ USARSPACE Program Management Review conducted six months later, the leading issue briefed was that the "ARSST must go beyond the CSP concept; [they] must be brokers for space force enhancement."[6]

Nevertheless, a heavy schedule of operational deployments to the field and a lack of resources prevented the ARSST from taking those steps in the institutional development process that would be necessary if the teams were to focus on space analytic support rather than the manning of space-related equipment. This situation began to change during the 1997-1998 time frame with the development of the ASSC concept. To implement this initiative, USARSPACE provided an influx of additional resources to the ARSST. These resources were used to develop a new concept of operations, establish a unit training program, and support the evolution of the ARSST into a full-fledged space analysis team. While much work remains to be done, by 1998 the ARSST leadership had identified Army key space support requirements, established priorities for ARSST near-term evolution, and developed a plan for implementation. As a consequence, the ARSST had a firm foundation for evolving into a more robust team that would be capable of supporting the full range of warfighter requirements.

However, while the additional resources provided by USARSPACE largely freed the ARSST from the tradeoff between providing deployment support or engaging in longer-term ARSST institutional development, longer-term issues remaiedn. For example, the ARSST TDA established a requirement for 34 soldiers, but only 21 were authorized in 1998. If not addressed, ARSST team members feared that the personnel shortfall could inhibit the future evolution of the ARSST and the ASSC. As described earlier, the ASSC concept represented a new approach to the recurring question of where the Army should focus its contingency space support efforts. Under that concept, ARSST teams had to be prepared to deploy simultaneously to support all types of operations, conducted by Army units at a number of echelons. If the ARSST was to successfully deploy multiple teams simultaneously and support units in operations ranging from theater campaign planning to special operations reconnaissance, it might require more resources than were needed when a single ARSST team deployed independently. Resource requirements could also be expected to increase as the ARSST and ASSC develop new capabilities to provide space analytical support to field units.

The Bottom Line: A Requirement for Resources

If the ARSST was to remain a valuable asset for the Army in both the near- and the long-term, Army decision makers concluded that sufficient resources had to be provided to avert a situation in which a tradeoff would be made between deployment support to the field and longer-term ARSST institutional development. The additional resources provided in the 1997-1998 time period allowed the ARSST to break out of the former cycle in which longer-term institutional development were often sacrificed for the sake of deploying teams to the field. In the meantime, however, the ARSST adopted a more aggressive concept of operations in which multiple teams would deploy simultaneously and new types of space analytic support would be provided to the field. These initiatives promised to yield great benefits to the Army.

The View from the Field: How Supported Units Rate Arsst Support

Units that received support from an ARSST in the past consistently rated the quality of ARSST support highly. In a field survey sent to officers who had trained with the ARSST, every respondent answered "yes" to the question, "If your unit deployed to war, would you request assistance from an Army Space Support Team?" Typical comments from the field include: "I still firmly believe that ARSSTs are truly a FORCE MULTIPLIER and bring a wealth of SPACE SYSTEMS support" and "I am a believer in the capabilities made available by the ARSST." On the other hand, the ARSST had little exposure across the Army as a whole. For example, in the Army's database of unit after-action reports and observations from exercises and CTC rotations, there were no references made to the ARSST. Similarly, while the ARSST was described in *FM 100-18: Space Support to Army Operations*, in 1998 there were no coordinating mechanisms or procedures for using an ARSST team or integrating space support into unit operations contained in other key Army manuals, such as *FM 101-5: Staff Organization and Operations*.

After-Action Reports and Observations From The Field

In discussions with Army officers with experience at the Corps and Division level, a strong dichotomy was observed between those personnel who had trained with an ARSST and those who had not. Those personnel who had experience working with an ARSST team were invariably strong supporters of the concept. They also had a better understanding of how space contributes to Army operations than their counterparts who had not trained with an ARSST. Military officers who had not worked with the Army Space Support Team generally believed that space support capabilities were limited to GPS position/navigation systems and theater-level satellite communications.

To gain a better understanding of how the "rank-and-file" Army viewed both space support and ARSST operations, a systematic search was conducted through the Army's database of unit after-action reports and observations from exercises and CTC rotations. This database was maintained by the Center for Army Lessons Learned (CALL) at Ft. Leavenworth on a restricted basis and could only be accessed by military personnel, DoD civilians, and others with a demonstrated requirement for access. The purpose of that database search was twofold: The first objective was to learn what units had written about space support in their after-action reports; the second objective was to gain an understanding of what space support materials would be accessible through established Army channels to the typical officer during an operational deployment or exercise, in a school setting, or while providing staff support for force development, doctrinal writing, or related efforts.

The most significant finding of the systematic database search was that there are no documents that directly mention or describe the ARSST. A search for information on the ARSST revealed 10 'hits' – none of which was applicable. Each of the hits resulted from the scanning in of poor quality documents into the *Center for Army Lessons Learned*, causing the computer search engine to return hits on material unrelated to the ARSST. As a result, an individual searching for data on the ARSST would instead receive information on TASOC facilities, bibliographical citations from a study of the efforts of continuous operations on both soldier and unit performance, a roster for the pre-combat inspection team during the 2nd Armored Cavalry Regiment's BOLD DRAGOON III Exercise "BEARHUNTER", and a standardized form for the servicing of clothes dryers, washing machines, and other appliances.[7]

Similarly, there was no information on systems used by the ARSST in the *Center for Army Lessons Learned* system, such as the SSP (Space Support Platform) and OMEGA (a GPS accuracy prediction tool). A search under SSP revealed resulted in 16 hits, none of which were applicable to the Army Space Support Team or its operations.[8] A search on OMEGA resulted in 30 hits, including one file describing the ARN-148 OMEGA GPS receiver mounted in a CH-47 helicopter, but no information on GPS accuracy.[9]

While no data on ARSST operations or systems was available in the *Center for Army Lessons* files, large quantities of information were uncovered on established space support systems, such as INMARSAT and GPS. Under INMARSAT, for example, 102 hits were registered.[10] This included a number of lessons learned from Army operations throughout the world. A military officer looking for background information on the use of INMARSAT terminals would find that during ABLE SENTRY in Macedonia, INMARSAT had proved to be "an ideal product for contingency operations" and had been used to support brigade task force operations, intelligence, and maintenance.[11] Furthermore, experiments were conducted with the Force Tracking System, designed to track logistical shipments with GPS positioning data and INMARSAT communications. Although this system had been designed to track shipments at sea, in Macedonia it was mounted on vehicles.[12] In Haiti, INMARSAT had been used extensively throughout the JTF 190 Headquarters, the 10th Mountain Division, and the United Nations forces. INMARSAT was considered so useful that it was recommended future communications packages for entry operations include INMARSAT terminals.[13] In addition, USARSPACE supported the Haiti deployment with INMARSAT, Mission Planning Rehearsal System, Terrain Reconnaissance Tool, and Multi-Spectral Imagery Processor. An observer from the *Center for Army Lessons Learned* concluded:

> "The availability of new technologies from ARSPACE improved the capability of the CJTF/MNF to accomplish its operational mission. This equipment allowed the SWO to more easily provide weather support, and its use by the terrain team allowed terrain products for operations to be prepared more easily, faster, and with accurate data."[14]

The military officer looking for background data on INMARSAT would also learn, among other things, that INMARSAT terminals had been used in Somalia for hospital operations, casualty reporting, equipment maintenance, and liaison with elements at Ft. Drum.[15] For early entry operations in Somalia, INMARSAT was viewed as a "critical asset" but one that also was "expensive, lacked in-country maintenance" and required "strong centralized control."[16] For U.S. support to United Nations peacekeeping operations in Cambodia, it was found that "The UN communications system could not be relied upon until very well into the mission . . . [but that] national rear link communications, via INMARSAT, were adequate for Contingent requirements up to the SECRET level."[17] During GUARDIAN RETRIEVAL, the Joint Operations Center "relied heavily on telephone comms (INMARSAT, DSN, MSE) for information flow and coordination."[18] However, the Joint Task Force J-2 had difficulty transmitting large graphics files via INMARSAT and it was recommended that the SIPRNET be used instead. Furthermore, it was recommended after GUARDIAN RETRIEVAL that the SETAF J2 acquire an INMARSAT to help "provide immediate SCI intelligence conductivity to the JTF."[19] For U.S. operations in Albania, INMARSAT had proven to be so useful that it was recommended that "INMARSAT link capability should be included on the first aircraft arriving in country."[20]

As the examples above illustrate, there is a large quantity of information on INMARSAT usage in the unit after-action reports and external observations collected by the Army. Only rarely, however, are the benefits of systems such as the INMARSAT and GPS attributed to USARSPACE. Furthermore, data regarding current ARSST operations and equipment is noticeably absent.

The Bottom Line: Officers Who Have Trained With An ARSST Are Impressed With The Value Of Space Support.

Officers who trained with an ARSST in the past consistently rated the value of that support highly. Unfortunately, the ARSST had little exposure across the Army as a whole. For the long-term, ARSST soldiers emphasized that space support must be incorporated into existing Army systems and processes for training, doctrine, and force development. In the near-term, leaders in the USARSPACE needed to continue "selling" the ARSST to the rank-and-file Army. A variety of initiatives were being pursued by the USARSPACE leadership in 1998 to accomplish this objective.

Space Support and Lessons Learned Analysis

As noted in the previous section, in 1998 little information on ARSST operations and capabilities was available in the Army's database of unit after-action reports, CTC observations, and exercise reports. This situation stemmed in large part form the lack of a formalized mechanism for collecting, analyzing, and disseminating lessons learned by the ARSST.

The Original ARSST Reporting and Collection Process

The original concept of operations for the ARSST (dated December 1994) included extensive reporting and collection requirements. Under that system, the following reporting requirements were established, with copies to be provided to both U.S. Army Space and Strategic Defense Command (now U.S. Army Space and Missile Defense Command) and HQDA:

1. Monthly reports by USARSPACE on the operational status and availability of each ARSST system, the status and location of ARSST personnel, and the readiness and availability of the ARSST teams.

2. Spot reports detailing personnel or equipment losses, equipment failures, impacting personnel actions, and mission conflicts.

3. "HOTWASH" reports within 2 hours of the completion of an ARSST mission.

4. Formatted after-action reports on all operational missions.[21]

Oral history interviews conducted with former and current ARSST Team Chiefs revealed that this process was never implemented. Although the ARSST teams produced written after-action reports for exercises that they supported, no evidence exists to suggest that these reports were indeed forwarded to USASSDC or HQDA. ARSST after-action reports were staffed through USARSPACE and approved by the USARSPACE Commander. However, there was no central repository for the retention and storage of ARSST after-action reports. In fact, when research was initiated for this history, each of the ARSST team members searched their personal files for copies of old after-action reports. Only seven were found.[22] In addition, there is no evidence that ARSST after-action reports were incorporated into the Army-wide lessons learned system. Simply stated, there has not been a concerted effort over the past five years to disseminate space support lessons learned. In fact, some of the ARSST Team Chiefs interviewed for this history stated that, at one point in time, a senior USARSPACE officer provided specific guidance to stop documenting lessons learned.

Implications of the Failure to Capture ARSST Lessons Learned

The results of the lack of a consistent and systematic process to capture, analyze, and disseminate lessons learned over the past five years of ARSST operations are as follows:

Army Space Support Team Personnel. The ARSST was a tight-knit organization in which lessons learned were quickly disseminated among team members by word of mouth. However, the personnel turnover rate among the teams tended to be high. This fact, coupled with the lack of a systematic training program for new ARSST personnel, resulted in the loss of many lessons learned over time.

U.S. Army Space Command. The ARSST served as the primary link between ARSPACE and the various warfighting headquarters. The USARSPACE Long Range Plan, as briefed during the May 98 IPR, identified the ARSST as the organization that provides "feedback to the ARSPACE staff on warfighting operational requirements to interject into the formal Army requirements process." Such input from the ARSST was also valuable for force development and training efforts involving space. However, without a systematic lessons learned process, ARSST soldiers feared that it might be difficult for the ARSST to fulfill this key role.

Army Training and Doctrine. The ARSST did not incorporate lessons learned on space (from the warfighter's perspective) into either the *Center for Army Lessons Learned* process or the U.S. Army Training and Doctrine Command school system. The only space support lessons learned analysis that was prepared for Army-wide dissemination is *The Ultimate High Ground! Space Support to the Army: Lessons from Operations DESERT SHIELD and STORM*, which was written in 1991. As noted earlier, an officer searching the Army's database of unit after-action reports in 1998 under the term "ARSST" would not find a single applicable reference. Instead, a series of unrelated documents and reports would be returned by the computer system. Furthermore, USARSPACE personnel interviewed noted that there was no systematic process whereby information gathered during ARSST deployments was provided directly to the TRADOC school system or incorporated into the space electives taught at the Army War College or Command and General Staff College. In short, the lessons learned during the prior five years of ARSST operations were not distributed throughout the "rank-and-file" Army.

The Bottom Line: A Systematic Process Should Be Established to Disseminate Space Support Lessons Learned Throughout the Total Army.

The Army employs a six-phase lessons learned process consisting of planning, collection, analysis, publication, distribution, and archiving. In 1998, the ARSST was collecting lessons learned and reporting them throughout Army Space Command after every mission. However, these lessons learned were not being developed for publication outside the Command, distributed to appropriate Army units, and archived for future use. Nor was a structured collection plan used by the ARSST to ensure that key issues were addressed and specified data was collected during an ARSST team deployment.

The Arsst and Space Education

All personnel interviewed for this history in 1998 stated their belief that the Army school system did not adequately prepare ARSST members to perform space analytic missions, nor did it sensitize warfighters to the importance and impact of space operations. ARSST personnel considered the development of Functional Area 40 as a key step toward solving these problems in the long-term. In addition, however, they saw a critical need for the Army to incorporate space into the professional education and development process for all leaders.

Current Space Education

The TRADOC space education program in 1998 consisted of two elective courses at Command and General Staff College, leading to the award of Additional Skill Identifier 3Y, and one elective course at the Army War College. There was no space instruction for company-grade officers and non-commissioned officers in the TRADOC school system. As a consequence, unless an officer had a particular interest in military space and opted to take the elective courses, he or she would not receive space training in a formal, school environment. A number of Army leaders were exposed to space when they receive support from an ARSST in the field. Unfortunately, the officers who take the CGSC and Army War College electives, or who have experience training with an ARSST, represented a tiny fraction of the total force.

For ARSST team members, there was little space training and education in the period from 1994 to 1997. Many ARSST team members noted that they had been deployed to the field within two to three weeks of assignment to USARSPACE. ARSST team chiefs were typically sent to the Joint Space Fundamentals Course and received some training on ARSST equipment and systems. However, all team chiefs interviewed in 1998 strongly emphasized that this level of education was inadequate to perform space analytical duties in the field. Non-commissioned officers focused on the manning of space support systems and were trained largely through an on-the-job process. ARSST NCOs tended to view this process as satisfactory for operating ARSST equipment, but insufficient for space analysis support duties.

The initiative that began in 1998 to provide training to ARSST personnel in a formal, systematic manner was seen as a positive step by all ARSST team chiefs interviewed during this history. They stated that the ARSST's continued evolution, as envisioned under the ASSC concept, remained dependent on the establishment of a good training and professional development program. The value of the training itself, however, was questioned by many ARSST team members. They argued that significant revisions and upgrades to the curriculum were required. Because both the ASSC concept and the supporting training process were still relatively new, it was not surprising that many ARSST team members argued for revisions to the training program. It should also be noted that the ARSST Branch Chief in 1998, Lieutenant Colonel LeRoy Maurer, had already taken steps to adapt the current training program in response to identified shortcomings and anticipated requirements.

Future Army Space Education

In 1998 the Army explored a number of initiatives for future space education, literacy, and training programs, such as the development of a Master of Military Arts and Sciences program with a focus on space operations. A full consideration of these initiatives lies beyond the scope of this history. However, it should be noted that ARSST soldiers interviewed for this history tended to share the following perspective. First, space education programs must be incorporated throughout the TRADOC school system, to include CAS3, Officer Advanced and Basic Courses, and advanced NCO courses. One former ARSST team chief added that space education should even be extended to the pre-commissioning process for officers. Second, there was a significant level of interest in Functional Area 40 activation and development. ARSST team chiefs often argued that their current duties were closely related to what an FA40 officer will do in the future when assigned to a Corps or Division staff. In addition, ARSST team chiefs felt that lessons learned during ARSST operations should be used to help guide the development of Functional Area 40. Third, as noted above, ARSST leaders in 1998 strongly believed that the education process for ARSST team chiefs required further development and expansion. Finally, many ARSST personnel argued that the ARSST teams could fulfill an important role in providing space education and training to soldiers in the field, if properly trained and resourced.

The Bottom Line: Continued Emphasis Should Be Placed Upon the Development of Space Education and Training Programs

Training and education programs in 1998 did not adequately prepare the Army to cope with space. In the long-term, the activation of the new Functional Area 40 was expected to help address that problem. In the short-term, ARSST leaders expected that the ARSST teams would continue to fill an indispensable role by helping to translate space capabilities into 'tools' for a supported unit. However, if the Army was to achieve the maximum value from space systems and capabilities in the future while minimizing the impact of adversary space usage, continued space education and training efforts would be essential. Initiatives within USARSPACE to enhance the quality of space training — not only for ARSST personnel but throughout the Army — were emphasized in 1998 as key priorities for the Command that should be adequately resourced by the Army.

School	Military Space Instruction
U.S. Army War College	1 Space Elective.
School of Advanced Military Studies	½ Day Familiarization Session, Periodically Conducted by USARSPACE.
Command and General Staff College	2 Space Electives.
CAS3	None.
Advanced Officer Courses	None known.
Basic Officer Courses	None known.
NCO Development System	None known.

Figure 18: Space Education in the Army's School System, 1998.[23]

The Arsst and Space Demonstration

All ARSST team members interviewed for this history believed that a primary role for the Army Space Support Team should be to provide field demonstrations of new space technologies and systems. However, as a general rule, ARSST team members did not believe that this function was being performed very well and noted that an improved process should be developed. In addition, they saw a need for a close relationship between the ARSST and the Space and Missile Defense Battle Laboratory.

The ARSST and Space System Demonstration Missions

From the standpoint of former and current ARSST team chiefs, the Army Space Exploitation Demonstration Program was not successfully equipping the teams with new systems and technologies in 1998. As early as January 1996, ARSST leaders were expressing concerns that the ASEDP process was not furnishing new systems for the teams to take with them to the field. Major Mike Jensen, the ARSST Division Chief at the time, noted that it was important to "[e]mphasize to the command that the Demo program must be providing ARSST new technology yearly to stay viable (LEOCOMM, GBS are good examples)."[24] ARSST personnel interviewed for this history were in agreement on three central points. First, they believed that the ARSST should serve as a conduit between the space demonstration effort conducted at the Space and Missile Defense Battle Laboratory (SMDBL) and the warfighter. Second, they agreed that the present space demonstration system had not fully satisfied the requirement to introduce new systems and technologies. Third, most believed that serious efforts to address this issue were being made at the SMDBL and were very hesitant to criticize the personnel involved in the program.

One typical ARSST team assessment of the space demonstration program was that

> "the idea was clearly a sound idea – that things would go through ASEDP and come through the ARSST teams. There were a couple of systems that went directly from ASEDP to fielding and there were other systems that just died. Priorities shifted, concepts changed, and we actually got left holding the bag with '94 equipment until very recently. We sort of lost a little bit of faith in the ASEDP system." He added, "There's clearly a need for it. There needs to be conduit between what is now the Battle Lab and the space support teams. One of the things I would have liked to have seen is the ASEDP folks and industry come to us and say: 'What do you need?' What we found is that nobody ever asked us what we thought we needed. Very rarely did anybody ever ask the guys out in the units what they needed. More often than not they came to us and said: 'Hey, you need this.'"[25]

From an historical standpoint, the initial level of interaction between the ASEDP and the ARSST was very high. The four original systems acquired for the COPS teams in 1994 had previously been demonstrated under ASEDP. Existing ASEDP training plans were adapted for COPS deployment purposes.[26] Furthermore, the concept of operations envisioned that teams would routinely be augmented by ASEDP equipment and personnel prior to deployment.[27]

In the period from 1995 to 1998, the level of interaction between the ARSST and the demonstration program declined. The ASEDP continued to provide new systems to the ARSST teams for demonstration in the field, such as the Laptop Visualization Device (LVD), Low-Earth Orbit Mobile Data Communications Capability (LEOCOMM), Global Broadcast Service (GBS), Direct PC, the Vehicular Data Communications and Positional Awareness Demonstration (VDCPAD), and the Attitude Determination Device (ADD). However, with the exception of ADD (which was demonstrated by Captain Cuthbertson and later selected for adoption into the next generation fire support vehicle[28]), in 1998 no ARSST team chief cited an example of a systematic transition of an ASEDP system through the ARSST to the field. This might have reflected the difficulties in measuring and quantifying the relationship between space demonstration efforts and subsequent adoption of the systems by the Army as a whole. A number of USARSPACE personnel argued that there has been a direct correlation between space demonstration efforts and unit demand for (and acquisition of) space systems, such as satellite weather receivers and satellite communications terminals. Others cautioned that no hard evidence had been developed that demonstrates a clear cause-and-effect relationship. In other words, other factors could be influencing the Army's interest in space systems and efforts to acquire them.

A full examination of the process of space demonstration to the field – and the correlation between this activity and subsequent Army decision making – lies beyond the scope of this history. It should be noted, however, that anecdotal evidence in the historical record suggested that there was a *relatively strong* correlation between the demonstration of new technologies by USARSPACE personnel and the subsequent adoption of space systems by warfighters. In the absence of evidence to the contrary, it is safe to assume that such a correlation indeed existed and that ARSST personnel performed an important duty when they brought new systems to the field. Furthermore, ARSST team members saw a clear benefit stemming from the ability of warfighters to experiment with new technologies and systems in an operational setting, suggest improvements, and even reject them outright before the Army had devoted a significant level of resources to acquiring the system.

The Bottom Line: The ARSST Should Continue To Demonstrate New Space Systems

The ARSST leadership in 1998 concluded that they could play a significant role for the Army as a conduit for bringing new technologies to warfighters. Although

ARSST personnel identified a number of weaknesses in program implementation and the value of the demonstration effort was somewhat difficult to quantify, the idea of using ARSST teams to demonstrate equipment was fundamentally sound. The Army needed to experiment with next-generation technologies and capabilities; the ARSST had the ability to bring these systems to the field effectively and at the lowest cost.

Summary

Army initiatives over the past twelve years to bring space technologies to field units clearly demonstrated the requirement for a deployable team of space experts capable of supporting tactical and operational missions. This team must be able to deploy directly into a theater of operations, integrate itself into the staff process and battle rhythm of the supported unit, and provide space analytic products and advice to the commander. In other words, the Army had a clear need for a team that could translate space capabilities into warfighting tools and ensure that space considerations were professionally addressed throughout all aspects of mission planning and execution.

The decision to activate an ARSST in 1994 marked a crucial step in the process of bringing space support to the warfighter. Over the next five years, ARSST teams deployed to support Army operations and exercises around the world, in the process incorporating space into the activities of units ranging from battalion to theater level. During this period, a number of recurring themes and issues were identified. First, the ARSST must be adequately resourced to support both deployment missions *and* longer-term institutional development activities. When resources were insufficient to accomplish both functions in the period between 1995 and 1997, the ARSST leadership was forced to focus on near-term deployment support missions while sacrificing longer-term institutional development. As USARSPACE implemented the Army Space Support Cell concept in 1998 — which promises to yield tremendous benefits for the Army — ARSST leaders emphasized the importance of sufficient personnel, funding, and equipment.

Second, units that received support from an ARSST consistently rated the value and importance of space support highly. However, only a small number of officers had an opportunity to train closely with ARSST personnel. USARSPACE, with assistance from senior leaders throughout USASMDC, continued to take steps to sensitize and teach the rest of the Army about the value of space. The ARSST represented a success story and provides an example of what can be accomplished for the rest of the Army. Closely related to this issue was a third key point — the fact that the five years of ARSST space support lessons learned had not been disseminated throughout the Army and, thus, were not available to inform Army training, doctrine, and force development efforts. This failure stemmed from the lack of a systematic process for collecting, analyzing, and disseminating lessons learned. Existing mechanisms within the USASMDC were examined for their relevance in addressing this issue, to include a systematic process for planning, collection, analysis, publication, distribution, and archiving lessons learned.

The fourth recurring issue in the history of ARSST operations was the lack of formalized spaced education and training for both the ARSST and the 'rank-and-file' Army. In the long-term, the activation of the new Functional Area 40 was expected to help address this problem. In the short-term, the ARSST would continue to fill an indispensable role by helping to translate space capabilities into 'tools' for a supported unit. However, if the Army was to achieve the maximum value from space systems and capabilities in the future while minimizing the impact of adversary space usage, continued space education and training efforts would be essential. Ongoing initiatives within USARSPACE to enhance the quality of space training — not only for ARSST personnel but throughout the Army — were identified as key priorities for the Command that should be adequately resourced by the Army.

Another key issue that had risen repeatedly since the activation of the teams in 1994 was the relationship between the ARSST and the space demonstration program. Although the ARSST originated as an offshoot of the Army Space Exploitation Demonstration Program, the level of interaction between the teams and the demonstration program diminished over the years. In 1998, the ARSST leadership repeatedly expressed concerns that the teams were not equipped with the latest space systems and technologies. Although there were a number of ongoing initiatives to address this issue in 1998 and the relationship between the ARSST and the demonstration program was expected to continue to evolve in the future, one point was clear — the ARSST teams were uniquely qualified to serve as a conduit for warfighter experimentation with new space capabilities.

---

[1] Femme Comp Incorporated, Satellite Communications Group, Draft Contingency Operations (Space) Concept of Operations (September 1994 Draft). Electronic copy of document on floppy diskette. Diskette found in ARSST Division files.

[2] Major Cafaro, U.S. Army Space Command, "Trip Report – Joint Task Force Support Hope, 29 July to 13 August 1994." 18 August 1994.

[3] Ibid.

[4] Meeting Notes, Major Foeller, U.S. Army Space Command, "Army Space Support to the Warfighter Review," 11 January 1996.

[5] Electronic Mail Message, Major Mike Jensen, ARSST Division Chief, "Future ARSST Issues." 8 January 1996.

[6] Major Foeller, U.S. Army Space Command, "Army Space Support Team Briefing at the HQ USARSPACE (Forward) Program Management Review." 12 July 1996.

[7] Unlimited content search conducted by James Hooper through the restricted Center for Army Lessons Learned database on 3 December 1998 under the term

"ARSST." A search under the term "Army Space Support Team" and "Space Support Team" proved to be overly broad. While these searches yielded a number of hits, none was applicable to the ARSST.

[8] Unlimited content search conducted by James Hooper through the restricted Center for Army Lessons Learned database on 3 December 1998 under the term "SSP." A search under the term "Space Support Platform" uncovered many more files but none of them appeared to be applicable to ARSST operations.

[9] Unlimited content search conducted by James Hooper through the restricted Center for Army Lessons Learned database on 3 December 1998 under the term "OMEGA" and "GPS."

[10] Unlimited content search conducted by James Hooper through the restricted Center for Army Lessons Learned database on 3 December 1998 under the term "INMARSAT." For GPS, literally hundreds of hits were registered.

[11] Center for Army Lessons Learned Database, "EXERCISE ABLE SENTRY AAR 930625-940106." Center for Army Lessons Learned Database, "CALL LESSONS LEARNED: OPN ABLE SENTRY, OOTW -- 9410."

[12] Center for Army Lessons Learned Database, "CALL LESSONS LEARNED: OPN ABLE SENTRY, OOTW -- 9410."

[13] Center for Army Lessons Learned Database, "HAITI IIR VOL 1 941201."

[14] Center for Army Lessons Learned Database, "HAITI OBSN AIRSPACE [sic] EQUIP USED BY THE CJTF-MNF." Captain Williams, Center for Army Lessons Learned, "OPERATION MAINTAIN DEMOCRACY: ARSPACE Equipment Used by CJTF/MNF HQs Staffs." Undated.

[15] Center for Army Lessons Learned Database, "SOMALIA TF MTN AAR 930213." Center for Army Lessons Learned Database, "CALL SOMALIA-LL-9112-9305."

[16] Center for Army Lessons Learned Database, "CALL SOMALIA-LL-9112-9305."

[17] Center for Army Lessons Learned Database, "PEACE UN PEACEKEEPING OPNS IN CAMBODIA 930622."

[18] Center for Army Lessons Learned Database, "GUARDIAN RETRIEVAL AAR-03, OPS."

[19] Center for Army Lessons Learned Database, "GUARDIAN RETRIEVAL AAR-07, INTEL, WEATHER."

[20] Center for Army Lessons Learned Database, "CALL IIR ALBANIA, NOMAD VIGIL."

[21] U.S. Army Space Command, Army Space Support Team (ARSST) Concept of Operations (CONOPS) (DRAFT). (Colorado Springs, Colorado: U.S. Army Space Command: 12 December 1994.)..

[22] After-action reports were found for ULCHI FOCUS LENS 98; 1st Infantry Division Warfighter Exercise; 2nd Battalion, 1st Special Forces Group JRTC Rotation 97-7; 3rd Battalion, 5th Special Forces Group AWE TF XXI exercise; ULCHI FOCUS LENS 97; YAMA SAKURA XXXI; and ULCHI FOCUS LENS 96.

[23] Dr. James Walker and James Hooper, "Lieutenant Colonel Bob Simmons and Lieutenant Colonel LeRoy Maurer Oral History Interview, ARSST Historical/Lessons Learned Study," 23 October 1998. This chart was developed by Lieutenant Colonel Simmons during the course of the oral history interview as he described the state of space education in the Army.

[24] Electronic Mail Message, Major Mike Jensen, ARSST Division Chief, "Future ARSST Issues." 8 January 1996.

[25] James Hooper, "Major Scott Cuthbertson Oral History Interview, ARSST Historical/Lessons Learned Study," 29 October 1998.

[26] Femme Comp Incorporated, Satellite Communications Group, Task Order Plan 95-08: Contingency Operations (Space) / COPS Documentation Development. 26 September 1994.

[27] Femme Comp Incorporated, Satellite Communications Group, Task Order Plan 94-08: Contingency Operations (Space) / COPS Documentation Development. 7 July 1994.

[28] James Hooper, "Major Scott Cuthbertson Oral History Interview, ARSST Historical/Lessons Learned Study," 29 October 1998.

CHAPTER FIVE:

FUTURE ARSST EVOLUTION

"The role of the Army in space is already evident – it has no role."

— B. Bruce-Briggs, 1986.[1]

"Assuming settlements on the moon, Mars, or wherever, would it not be appropriate for the Army to maintain a space version of its current Earth missions?"

— Major Sherwood C. Spring, U.S. Army, 1983.[2]

If decision-makers are to make informed choices, they must possess a clear understanding of the past. The primary goal of this analysis of the Army Space Support Team has been to support decision-making—both present and future—by outlining the organizational and intellectual evolution of the ARSST, identifying trends and issues of significance, and explaining how important problems were approached and why key decisions were made.

As the quotes at the top of this page illustrate, a number of wild predictions have been made about the Army's role in space in the past. No such predictions will be made in this chapter. Instead, the following questions will be addressed:

- In the past, what has the ARSST long range vision been? How have ARSST personnel looked at future space support operations?

- What are the major assumptions underlying current ARSST long range planning?

- What concepts for future ARSST organization and operations are currently being discussed and explored?

THE ARSST LONG RANGE VISION, 1996-1998

In the period from 1986-1998, the Army actively experimented with tactics, techniques, and procedures for exploiting space systems and technologies. Members of the Army Space Support Team played a key role in this process since 1994. Throughout, ARSST personnel were cognizant of two significant facts. First, space technology and capabilities were rapidly evolving. Second, to keep pace with this evolution the ARSST must continue to adapt and grow. As a consequence, the officers and NCOs assigned to the ARSST spent a tremendous amount of time thinking about the future.

ARSST Long Range Vision: January 1996

The first far-reaching vision of future ARSST roles, missions, and operations was presented by Major Jensen (ARSST Division Chief) after the teams had completed their first year of field operations. In Major Jensen's vision, the future role of the ARSST would be to provide multi-dimensional space support to the Army, to include operational support, space analysis, force development, and training. On an operational level, the ARSSTs would continue to provide rapidly deployable space support for the Army and would be responsible for helping supported units develop and execute operations plans. ARSSTs would support Army units from Brigade to Corps level. The ARSST would also participate in Army force development efforts, helping to "test and evaluate Force Development employment and organizational concepts." Finally, the ARSST would play a leading role in the space education of the Army by providing technology demonstrations and equipment training, to include a "'Green Suit' education program at TRADOC schools."[3]

ARSST Long Range Vision: July 1996

The need for the ARSST to continue to evolve to perform new roles and missions, which was identified by Major Jensen in January 1996, was reemphasized during a Program Management Review conducted by USARSPACE in July. During this review session, the ARSST discussed the need for the teams to evolve so that they could "be brokers for space force enhancement."[4] It was also expected that the ARSST teams would "continue to serve as an operational exploitation/demonstration platform introducing and supporting the warfighter with new technology."[5] Given this long range forecast, the ARSST Division saw a need to be integrated into the planning and process for major Corps-level exercises and contingency missions. In addition, the ARSST teams would be responsible for educating Corps staffs on Army space-based force enhancement capabilities. Finally, the ARSSTs would need to take steps to "integrate current and future ARSPACE space force enhancement capabilities at Corps level and below."[6]

ARSST Long Range Vision: 1997

The ARSST continued to evaluate future possibilities for the evolution of the teams in 1997. A number of areas for future expansion of the ARSST role were foreseen. First, USARSPACE envisioned an evolution of the ARSST into "a 'one stop shop' with weather, imagery, missile defense, space expertise, and communications." Second, the ARSST would have to develop an improved ability to conduct joint operations, to include mechanisms for coordinating with the Joint Space Support Teams and other space support assets. Third, the ARSST Division saw a need to support units in the field from Combatant Command to Division level. Fourth, the ARSST would continue to bring the latest technology to the field, whether it was acquired through ASEDP or a materiel developer. These technology demonstrations were expected to include systems capable of faster data transfer, direct downlink of imagery, and enhanced communications. In addition, the ARSST would experiment with techniques to integrate "black" and "white" space capabilities. Finally, the ARSST would seek to play a key role in the space education of the Army.[7]

ARSST Long Range Vision and Planning Thrusts: 1998

In 1998, the ARSST participated in the development of the USARSPACE Long Range Plan. While developing input for this plan, the ARSST assumed that no significant changes in the mission would take place in either the mid-term (1-5 years in the future) or the long-term (5-12 years in the future). It was expected that the ARSST would "continue to maintain the capability to rapidly deploy worldwide to provide space force enhancement to Army units during contingency operations and exercises."[8] While no major changes in the ARSST mission were anticipated, it was expected that the continued evolution of space systems would influence the type of support provided by the ARSST. Specifically, ARSST capabilities were expected to focus increasingly on space analysis missions. In the meantime, ARSST equipment would become smaller and easier to integrate into the command and control networks of supported units. Finally, many functions currently performed by the ARSST, such as production of high quality multi-spectral imagery, would likely be integrated into supported units as an internal capability.

In May 1998, an in-process review of the USARSPACE Long Range Plan was conducted. During this review, a series of long range planning thrusts were presented. For the ASSC, seven key thrusts were identified: First, it was recommended that two ASSCs be forward-deployed, with one stationed in Korea and a second ASSC in Europe. The second ASSC thrust was the designation of the Army Space Support Cell as the focal point for injecting USARSPACE input into the theater planning process. As such, the ASSC would function as a liaison element for all space and missile defense support. The third long range planning thrust was the integration of the ASSC into the Theater Crisis Action Team, ensuring that space capabilities were integrated into all elements of a theater headquarters planning process. The fourth recommendation was that the ASSC be assigned the mission of providing logistics support for all SMDC assets in theater. The fifth long range planning thrust was ASSC coordination with in-theater staffs to provide training and ensure that space events and considerations were incorporated into exercises. Sixth, the need for ASSCs to participate in theater exercises was emphasized. Such participation would ensure that space events were properly simulated. Finally, the ASSC recommended that a USARSPACE Battle Staff be established to support military operations. This staff was intended to function as a cohesive planning and coordinating element, with the capability to support all levels of conflict, contingency missions, crises, and exercises.[9]

During the May 1998 in-process review, a number of key long range planning thrusts were also identified for the ARSST. The first thrust presented was the need to integrate the ARSST teams into BCTP and CTC rotations. Second, it was recommended that the ARSST teams be used to introduce new equipment and space products to supported units. This would ensure that USARSPACE continued to provide cutting-edge technology to the field. Third, the ARSST cited a need to develop and conduct advanced training for ARSST personnel, to include both individual and collective training tasks. Training was needed to educate newly assigned personnel on essential ARSST functions and to maintain the proficiency of experienced personnel. In addition, training programs needed to be updated as new hardware and software were acquired. The fourth long range planning thrust discussed at the review was the development of an internet homepage to provide information on ARSST capabilities. The fifth planning thrust presented during the review was the need to exploit the capabilities of USSPACECOM and the other Services. The intent of this thrust was to leverage all of these capabilities on behalf of ground forces. The final ARSST long range planning thrust was the use of the ARSST teams to provide feedback on warfighter operational requirements. This data would be integrated by USARSPACE into the Army's formal requirements process.[10]

> **1998 Long Range Planning Assumptions.**
>
> • **The space capabilities of United States adversaries will increase.**
>
> • **The dependence of the United States on space systems will increase (RISTA, navigation, targeting, communications, etc.)**
>
> • **Highly capable space systems will be available commercially, and might be available to an adversary during hostilities.**
>
> • **Commercial satellite communications capabilities will continue to improve.**

The ARSST Long Range Vision: Common Themes (1996-1998)

A number of visions for future ARSST roles, missions, and operations were considered by the ARSST from 1996 to 1998. Although there was significant evolution in the manner in which this vision has been presented, three common elements were present in each iteration: First, each of these visions assumed that the primary ARSST mission would continue to be deploying to the field to provide operational space support. Second, each of these visions assumed that the ARSST role should not be limited to manning equipment. Instead, the ARSST must be capable of conducting space planning and analysis. Third, it was anticipated that the ARSST teams would continue to serve a key role in providing equipment demonstrations and space education to the Army.

ARSST Long Range Planning Assumptions, 1998

In developing input for the USARSPACE Long Range Plan in February 1998, the ARSST assumed that it would have to react to four significant trends in the military space environment. First, it was assumed that the potential space capabilities of adversary forces would continue to increase. Second, the reliance of the U.S. and its potential coalition partners upon space-based capabilities would also continue to rise, particularly for intelligence, navigation, targeting, munitions guidance, and communications support. Third, commercial space capabilities would continue to evolve and expand. Potential adversaries might be able to employ commercial systems and capabilities to influence the course of events on a battlefield. Finally, it was assumed that satellite communications systems would continue to improve, providing new command and control options for both friendly and adversary forces.

Each of the four assumptions used as a basis for ARSST long range planning reflected a reasonable extension of current and ongoing trends in the military space environment. The list of foreign countries that owned and operated space systems in 1998 included Russia, China, India, France, Israel, Japan – and continues to grow. In addition, a number of other countries had demonstrated an interest in similarly acquiring space systems and capabilities. As a result, the Defense Intelligence Agency expected that nearly forty countries will have their own satellite systems by the year 2018.[11]

The second key long range planning assumption – a continued increase in the reliance of the United States on space systems and capabilities – also represented an ongoing trend in the military space environment. The United States had historically led the world in the development and use of military space technology. As the U.S. military embraced the future espoused in *Joint Vision 2010*, the role of space in delivering Information Superiority was expected to become even more critical. Command and control, communications, intelligence, surveillance, reconnaissance, and indicators and warning systems would all be heavily space-dependent. Furthermore, potential adversaries had noted the U.S. dependence on space. During the Cold War, the Soviet military incorporated space denial operations into its strategic doctrine; emerging military powers, such have China, had similarly begun thinking about vulnerabilities stemming from U.S. dependence on space. For example, military analysts in China in 1998 contended that the neutralization of U.S. satellite systems offers one asymmetrical approach to warfare that "could cripple the United States at a low cost to China."[12]

The third long range planning assumption identified by the ARSST – an increase in the capabilities of commercial space systems and the consequent potential for an adversary to employ those capabilities to influence the course of events on a battlefield – represented another continuation of the current trend lines. While the commercial space industry in the United States had taken a leading role in developing multi-spectral imagery systems, a number of foreign countries had also developed or were in the process of developing commercial imaging satellites (e.g., the French SPOT 4 and 5, the Indian IRS-1C and IRS-1D, the Korean KOMSAT, and the Japanese ADEOS).[13] The Defense Intelligence Agency expected that, by the year 2018, twelve commercial consortia would offer products and service with significant potential for battlefield application.[14] Some military space analysts further predicted that the capabilities of commercial imaging satellites would evolve within 10 years to the point where they could offer a customer imagery at a resolution of one meter or better, possibly available through direct tasking and downlink.[15]

The fourth ARSST long range planning assumption – that the capabilities of satellite communications systems would continue to improve, providing new options for both friendly and adversary forces – was tied to long-term, structural changes presently taking place in the global telecommunications industry. A number of satellite communications initiatives in 1998, such as Iridium, GlobalStart, Odyssey, and Teledesic, offered low-cost data and voice connections to commercial customers. The United States military had already made heavy use of existing commercial satellite communications systems, such as INMARSAT, to support deployments in Saudi Arabia, Somalia, Bosnia, Haiti, and other locations. Adversary forces, who could expect their military command and control systems to be heavily targeted by the United States in any conflict, might decide to similarly exploit commercial satellite communication systems.

Visions for Long Term Space Support Evolution

In 1998 the Army was deeply engaged in a number of DTLOMS initiatives designed to exploit the capabilities offered by existing and future space technologies. These initiatives, when considered in tandem, represented a significant expansion of the role that space-borne systems were expected to play in Army operations in the future.

From a doctrinal standpoint, TRADOC planners assumed that space systems would play a magnified role as the Army evolves into Force XXI and the Army After Next. It was anticipated that the Army would place increased reliance on space-based capabilities (including civilian systems) to support command and control, communications, intelligence, surveillance, and weapons targeting. Furthermore, TRADOC emphasized the need for the Army to cope with the use of advanced space capabilities, both military and civilian, that might be exploited by an adversary in the future.[16] From a leadership development and training perspective, the Army took steps to activate the new FA40 functional area (Space Operations Officer) to deal with the warfighting implications of space operations.

From the standpoint of materiel development, the Army began to explore the potential for integrating space capabilities into larger warfighting systems. For example, the Army explored the development of a "tactical internet" that would link each soldier on the battlefield and permit data to be shared instantaneously. As part of the tactical internet concept, GPS systems would be used to track the position of all U.S. units automatically. In the meantime, satellite systems would operate in conjunction with unmanned aerial vehicles, reconnaissance aircraft, and special operations forces to identify enemy movements. After advanced sensor systems detected enemy units, the enemy would be attacked at long range by precision-guided artillery (possibly enhanced with GPS guidance support). In the meantime, an advanced digital communications system would permit soldiers on the ground to share information, giving U.S. forces the agility required to outmaneuver an enemy force, and allow logistics support units to track the fuel and ammunition usage of maneuver forces automatically.[17]

In 1998, the 'tactical internet' was viewed as the potential next wave in providing space support to the Army, offering the seamless integration of space capabilities, such as GPS, into larger warfighting systems. This trend was also evident in a number of ongoing materiel development programs. For example, the Joint Warning and Reporting Network (JWARN), designed to detect chemical and biological attacks, integrated handheld detectors, GPS receivers, and modeling and simulation software. JWARN was intended to distribute reports on the location and type of a biological or chemical attack automatically, forecast how the agent might be affected by weather conditions, and track any movement.[18] The ATACMS Block II system would use GPS for enhanced accuracy.[19] It was even proposed that individual soldiers be equipped with space systems. Under one concept for space support to infantry units,

> "each rifleman would have a GPS terminal, a radio and computer built into his backpack and a monocle eyepiece attached to his helmet through which he could see a digital battlefield map or the view through the night-vision telescopic sight mounted on his rifle. By aiming the rifle with the eyepiece, he would be able to shoot around a corner while exposing only his forearms."[20]

These initiatives and ideas represented a significant expansion of the role that space-borne systems were expected to play in supporting Army operations in the future. They also highlighted the Army's need for space experts able to translate space capabilities into 'tools' for the ground commander.

The Long Term View from the ARSST: Areas of Consensus

Personnel assigned to the ARSST, interviewed in 1998, had thought deeply about tactics, techniques, and procedures for applying space in support of future Army operations. In addition, ARSST personnel considered a number of roles and organizational constructs that might be used by the ARSST to help supported units accomplish their missions. There was a strong degree of consensus among ARSST personnel on key aspects of the future evolution of the teams, as revealed in oral history interviews conducted with the current ARSST Branch Chief, all current ARSST team chiefs, many of the non-commissioned officers assigned to the ARSST, military officers formerly assigned to the ARSST, and civilian personnel who were involved in the development of the team from 1994-1998.

First, all ARSST personnel saw a need for the Army to be involved in space. Everyone who was interviewed as part of this history believed that the Army received clear benefits from the use of space-based technologies and systems. Second, there was a strong consensus among ARSST personnel that the role of the teams must be expanded beyond manning equipment and that the capability to conduct space analytic support must be developed. For example, Lieutenant Colonel Bob Simmons of U.S. Army Space Command suggested that one long term space analytical role for the ARSST would be to develop a "space estimate" for the supported commander as part of a formal staff process.[21] Other personnel assigned to the ARSST referred to this process as 'space intelligence preparation of the battlefield.'[22] Despite the differences in the terminology that was used, however, all ARSST personnel viewed this capability as a key to the Army of the future.

As part of the ARSST's evolution into a space analysis-oriented organization, ARSST personnel also saw the need to develop new capabilities to support field unit. Examples cited included the need to provide a supported commander with information on the specific capabilities of U.S., adversary, and neutral satellite systems, the effects of space weather on friendly operations, and GPS accuracy impacts. ARSST personnel asserted that these analytic tools could be used to enhance the operations of a supported unit, particularly in the future as increasingly capable space systems were introduced.

As one example of a space analysis capability that currently does not exist in the Army, Lieutenant Colonel Simmons noted that USARSPACE did not know in 1998 which specific military systems and staff processes were related to a space capability. As a consequence, the ARSST teams were unable to provide specific analytic support to a unit on how, for instance, variations in GPS accuracy might affect the accuracy of an ATACMS strike. Lieutenant Colonel Simmons and Lieutenant Colonel LeRoy Maurer of USARSPACE suggested that one analytic role for the ARSST would be to develop the capability to advise a supported commander on which of his systems were reliant on space and how changes in the space environment or satellite infrastructure (either as the result of natural phenomena, enemy action, or U.S. decisions) would affect those systems.[23]

All ARSST personnel interviewed, without exception, anticipated a continued need for the ARSST to provide equipment demonstrations and space education to the Army. Lieutenant Colonel Maurer noted: "The technology is going to change and until it's folded into the Army – if it's a prototype and it has merit – I think the ARSST is exactly the right place to put it. We can do the proof of principle and see what the merit is."[24] Other ARSST personnel reiterated the same theme. For example, Captain David Strombeck emphasized: "The Battle Lab should be getting the unique capabilities and the ARSST should be demonstrating it."[25]

One critical warfighting need emphasized by ARSST personnel was the ability to provide unclassified direct tasking/direct downlink imagery at resolutions of 10 meters or better. A number of ARSST personnel talked at great length about the importance of acquiring such a capability for the Army. Lieutenant Colonel Maurer noted: "Eagle Vision II is a prime example. I would like to take that under the ARSST team. It gives me direct downlink capability. What a great asset if the balloon goes up for a space team to have that and to be able to produce a real-time space product for a tactical commander."[26]

One issue that all current ARSST team chiefs emphasized repeatedly and unequivocally was the need for

ARSST Future Evolution: Areas of Consensus among Current Personnel.
• The Army needs to be involved in space.
• The ARSST must evolve into a space analysis-focused organization, capable of providing a 'space estimate' or 'space IPB.'
• The ARSST must be able to provide analysis of friendly, neutral, and adversary satellite systems.
• The ARSST must be able to assess space weather impacts and GPS accuracy impacts.
• The ARSST must be able to advise a commander on how space might influence all aspects of his operations, both positively and negatively.
• The ARSST should be used to conduct demonstrations of cutting-edge technologies and systems. Of particular importance is the acquisition of high-resolution, real time (or near-real time) unclassified imagery.
• The current ARSST capability to produce multi-spectral imagery products essentially duplicates a capability that already exists in supported units.

the Army Space Support Team to move away from the focus on production of multi-spectral imagery maps for supported units. The ARSST team chiefs viewed this support as a redundant capability that is largely duplicative of the work performed by engineer topographic analysts already assigned to Corps and Division headquarters. Even though supported units use ARSST-produced imagery and the ARSST teams can often provide a somewhat superior multi-spectral imagery product to the supported unit, ARSST personnel emphasized the need for the teams to evolve beyond producing topographic imagery into a focus on providing space analytic support.

The Long Term View from the ARSST: Unresolved Issues

Although there was a remarkable degree of consensus among ARSST team members regarding the future evolution of the teams, some issues of disagreement remained. First, a number of concepts for the integration of "black" (classified) and "white" (unclassified) space products had been discussed by the ARSST. Many ARSST personnel viewed this as an initiative that offers significant potential for the Army. They believed that black-white space integration should be pursued and implemented by the ARSST as soon as possible. On the other hand, other

ARSST personnel argued that, while classified military space systems were acquired by the USARSPACE Office, the operators were Military Intelligence analysts. As a consequence, before black-white space integration could proceed, agreement must be

reached not only with the National Reconnaissance Office but also within the Army. With ARSST personnel deploying on an average of 140 days per year, it was also argued that the ARSST could not serve as the focal point for developing an approach for black-white space integration. The bottom line on black-white space integration was that the ARSST leadership had identified this as an area meriting continued development but had not been able to pursue it as a top priority for the teams by 1998.

There was also some disagreement within the ARSST regarding the need to develop a self-sustainment capability for the teams. Difficulties in obtaining support while deployed to the field were repeatedly cited by the ARSST, particularly regarding the transmission of large imagery files. In the past, ARSST leaders conducted research into the costs and benefits of integrating all ARSST systems into a self-sustained tactical vehicle. During ULCHI FOCUS LENS 98, there was also some experimentation in using the ASSC as a coordinating mechanism for logistical support. Some ARSST team members in 1998 expressed a lukewarm attitude toward this issue, however. In the after-action review from ULCHI FOCUS LENS 98, the ARSST Branch Chief noted that the teams had demonstrated the ability to operate independently and, therefore, support from the ASSC was largely unneeded. In the period from 1995 to 1998, a number of factors prevented the integration of ARSST systems into a self-sustained tactical vehicle. These included the high cost of purchasing an equipment shelter, maintaining the vehicle, and deploying the tactical vehicle overseas. In addition, it was argued that space analysis support, unlike the production of hard products, does not require a large team of personnel equipped with large amounts of equipment. Instead, an Army space analyst would be able to deploy to support a unit carrying only a laptop computer.

A third area of disagreement regarding the future evolution of the ARSST stemmed from the level at which an ARSST team should focus its support. In the past, the ARSST teams had been affiliated with a Corps Headquarters and the Corps staff served as the focal point for space support. ARSST team members in 1998 generally believed that Corps-level support should remain the focus of ARSST doctrine. With the development of the Army Space Support Cell, however, it was argued that the focal point for ARSST support might be changed to the Division Headquarters. Experience during the 1st Infantry Division BCTP was cited as a justification for restructuring the ARSST to focus on division-level missions.

Finally, some analysts outside USARSPACE suggested that the ARSST may be able to fulfill a long term role as a space liaison capability that could be deployed in support of U.S. allies and coalition partners. A possible model for developing such a capability was provided by the U.S. Air Force experience in providing air support planning to coalition forces during Operation DESERT STORM. In 1990, U.S. Air Force Tactical Air Control Parties (TACPs) were assigned to Arab coalition forces – the 20th Saudi Mechanized Brigade and 4th Armored Brigade, the Kuwaiti Liberation Brigade and 35th Martyr Armored Brigade, the Syrian 9th Armored Division, and the Egyptian 3rd Mechanized Division and 4th Armored Division. The TACPs were assigned three primary missions: [1] advise the supported commander and staff on the uses of air power, [2] control Allied close air support missions; and [3] train supported forces to develop "a long-term, forward air control capability."[27] Throughout the ground offensive, the TACPs coordinated air support and aerial reconnaissance missions and also provided communications links to other coalition forces.[28] A similar space support role for coalition forces might be supported by an ARSST team in the future. However, before such a role could be assumed by the ARSST, procedures would have to be developed for the release of information that is currently restricted to U.S. personnel only. In addition, the ARSST would likely require a significant infusion of resources to accomplish such a mission. ARSST personnel, who were operating in 1998 with limited resources, generally did not view the addition of such a new mission with favor.

Future Organizational Constructs

In discussions with ARSST personnel in 1998, a number of visions for future Army space support were described. These visions of future space support, although geared towards the long term (5-12 years), were significant because they reflect what the few officers in the United States Army with operational space support experience viewed to be the optimal end-states for ARSST organization and operations. These long term visions were also important because they added a broader context to contemporary decisions which, through design or by accident, were anticipated to set the parameters for continued evolution of the ARSST.

For convenience, the long term ideas discussed by ARSST personnel have been grouped into three categories, each of which will be discussed separately. The first long term vision saw the ARSST providing a deployable unit of space support personnel equipped with a full suite of equipment that is mounted in a tactical vehicle. ARSST equipment would consist of state-of-the-art space systems that had not been provided to field units, either because of its high cost or the fact that the technology had only been recently developed. An example of the type of equipment that would be manned by the ARSST would be a satellite system capable of direct tasking and direct downlink of high-resolution, unclassified imagery. The tactical vehicle used by the ARSST would be designed to act as a tactical operations center for performing space analytic functions on a battlefield, to include the development of a 'space estimate' for the supported commander,

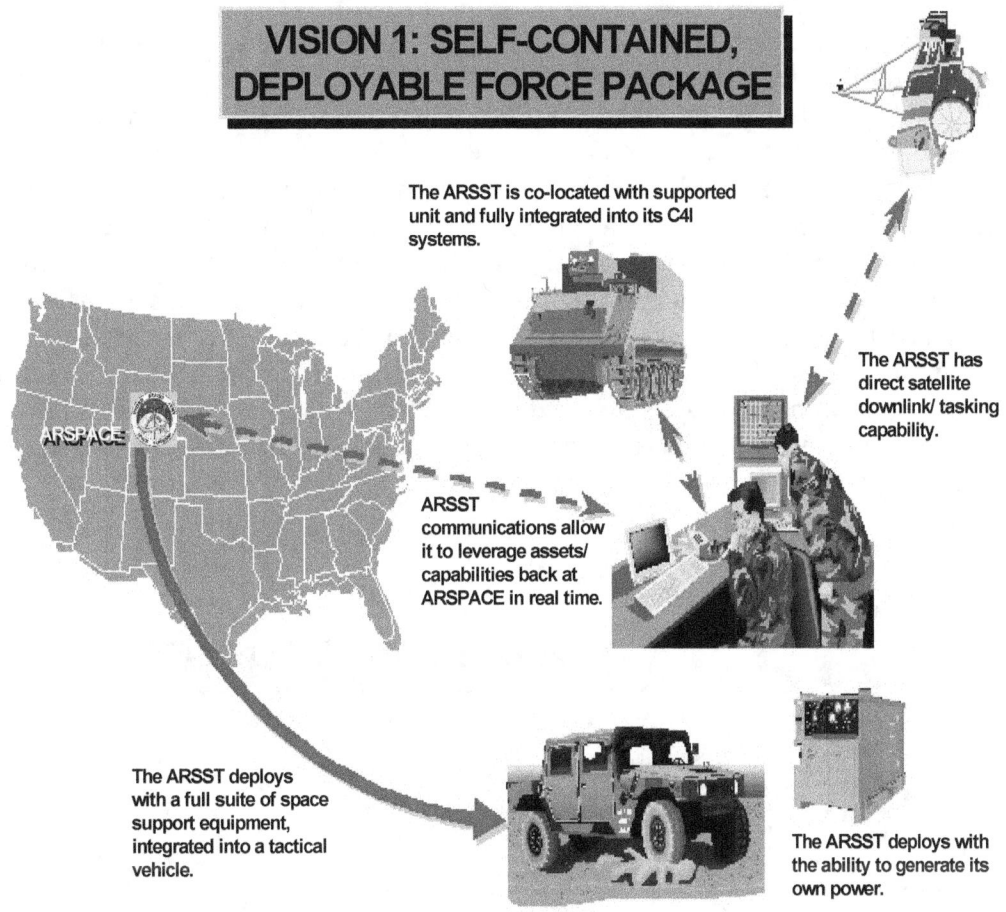

Figure 19: Future ARSST Organizational Construct – Self-Contained Deployable Force Package.

and would be capable of immediate integration into the command, control, communications, computers, and intelligence (C4I) systems of the supported unit. In addition, the deployed ARSST team would be integrated into the C4I network at U.S. Army Space Command and would be capable of leveraging space support tools throughout USSPACECOM. One model cited by some individuals for this long term vision was the Army Space Command's development of a Force Projection Tactical Operations Center to support theater missile defense operations in the field.

Under a second long term vision for ARSST operations, a space liaison officer would deploy to a supported unit rather than a full ARSST team. The primary function of this liaison officer would be to provide planning and space analytic support to the supported commander and his staff. All production functions would remain at the U.S. Army Space Command in Colorado Springs, where they could be easily accessed by the space liaison officer over established communications networks. In essence, the space liaison officer would serve as the space advisor to a supported unit and would coordinate with other organizations to provide any additional space support or products that might be required.

Under the third long term vision for ARSST evolution, structural changes in the Army would necessitate a redirection of the ARSST role away from operational support. This shift would result from the activation of the FA40 functional area, the assignment of Space Operations officers to Corps and/or Division staffs, and the incorporation of space education programs throughout the Army's training and career development process. With a Space Operations officer permanently assigned to the staff, a Corps or Division headquarters would no longer require operational support from an ARSST. Instead, ARSST teams would be used only to demonstrate new systems and technologies to the field and provide advanced training to units and soldiers. USARSPACE would not have a direct operational presence at Corps and Division headquarters but would be available to provide additional space production support if requested by a unit's Space Operations officer.

Figure 20: Future ARSST Organizational Construct – One Man with a Laptop.

Technological Trends. The evolution of government and commercial space technologies would continue to be a determining factor in the continued evolution of the ARSST. If space systems and capabilities continued to evolve at a rapid pace, the ARSST would likely fill a long term critical warfighting need by interjecting new and advanced capabilities into a commander's planning cycle and operations. Eagle Vision II was repeatedly cited as the type of capability that might be brought to the field by an ARSST team in the future. As a general rule, it was expected that there would be a greater need for space support from an ARSST in the long term if advanced and new space technologies continued to be rapidly introduced on the commercial market; if the costs of these new technologies and systems remained high; if the systems were technically complex; if special training and expertise was needed to understand and employ these systems; and if the systems had applications that extended across a number of functional areas, rather than supporting just a small niche requirement. If the converse situation was true, there would be a reduced requirement for ARSST support in the long term.

Each of the three visions for long term ARSST evolution offered a useful glimpse into how the Army might be provided space support in the future. When considered within the context of the Army's experience in applying space systems and technologies over the period from 1986 to 1998, the ongoing experimentation with the ASSC concept, and continuing trends in the military space environment, all three of the long term visions appeared to offer a reasonable approach to the Army's long term need to address the warfighting implications of space. Ultimately, however, the manner in which the ARSST would evolve was expected to be driven by four key factors, each of which lie beyond the complete control of USARSPACE.

Threat Trends. The amount of emphasis that the Army placed on space analytic support in the long term was expected to be driven in large part by the threat posed in the future. If adversaries developed a demonstrated capability to destroy, degrade, or disrupt space systems used by the Army for important tactical and operational warfighting purposes, commanders would demand more space support from USARSPACE. Similarly, if an adversary gained the capability, for example, to download high-resolution imagery in a timely manner, provide this data to its tactical and operational commanders, and use it on the battlefield, the Army would place increased emphasis on space analysis and support. On the other hand, if the threat posed by an adversary was perceived to be hypothetical or unimportant, it was unlikely that commanders would devote the resources required to implement some of the long-term visions discussed by ARSST personnel.

The New FA40 and the Role of the Space Operations Officer. The third key driver of ARSST evolution in the long term was defined as the manner in which the new FA40 functional area was implemented by the Army and the reception that the Space Operations officer received when assigned to a unit. If a Space Operations officer was able to fulfill all of the operational needs of his unit, the requirement for an ARSST to provide operational support might be significantly reduced. However, if there were certain operational requirements that the assigned

Space Operations officer was unable to address, the ARSSTs would need to evolve to satisfy those requirements. Finally, if the Army was unable or unwilling to assign Space Operations officers to all units requiring space analytical support, the need for USARSPACE to maintain a deployable ARSST capability would remain.

Resources. In an environment of tight Army budgets and limited personnel, perhaps the most significant factor governing the long term evolution of the ARSST would be the level of resources available. As in the past, resource levels would continue to exert a decisive influence on how many personnel the Army assigns to space support functions (either on the ARSST or as Space Operations officers at the Corps and Division level); the quantities and types of space systems that could be procured; whether enough space systems would be available to equip all field units or if only a few systems could be purchased to support the entire Army; how many and what types of field deployments USARSPACE could support; and whether or not space support equipment was integrated into a tactical vehicle or not.

Summary

As the ARSST conducted long range planning in the 1995 to 1998 period, a number of common themes were stressed. Most importantly, the ARSST anticipated a continued warfighting requirement for operational space support. In addition, ARSST long range planning emphasized the need to conduct space systems demonstrations, support Army space education, and explore new force development and technological concepts.

ARSST long range planning in 1998 was based upon four key assumptions. First, the space capabilities of U.S. adversaries would continue to increase. Second, the dependence of the United States upon space systems—both commercial and military— would also rise. Third, commercial space capabilities would expand, with a number of implications for military operations. Finally, satellite communication systems and capabilities would be revolutionized, introducing a number of new factors for military command and control. Given these trends, ARSST personnel in 1998 believed that the Army needed to be closely involved in exploiting space systems and capabilities in the future. To support that requirement, the ARSST must evolve into a space analysis-focused organization, capable not only of translating space capabilities into tools for the supported commander but also of understanding the threat from neutral and adversary space systems, fully exploiting the capabilities of U.S. and commercial space systems, anticipating space environmental impacts, proactively identifying and addressing U.S. vulnerabilities and opportunities, and developing a 'space estimate' for incorporation into the warfighter's planning process.

 Looking at the long term trends in the military space environment and the Army's requirements for space support, personnel assigned to the ARSST described three future organizational constructs for the teams. Under the first concept, the ARSST would continue to deploy as a task-organized team of space personnel, but would have self-contained and integrated equipment, mounted in a tactical vehicle.

Under the second concept, technology would evolve to the point where a single soldier would be capable of providing the full spectrum of space support through a small laptop computer. Under a third vision of long term ARSST evolution, the successful implementation of space education throughout the Army coupled with the assignment of space operations officers on Corps and Division staffs would render the ARSST unnecessary. In other words, space analysis would be part of every Division and Corps Headquarters' integral capabilities.

Each of the visions for future evolution of the ARSST was dependent upon a number of variables—the future threat, the evolution of space technology, the development of Functional Area 40 and the introduction of a space operations officer to the field, and the level of resources allocated to space support and space operations by the Army. No matter how the military space environment evolves in the future or how the Army organizes the ARSST to address it, however, one fact remained unchanged: The Army Space Support Team experience established a firm foundation for the application of space on behalf of the warfighter. For years to come, this experience will guide how the Army addresses space at the tactical and operational levels of war.

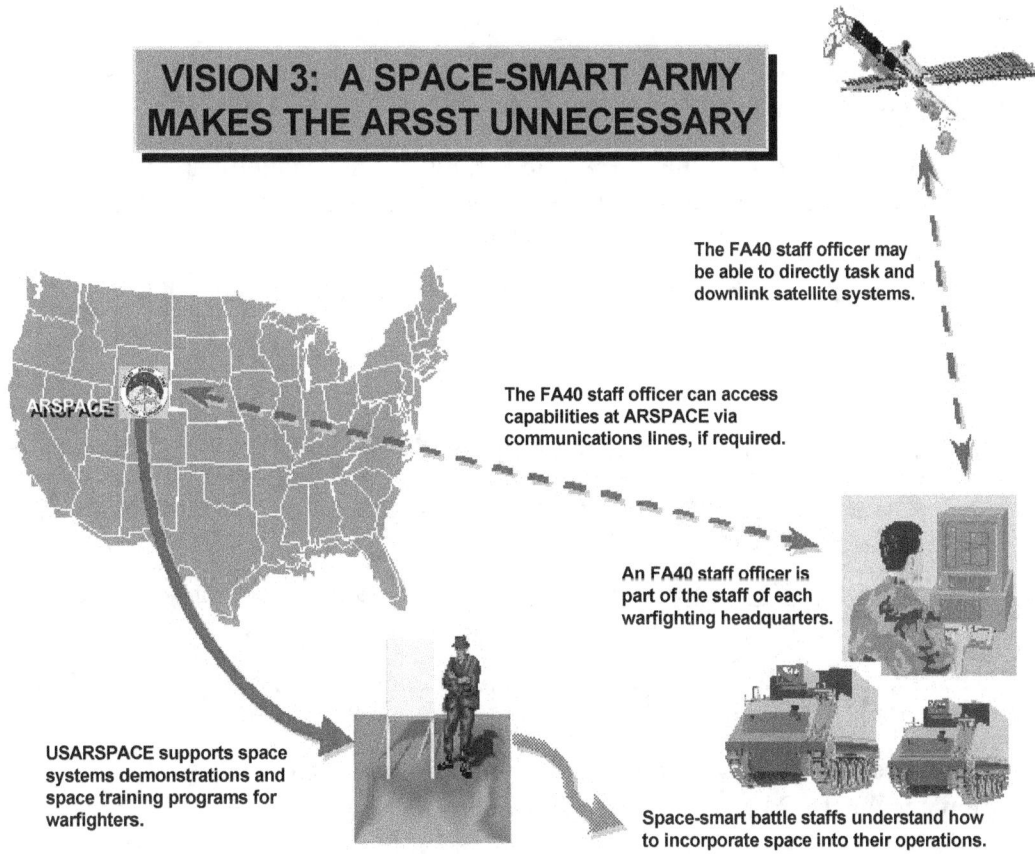

VISION 3: A SPACE-SMART ARMY MAKES THE ARSST UNNECESSARY

The FA40 staff officer may be able to directly task and downlink satellite systems.

The FA40 staff officer can access capabilities at ARSPACE via communications lines, if required.

ARSPACE

An FA40 staff officer is part of the staff of each warfighting headquarters.

USARSPACE supports space systems demonstrations and space training programs for warfighters.

Space-smart battle staffs understand how to incorporate space into their operations.

Figure 21: Future ARSST Organizational Construct – A Space-Smart Army Makes the ARSST Unnecessary.

[1] B. Bruce-Briggs, "The Army in Space: New High Ground or Hot-Air Balloon?" Military Review (December 1986), p. 48.

[2] Major Sherwood C. Springs, "The Army in Space." [Undated article provided to Brigadier General(P) Colin L. Powell on 15 June 1983 by Lieutenant Colonel James W. Labounty].

[3] Meeting Notes, Major Foeller, U.S. Army Space Command, "Army Space Support to the Warfighter Review," 11 January 1996.

[4] Major Foeller, U.S. Army Space Command, "Army Space Support Team Briefing at the HQ USARSPACE (Forward) Program Management Review." 12 July 1996.

[5] Memorandum, U.S. Army Space Command, MOSC-OO-C, to TSOC PAT, ATTN: Mr. Jim Taylor, SPJTSOC, Subject: ARSPACE ARSST Information. 17 July 1996.

[6] Major Foeller, U.S. Army Space Command, "Army Space Support Team Briefing at the HQ USARSPACE (Forward) Program Management Review." 12 July 1996.

[7] U.S. Army Space Command Briefing, "Forward Deployment of ARSST: A One Stop Shop is Our Goal," Undated.

[8] U.S. Army Space Command, "ARSST Long Range Planning Input," February 1998. A copy of this document in electronic format was found on a floppy disk in the ARSST program files at Colorado Springs, Colorado.

[9] U.S. Army Space Command Briefing, "Long Range Plan," May 1998.

[10] Ibid.

[11] Ibid.

[12] Reuters, "China, Others Spot U.S. Computer Weaknesses: CIA." 26 June 1998.

[13] U.S. Army Space Command (Forward), Space Support Reference Book, 20 August 1997, p. MSI-48.

[14] Armed Forces Newswire, "DIA Says Days of U.S. Hegemony in Space Are Numbered." 2 February 1998.

[15] Dr. James Walker and James Hooper, "James H. Williamson Oral History Interview, ARSST Historical/Lessons Learned Study," 22 October 1998.

[16] Bob Brewin, "Army Views Space As Ultimate 'High Ground.'" Federal Computer Week. 24 March 1998.

[17] CQ Washington Alert, "Modern Army Prepares for War on Two Fronts: Present, Future." 8 August 1998.

[18] Daniel M. Verton, "Interagency Office to Respond to WMD; Marines Also Launch System to Detect Biological, Chemical Agents." Federal Computer Week. 6 April 1998.

[19] Dr. James Walker and James Hooper, "Lieutenant Colonel Bob Simmons and Lieutenant Colonel LeRoy Maurer Oral History Interview, ARSST Historical/Lessons Learned Study," 23 October 1998.

[20] CQ Washington Alert, "Modern Army Prepares for War on Two Fronts: Present, Future." 8 August 1998.

[21] Dr. James Walker and James Hooper, "Lieutenant Colonel Bob Simmons and Lieutenant Colonel LeRoy Maurer Oral History Interview, ARSST Historical/Lessons Learned Study," 23 October 1998.

[22] Dr. James Walker and James Hooper, "Captain Gerry Skaw and Sergeant First Class Howard Smith Oral History Interview, ARSST Historical/Lessons Learned Study," 22 October 1998.

[23] Dr. James Walker and James Hooper, "Lieutenant Colonel Bob Simmons and Lieutenant Colonel LeRoy Maurer Oral History Interview, ARSST Historical/Lessons Learned Study," 23 October 1998.

[24] Dr. James Walker and James Hooper, "Lieutenant Colonel Bob Simmons and Lieutenant Colonel LeRoy Maurer Oral History Interview, ARSST Historical/Lessons Learned Study," 23 October 1998.

[25] Dr. James Walker and James Hooper, "Captain David Strombeck and Staff Sergeant William Bates Oral History Interview, ARSST Historical/Lessons Learned Study," 23 October 1998

[26] Dr. James Walker and James Hooper, "Lieutenant Colonel Bob Simmons and Lieutenant Colonel LeRoy Maurer Oral History Interview, ARSST Historical/Lessons Learned Study," 23 October 1998.

[27] Aviation Week & Space Technology, "U.S. Close Air Support Teams to Aid Arab Coalition Forces." (Vol. 134, No. 7, 18 February 1991), p. 63.

[28] David A. Fulghum, "Allied Air Power, Forward Controllers Back Arabs to Make Their Drive Succeed," Aviation Week & Space Technology (Vol. 134, No. 16, 22 April 1991), pp. 70-73.

CHAPTER SIX:

CONCLUSIONS

When this history was initially written, a number of observations and conclusions were put forward regarding the Army space support experience from 1986 to 1998. Much has changed since that time and, in the new military environment of 2003, it is useful to reexamine some of the original observations in light of subsequent developments in Army space support. This is particularly important given the context of ongoing efforts to transform the Army for the future as well as the rapidly evolving requirements of the current national security environment, both of which generate new demands for Army space capabilities.

The establishment of the Army Space Institute in 1986 proved to be the critical first step in a long, systematic Army effort to leverage space systems and technologies to support tactical operations more effectively. The activation of the Army Space Demonstration Program in 1987, later designated the Army Space Exploitation Demonstration Program, proved invaluable because it allowed soldiers to experience first-hand the potential benefits offered by space capabilities. The activation of Army Space Command (ARSPACE) in 1988 marked a third crucial step in the evolution of the Army space support organization. Taken together, these early initiatives established a firm foundation for the later application and expansion of Army space support capabilities.

The first Gulf War represented a watershed event in the history of Army space support by demonstrating to both soldiers and commanders the benefits of space capabilities on an actual battlefield. The Army leveraged space in Operation DESERT SHIELD/DESERT STORM on a number of levels, to include GPS position/navigation support, satellite weather data, satellite communications, multi-spectral terrain imagery, and a ballistic missile warning capability to tactical commanders. During this conflict, however, it also became apparent that few tactical commanders understood the full potential and limitations of space support capabilities, or knew how to employ space assets in the most effective manner. The first Gulf War made clear the requirement to normalize space in the Army.

After the first Gulf War, the Army space support program experienced a period of energetic development. In these formative stages, the leadership provided by certain key individuals shaped Army space support efforts and established a foundation for the long-term success of the program. For example, U.S. Army Chief of Staff General Gordon R. Sullivan incorporated space support systems and capabilities into the Army's "Louisiana Maneuvers" experiments of the early 1990s. Similarly, the direction and management provided by then-BG Edward G. Anderson III (Combined Arms Center, U.S. Training and Doctrine Command) and then-Major General Jay Garner (Assistant Deputy Chief of Staff for Operations and Plans, Force Development) proved instrumental. Their leadership helped shape the Army's decision to field a Commercial Space Package (CSP) and subsequently activate a contingency space support capability at ARSPACE. In 1994, thanks to the proactive efforts of such Army leaders, the Army activated a deployable space support team (COPS) at Colorado Springs. The COPS team was the Army's first dedicated space support organization and the predecessor of the ARSST.

ARSST teams deployed in support of field units for the first time on 1 January 1995. Over the course of that year, the ARSST supported six Corps and Joint Task Force-level exercises, three Division-level exercises, and three Special Operations exercises. In addition, the ARSST conducted an estimated 13 equipment demonstrations and sent personnel to support three Force Projection Tactical Operations Center (FP TOC) exercises. The frequency and length of ARSST deployments resulted in a high level of unit operations tempo, in which the soldiers of the ARSST averaged more than 140 deployment days per year. Furthermore, the ARSST's intense level of deployment support continued in subsequent years, including a 1996 deployment to Bosnia to support the 1st Infantry Division (Mechanized) in Tuzla, Bosnia, marking the first time that an ARSST deployed in support of an actual contingency mission rather than a training exercise. The demand for ARSST support was generally greatest from the XVIII Airborne Corps and Army special operations forces. Every deployment brought with it new lessons in terms of ARSST capabilities and configuration and, from 1995 to 1998, the concept of operations for ARSST employment evolved significantly.

In these early years, the Army's space support concept was repeatedly refined, reshaped, and reconfigured. This evolution was guided by the contributions of several leaders, to include Lieutenant General Don Lionetti, Lieutenant General Jay Garner, and Lieutenant General Edward G. Anderson III in their roles as Commanding General, U.S. Army Space and Strategic Defense Command (USASSDC). Their legacy has been carried forth since USASSDC was transformed in 1997 to become today's U.S. Army Space and Missile Defense Command (USASMDC). Under the leadership of Lieutenant General John Costello and Lieutenant General John M. Cosumano, USASMDC has continued to provide the leadership and direction necessary to refine the Army's space support capabilities and to integrate them into the process of Army Transformation.

An issue of particular importance for the Army has been the process of "normalizing space." The *Army Space Policy* of 1994 emphasized the importance of seamlessly integrating space capabilities into Army operations and established a number of goals to support that objective. In 1998, this history of the ARSST emphasized the significant progress that had been made by the Army towards deploying a variety of new space capabilities and integrating them into the operations of units at the tactical level. Importantly, in the five years since the original publication of the history, the Army has largely accomplished its goal of normalizing space. This progress has been achieved in large part as a result of Army Space Support Team operations and experience. As the Army of 2003 transforms itself for the future, however, the integration of advanced space-based capabilities into land force operations will assume even larger importance. The

Objective Force envisioned under the Army Transformation Campaign Plan is a fully space-enabled land force that will routinely exploit an overhead constellation of military and civilian space platforms. The Army's Objective Force will rely upon these platforms to provide a range of capabilities, to include intelligence, surveillance, and area reconnaissance, long haul communications, positioning and navigation, targeting, and missile defense early warning support.

If space systems and services are to satisfy the needs of the Army's Objective Force, they must be responsive, accurate, timely, and capable of dynamic interaction with other battlefield systems. The Army is currently pursuing and advocating a number of space-based capabilities to meet these military demands. These include space-based intelligence, surveillance, and reconnaissance sensors (ISR) capable of in-theater tasking, processing, and exploitation by Army forces; dynamic bandwidth satellite communications systems that are seamlessly integrated; tactically relevant space control capabilities to ensure continued access to space-based systems while, if necessary, negating enemy space capabilities; advanced missile warning and tracking systems; precise and jam-resistant position, navigation, and timing services; and new sensor systems to provide advanced weather, terrain, and environmental monitoring to Army forces.

As part of the Army's effort to transform itself for the future, the space requirements of the future Objective Force are being developed with reference to the six critical operational goals for defense transformation outlined in the 2001 Quadrennial Defense Review, to include the goal of "Enhancing the capability and survivability of space systems and supporting infrastructure." The Army is also working to integrate space capabilities across all thirteen Lines of Operation (LOs) outlined in its Transformation Campaign Plan. Importantly, the U.S. Army Space and Missile Defense Command has been designated the Army's "vertical integrator" for Space, responsible for ensuring that each of the thirteen "horizontal" LOs properly address space-specific issues and requirements.

In addition to these changes, there have been several other important developments in the organization and employment of Army space support capabilities since the original 1998 publication of this history. For example, in October 1999 Congress chartered a *Commission to Assess United States National Security Space Management and Organization.* The Commission, chaired by Donald Rumsfeld and commonly referred to as the Rumsfeld Space Commission, was tasked to undertake a comprehensive examination of the future impact of space on the U.S. military and recommend improvements in the organization and management of DoD space activities. In January 2001, the Commission reported that the Department of Defense lacked the senior-level focus and accountability required to provide oversight and guidance over national security space operations. It also proffered a series of recommendations for reorganizing and realigning management responsibilities within Department of Defense, the Services, and the intelligence community. In response to these recommendations, the DoD announced a series of initiatives, ranging from the designation of the Department of the Air Force as the DoD Executive Agent for space to the establishment of a new Major Force Program (MFP) for Space.[*]

Also included in the Rumsfeld Space Commission report was an emphasis on the need for a cadre of space-qualified officers capable of integrating space activities into military operations. That finding reinforced the importance of ongoing efforts within the Army to establish a new officer functional area for space operations, classified as Functional Area 40 (FA40). Today, FA 40 space operations officers serve as the primary focal point for the integration of space capabilities in the military decision making process of Corps and Division headquarters. The presence of FA40 officers on warfighting staffs provides commanders with the familiarity and the expertise to fully exploit space-based assets and space products, significantly enhancing the command's warfighting capabilities. Additionally, FA 40 officers are assigned to key billets at the Combatant Commands, the Joint Staff, the Office of the Secretary of Defense, various multi-service space organizations, and the National Reconnaissance Office, where they provide invaluable expertise for decision-making while ensuring that Army requirements and operating capabilities are integrated throughout the national security space community.

Moving beyond the first units established by U.S. Army Space Command in the mid-1990s, the Army has since established a robust force structure that includes three space battalions. In 1999, the Army activated the 1st Space Battalion, consisting of an Army Space Support Company (ARSSC), a Theater Missile Warning Company, and an electronic warfare detachment. The ARSSC included five Army Space Support Teams, each of which continued their historical mission of supporting warfighting units by providing space capabilities, expertise and products. The new Theater Missile Warning Company was assigned responsibility for operating the Joint Tactical Ground Station (JTAGS), operated by the Army and the Navy to provide in-theater early warning of missile launches. The 1st Space Battalion also developed a Space Control and Electronic Warfare Detachment (SEWD), responsible for conducting space control missions.

Another key milestone in the development of Army space support force structure was achieved in 2001 with the activation of the 193rd Space Battalion, Colorado Army National Guard. The 193rd Space Battalion provides Army Space Support Teams and Space Operations officers to support Army and joint operations. The 1st and 193rd Space Battalions joined the Army's longest serving space battalion, the 1st Satellite Control Battalion, which remained responsible for operating Defense Satellite Communications System (DSCS) Ground Stations in support of U.S. military forces deployed around the world. In April 2003, all three battalions were placed under the command of the new 1st Space Brigade (Provisional). This provisional brigade was charged with the mission to "conduct continuous, global space support, space control and space force enhancement operations in support of U.S. Strategic Command and Supported Combatant Commanders, enabling the delivery of decisive combat power." The formation of the 1st Space Brigade was important not only because it represented another step in the evolution of Army space capabilities; it also provided a basis for the potential establishment of a composite combat organization in the future that integrates space, missile defense, and information operations formations. Such a development may also include the creation of new Army space control units that provide space electronic warfare support and conduct space counter surveillance and reconnaissance missions.

Changes in the Unified Command Plan (UCP) also promised to impact the Army's space mission in the future. In 2002, a significant realignment of the U.S. military command structure was made to accommodate the establishment of a new Combatant Command, U.S. Northern Command (USNORTHCOM). This command was assigned responsibility for the continental defense of the United States and for providing military assistance to civilian authorities. Geographical areas of responsibility were realigned between U.S. Joint Forces Command (USJFCOM), U.S. European Command (USEUCOM), and USNORTHCOM. Most importantly from the standpoint of the Army space support operations, U.S. Space Command (USSPACECOM) and U.S. Strategic Command (STRATCOM) were merged into a single command to eliminate redundancies in the command structure and streamline the decision making process. As a result of this merger, USSTRATCOM was tasked with a variety of new responsibilities, to include military space operations, information operations, computer network operations, and strategic defense and attack missions. Another consequence of the USSPACECOM merger with USSTRATCOM was that U.S. Army Space and Missile Defense Command was designed to serve as the Army Service Component Command to USSTRATCOM.

These organizational developments have been accompanied by a number of Joint and Army doctrinal changes since this history was originally written in 1998. For example, a number of long-standing operational issues between the Services were resolved and *Joint Publication 3-14: Joint Doctrine for Space Operations* was published in August 2002. This doctrinal publication highlighted the dependence of joint warfighters on space capabilities and established guidelines for joint military operations in four space mission areas: force enhancement, space control, space support, and force application. Concurrent with these joint efforts, the Army strove to update and revise its doctrine for space operations, as reflected by the publication of new field manuals such as FM 40-1, *Joint Tactical Ground Station Operations* and the development of FM 3-14, *Space Support to Army Operations* and FM 3-14.6, *Army Space Support to Corps and Divisions*. The Army also integrated space capabilities and considerations in a number of its key doctrinal publications, to include FM 5-0, *Army Planning and Orders Production*; FM 6-0, *Command and Control*; and FM 7-15, *Army Universal Task List*.

All of the innovations outlined in the preceding paragraphs were shaped by the early work of the ARSST teams. In addition to influencing changes in Army space doctrine, organization, training, and capabilities, however, the ARSST teams continued to make concrete contributions on the ground, and have deployed in support of every contingency operation since Operation DESERT STORM. ARSST soldiers from both the 1st Space Battalion and the 193rd Space Support Battalion have deployed in support of Operation ENDURING FREEDOM and Operation IRAQI FREEDOM. During these conflicts, ARSST soldiers provided a range of products and services to combat units, ranging from multi-spectral imagery and mapping products and GPS jamming support to providing technical advice and training for the operation of commercial Blue Force Tracking devices and submitting satellite tasking requests to help units identify minefields and navigate on the battlefield. In addition, the ARSST teams have continued to provide exercise and training support to Army and joint units, ranging from deployments to Southwest Asia in support of the INTERNAL LOOK and LUCKY SENTINEL exercises, to Poland in support of exercise VICTORY STRIKE. More recently, the MILLENIUM CHALLENGE 02 exercise demonstrated the validity of several SMDC initiatives, including the Tactical Space (TACSPACE) initiative evaluating space support to the military decision making process provided by a six-man space support element (SSE).

When this history was first published, the authors suggested several possible scenarios for the future evolution of the ARSST. The first of these suggested that the ARSST might deploy as a self-contained force, with a full suite of space support equipment, its own power source, and a direct satellite link capability, all integrated into a tactical vehicle. In this scenario the ARSST would be co-located with the supporting unit and would be capable of serving as a "one stop shop" for space support capabilities. In the second scenario, the ARSST would be replaced by a single space liaison officer (SLO) equipped with a laptop loaded with relevant space analysis systems. In this scenario, the SLO would be co-located with the supported unit, which would be responsible for providing all supply, transportation, and other logistic support. The SLO would request assistance from U.S. Army Space Command to provide any additional support that he could not personally furnish. The final scenario envisioned placing FA40 staff officers in each warfighting headquarters, rendering the staffs "space-smart" and making the ARSSTs largely unnecessary. As events turned out, the configuration of space support in 2003 represented a combination of some of the above scenarios: ARSSTs deploy as a team to provide space support in response to specific contingencies and augmentation requirements while FA40 space operations officers maintain a permanent presence on headquarters staffs, ensuring that commanders understand and are able to take full advantage of space assets and fulfilling liaison roles when appropriate.

The pace of change and innovation in Army space support has been particularly dramatic in recent years. The establishment of the FA40 Space Operations Officer functional area, the continued development and implementation of Army space doctrine, and numerous real-world experiences with Army space tactical and operational integration, suggest that the desired goal of space normalization has been largely achieved. As a result, the ARSST teams have now largely transitioned from a posture of providing training and demonstration support to one of active participation in operational missions. One chapter has ended in the history of Army space and the ARSST teams, but another is well underway.

---

* Major Force Programs aggregate a series of related DoD budget items. MFPs track the resources employed to support a macro-level DoD mission, such as special operations.

BIBLIOGRAPHY*

ARTICLES (by date)

Bruce-Briggs, B. "The Army in Space: New High Ground or Hot-Air Balloon?" *Military Review* (December 1986).

Siegel, Major Steven C., "Army Space Institute." *Army Trainer* (Summery 1987).

Shepherd, Marquis. "Army Unit To Bring Technology Of Space Down To Earth For Troops," *Kansas City Times* (13 January 1988).

"Desert Shield Prompts Acceleration of AMRAAM, SFW Testing." *Aerospace Daily* 155, no. 56 (19 September 1990).

"Army Space Command Demo Efforts Go Operational in Desert Shield." *Aerospace Daily* 156, no. 34 (20 November 1990).

"Iraqis Still Receive Weather Data from U.S. Satellites." *Aviation Week & Space Technology* 134, no. 3 (21 January 1991).

Covault, Craig. "USAF Missile Warning Satellites Providing 90-Sec. Scud Attack Alert." *Aviation Week & Space Technology* 134, no. 3 (21 January 1991).

"U.S. Close Air Support Teams to Aid Arab Coalition Forces." *Aviation Week & Space Technology* 134, no. 7 (18 February 1991).

"Spacecraft Played Vital Role in Gulf War Victory." *Aviation Week & Space Technology* 134, no. 16 (22 April 1991).

Fulghum, David A. "Allied Air Power, Forward Controllers Back Arabs to Make Their Drive Succeed." *Aviation Week & Space Technology* 134, no. 16 (22 April 1991).

Moore, Captain George M., Colonel Vic Budura, Joan Johnson-Freese. "Joint Space Doctrine: Catapulting into the Future." *Joint Forces Quarterly* (Summer 1994).

Allard, C. Kenneth. "Lessons Unlearned: Somalia and Joint Doctrine." *Joint Forces Quarterly* (Autumn 1995).

Caton, Jeffrey L. "Joint Warfare and Military Dependence on Space" *Joint Forces Quarterly* (Winter 1995-96).

White, Ed. "Space Support is Current Revolution in How Army Fights and Wins Land Conflicts." *The Eagle* 3, no. 5 (Sep/Oct 1997).

Tilelli, General John H. "Ulchi-Focus Lens '97: Putting JV 2010 into Practice." *Joint Forces Quarterly* (Autumn/Winter 1997-98).

Brewin, Bob. "Army Views Space As Ultimate 'High Ground.'" *Federal Computer Week* (24 March 1998).

Verton, Daniel M. "Interagency Office to Respond to WMD; Marines Also Launch System to Detect Biological, Chemical Agents." *Federal Computer Week* (6 April 1998).

"Modern Army Prepares for War on Two Fronts: Present, Future." *CQ Washington Alert* (8 August 1998).

"Joint ROK, US Military Exercise Due in Texas." <u>*Korea Times*</u> (6 December 1998).

Reports, Manuscripts, and Other Materials (available in the files of the USASMDC Historical Office)

10th Mountain Division (Light), *US Army Forces, Somalia: After Action Report Summary* (2 January 1993).

Army Space Institute/TPIO Space. *Historical Review 1990.* Ft. Leavenworth, Kansas: Army Space Institute (1990).

Battle Command Battle Laboratory. *Louisiana Maneuver General Officer Working Group Briefing* (9 September 1993).

Brown International, "Draft Army Space Support Cell Concept of Operations." Undated.

Cafaro, Major. U.S. Army Space Command. *Trip Report – Joint Task Force Support Hope, 29 July to 13 August 1994* (18 August 1994).

Center for Army Lessons Learned, *The Ultimate High Ground! Space Support to the Army: Lessons Learned from Operations DESERT SHIELD and STORM.* Ft. Leavenworth, Kansas: Center for Army Lessons Learned Newsletter, no. 91-3 (October 1991).

Femme Comp Incorporated, Satellite Communications Group. *Task Order Plan 94-08: Contingency Operations (Space) / COPS Documentation Development* (7 July 1994).

Femme Comp Incorporated, Satellite Communications Group. *Contingency Operations – Space (COPS) Standard Operating Procedures (SOPS) Initial Draft.* (16 August 1994).

Femme Comp Incorporated, Satellite Communications Group. *Task Order Plan 95-08: Contingency Operations (Space) / COPS Documentation Development* (26 September 1994).

French, Jr., Lieutenant Colonel(P) John R. *U.S. Army Space Institute Semiannual Historical Report 1 July – 31 December 1986.* Ft. Leavenworth, Kansas: Army Space Institute (26 January 1987).

Headquarters, United States European Command, *Operation Support Hope 1994 After Action Report.* U.S. Army Peacekeeping Institute (1994).

Headquarters, Department of the Army. HQDA Program Release Worksheet for Input into the Program Budget Accounting System to SAFM-BUI-I from SARD-RR (30 March 1994).

Hooper, James, Joe Kupsky, and James Walker. *The Data Collection Exercise: Army Leadership at the Cutting Edge of Space Control.* Huntsville, Alabama: U.S. Army Space and Missile Defense Command (July 1999).

Hooper, James, Todd Clark, and James Walker. *The Joint Tactical Ground Station: Fielding and Operational Lessons Learned.* Huntsville, Alabama: U.S. Army Space and Missile Defense Command (April 2000).

Kelly, Ricky B. *Centralized Control of Space: The Use of Space Forces by a Joint Force Commander.* Maxwell Air Force Base, Alabama: School of Advanced Airpower Studies (22 September 1994).

Kiker, Ed. *Informal Thoughts on the Status of the Army Space Institute* (1992).

Korpsel. Major and Mr. Freeman, *Input to LAMP: Space Support for Desert Shield.* Ft. Leavenworth, Kansas: Army Space Institute (September 1990).

McIlnay J.G., W.T. Brandon, and D.F. Collette. *Communications Alternatives for U.S. Army Space Command Space Support Teams.* Bedford, Massachusetts: MITRE Center for Air Force C3 Systems (February 1998).

Minnon, Major. *Information Paper – Manpower Requirements for Contingency Space Capabilities and Commercial Space Package* (18 February 94).

Proctor, Colonel Jerry V. *All Source Analysis System Information Briefing.* ASAS User's Conference (6 August 1998).

SD/CWN Headquarters Space Division (AFSC), Los Angeles Air Force Base. *Multiservice Test and Evaluation Master Plan for the NAVSTAR Global Positioning System User Equipment.* Los Angeles Air Force Base, California: SD/CWN Headquarters (November 1987).

SD/YEA Headquarters Space Division, Los Angeles Air Force Station. *NAVSTAR Global Positioning System Coordinated Test Program – II: Test and Evaluation Master Plan Army Annex.* Los Angeles Air Force Station, California: SD/YEA Headquarters (July 1982).

Skaw, Captain Gerald R. U.S. Army Space Command. *After Action Report, YAMA SAKURA XXXI* (25 February 1997).

Slaven, Captain George E. *What the Warfighter Should Know About Space: A Report on U.S. Space Command Joint Space Support Teams.* Maxwell Air Force Base, Alabama: Air War College Air University (April 1997).

Springer, Lieutenant Colonel Francis J. *Independent Operational Assessment of the NAVSTAR Global Positioning System (GPS) Army User Equipment (AUE) Operational Test II, November 1985/January 1986.* Falls Church, Virginia: U.S. Army Test and Evaluation Agency (3 April 1986).

Stahl, Lieutenant Colonel David T. 10th Mountain Division Operations in Haiti: Planning/ Preparation/Execution; August 1994 Thru January 1995.

Tovar, Wencis R. *Combined Arms Center Annual Historical Review: Army Space Institute Input.* Ft. Leavenworth, Kansas: Army Space Institute (4 August 1989).

U.S. Army Combined Arms Combat Development Activity. *The Army Position and Navigation Master Plan.* Ft. Leavenworth, Kansas: Combined Arms Combat Development Activity (May 1986).

United States Army Signal Center and Fort Gordon. *Operational Issues and Criteria for the Operational Test IOTE of the NAVSTAR Global Positioning System (GPS) Army User Equipment (AUE) Manpack/Vehicular Set.* Final draft. Ft. Gordon, Georgia. (9 August 1987).

United States Army Space Command. *Fact Sheet: U.S. Army Space Command.* Directorate of Public Affairs (7 April 1988).

United States Army Space Command. *USARSPACE Information Paper.* Peterson AFB, Colorado: U.S. Army Space Command (31 July 1989).

United States Army Space Command. *Army Space Support Team (ARSST) Concept of Operations (CONOPS).* Draft. Colorado Springs, Colorado: U.S. Army Space Command (12 December 1994).

U.S. Army Space Command. Army Space Support Team Division. *ARSST Deployment Schedule* (10 April 1995).

U.S. Army Space Command. Army Space Support Team Division. *ARSST Deployment Schedule* (8 May 1995).

U.S. Army Space Command. Army Space Support Team Division. *ARSST Deployment Schedule* (22 May 1995).

United States Army Space Command. *Army Space Exploitation Demonstration Program.* Public Affairs brochure. Colorado Springs, Colorado: U.S. Army Space Command (6 October 1995).

U.S. Army Space Command, Army Space Support Team Division, "ARSST Deployment Schedule." 19 June 1995.

U.S. Army Space Command. *Description/Specification/Work Statement: Upgrade to the Space Support Platform Plus.* Undated.

U.S. Army Space Command. *Final Training Support Package for the High Resolution Satellite Receiver* (27 February 1995).

U.S. Army Space Command. *Tactical Weather System (TWS) Program of Instruction (POI)* (12 September 1996).

U.S. Army Space Command, Revised Draft: Training Support Package for Mission Planning Rehearsal System (MPRS) (2 December 1994).

United States Army Space Command (Forward). *Space Support Reference Book* (20 August 1997).

U.S. Army Space Command (Forward). *The Army Tactical Missile Defense Element Handbook.* Undated.

U.S. Army Space Institute, *Unit and Sustainment Training Support Package for the Small Lightweight Global Positioning System Receiver (SLGR).* Ft. Leavenworth, KS: U.S. Army Space Institute (28 September 1990).

U.S. Space Command. *USSPACECOM Regulation 11-5: USSPACECOM Support to Theater Operations Management Program.* Peterson Air Force Base, Colorado: Headquarters United States Space Command (14 April 1993).

U.S. Space Command. USCINCSPACE. *UMD38-2: SPACE SUPPORT TEAM OPERATIONS* (Colorado Springs, Colorado: Headquarters, United States Space Command) (2 January 1996).

United States Naval Observatory. *GPS System Description* (12 June 1998).

Walker, Dr. James. U.S. Army Space and Strategic Defense Command. *3QFY97 USASSDC Command Achievements and Initiatives Report* (1997).

Oral History Interviews:

Mr. James H. Williamson (by Dr. James Walker and James Hooper, 22 October 1998).

Major Michael McFarland, Sergeant Eric Herrmann, and Staff Sergeant Mark Stroup (by Dr. James Walker and James Hooper, 22 October 1998).

Captain Gerry Skaw and Sergeant First Class Howard Smith (by Dr. James Walker and James Hooper, 22 October 1998).

Captain David Strombeck and Staff Sergeant William Bates (by Dr. James Walker and James Hooper, 23 October 1998).

Lieutenant Colonel Bob Simmons and Lieutenant Colonel LeRoy Maurer (by Dr. James Walker and James Hooper, 23 October 1998).

Lieutenant Colonel Frankie D. Moore (by Dr. James Walker and James Hooper, 23 October 1998).

Mr. Gary Baumann (by Dr. James Walker and James Hooper, 23 October 1998).

Major Scott Cuthbertson (by James Hooper, 29 October 1998).

Major Gwynne T. Burke (by James Hooper, 5 November 1998)

APPENDIX ONE: ARSST EQUIPMENT

This annex provides a summary of the key equipment and systems used by the Army Space Support Team. The annex is divided into three major sections, as described below:

- The first section provides a summary of the systems acquired as part of the Commercial Space Package, to include the High Resolution Weather Satellite Receiver, the Mission Planning Rehearsal System, INMARSAT communications terminals, and the Multi-Spectral Imagery Processor.

- The second section provides a brief description of key equipment upgrades and new space support systems used to equip the ARSST in the period from 1996 to 1998, to include the Space Support Platform, the Space Support Platform Plus, the Multi-Source Tactical System, the Laptop Visualization Device, and the All Source Analysis System—Warlord.

- The last section of this annex provides a summary of Army Space Support Team communication architectures and approaches.

The Commercial Space Package

The Army Space Support Team was equipped in 1994 with four space systems that had been acquired as part of the Army's Commercial Space Package (CSP) initiative. As described in pages 2-4 to 2-14 of this study, the CSP used commercial off-the-shelf (COTS) systems to provide a near-term, but limited, space support capability for Army operations and deployments.

The four CSP systems provided to the ARSST were designed to fulfill key weather, imaging, communications, and topographic support requirements identified by the Army during DESERT SHIELD/DESERT STORM and subsequent deployments to Somalia, Haiti, Zaire, and Bosnia. First, the ARSST was equipped with two satellite weather receivers, allowing it to downlink weather information directly. With this capability, the ARSST could support operations in remote locations with day-to-day weather information. Second, 5 Mission Planning Rehearsal Systems (MPRS) were provided to the ARSST, allowing supported commanders and staffs to review terrain in areas of future operations. With the MPRS, an ARSST could provide three-dimensional imagery maps or conduct terrain 'fly-throughs' for the supported unit. Third, a critical need for additional satellite communications support had been identified during previous Army deployments. To address this requirement, the ARSST was equipped with twelve INMARSAT man-portable terminals, providing near-global communications using secure voice, data, or fax transmissions. Finally, the ARSST was equipped with two Multi-spectral Imagery Processors, allowing it to transform imagery from commercial satellite systems into digital and paper maps, complete with a military grid reference system.[1]

The High Resolution Weather Satellite Receiver (HRWSR)

The HRWSR was designed to acquire data from existing military (Defense Meteorological Satellite Program, or DMSP) and civilian (Television Infrared Orbital Satellite, or TIROS) weather-sensing space platforms. Those satellites were designed to provide images of earth in five regions of the visible and infrared electromagnetic spectrum, with a ground resolution of .06 kilometers. Additional instruments on these satellites could sense critical weather elements such as atmospheric winds, surface and upper-air temperatures, pressure fields, and humidity. Using this satellite weather data, the HRWSR terminal could process and display weather imagery (to include three-dimensional cloud formations), present the spatial location of soil moisture, and provide a database for use in the planning of future operations.[2]

The basic HRWSR system processing unit included a SUN Sparc 10 processing unit with 64 Megabytes of Random Access Memory

Artist's Rendition of a DMSP Satellite in Orbit.

Background: DMSP.

The Defense Meteorological Satellite Program (DMSP) was designed to gather weather data from around the world and transmit it to ground stations supporting U.S. military operations. DMSP has been collecting weather data for U.S. military operations for more than two decades. DMSP satellites typically operate in two-satellite constellations in sun-synchronous, circular polar orbits. The design life of a DMSP satellite is approximately three to four years.

(RAM) and a SeaSpace frame synchronizer card with TeraScan Version 2.X software. For storage and data retrieval, the system included three disk drives (424 Megabyte internal, two 1 Gigabyte external), an archive tape system (4mm tape drive with 2.6 Gigabyte capacity), and a CD-ROM drive for master software or database retrieval. As initially configured, the HRWSR system included a 1 meter antenna dish with 56" radome, an antenna base, a receiver, and quick disconnect antenna cables. Removable camouflaged antenna covers (1 desert, 1 woodland) were included with the receiver package.[3] The HRWSR receiver was also deployed with a GPS antenna to permit rapid deployment and an Uninterruptable Power Source (UPS) line filter to allow graceful degradation with loss of power.[4] Other elements of the HRWSR included a monitor, a color printer, and a KG-44

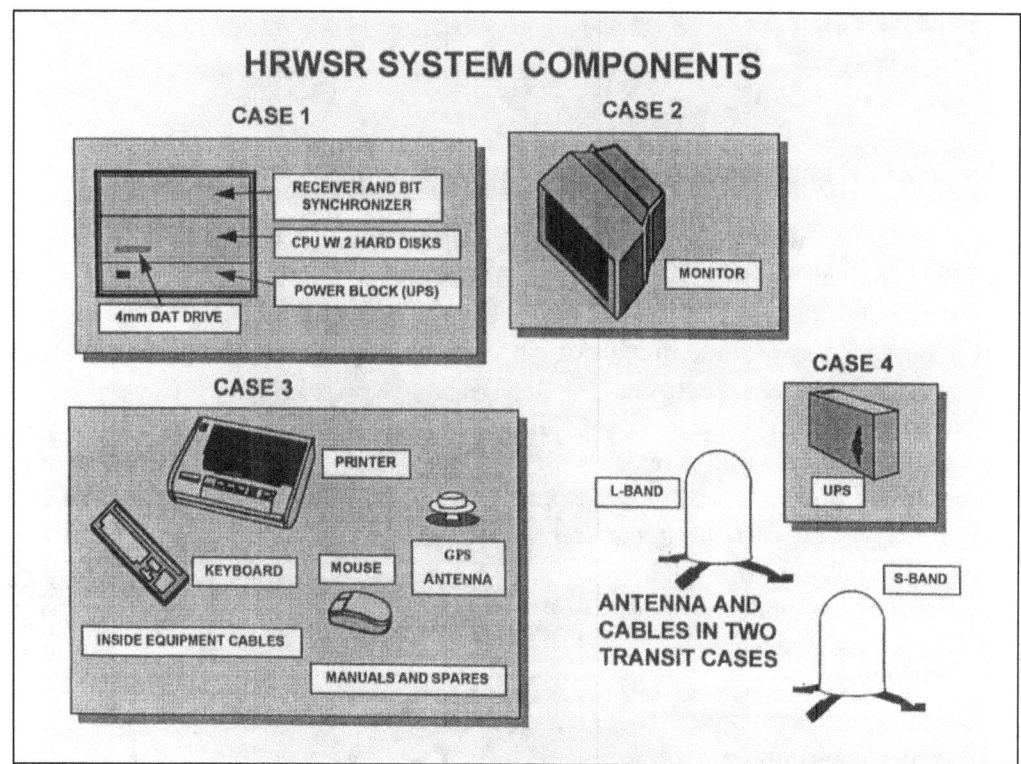

Figure A-1: Components of the High Resolution Weather Satellite Receiver (as presented in the February 1995 HRWSR Training Support Package).

encryption device (required to access DMSP satellite transmissions).

Prior to the deployment of ARSST personnel in early 1995, a training support package was developed for the HRWSR. The training package, promulgated in February 1995, contained eleven key training blocs and a test section. The first training bloc provided an overview of the HRWSR. Subsequent training blocs provided additional information on the operation of the system, including procedures for setting up and initializing the HRWSR, entering orbital elements, and scheduling satellite passes. Additional training blocs addressed data processing, troubleshooting and file management, tape operations, and printing output.[5] As the Army Space Support Team gained experience during deployments to the field, the HRWSR training program continued to evolve. By 1996, a three day program of instruction had been developed for soldiers assigned to the ARSST. During the first day, the students received instruction on weather satellite characteristics, HRWSR set-up, decryption equipment handling, UNIX commands, entering orbital elements, and scheduling satellite passes. During day two, the students learned how to process and view satellite weather imagery, enhance imagery and develop overlays, and perform advanced system processing. Training on advanced processing techniques continued on the third day, followed by instruction on HRWSR enhancements and legends and techniques for exporting imagery files.[6]

The Mission Planning Rehearsal System (MPRS)

The second major system acquired for the ARSST as part of the Army's Commercial Space Package was the Mission Planning Rehearsal System. The MPRS was designed as a situational awareness tool, using imagery and data from multiple sources to allow a supported commander to visualize operations on the actual terrain before being committed to action.[7]

The MPRS used space-derived imagery from multiple sources, including the civilian Landsat and SPOT satellites, to develop three-dimensional interactive terrain perspectives of an area of operations. With software such as Autometric's *Wings Mission Rehearsal*, the Mission Planning Rehearsal System could then be used by the supported unit to 'fly through' the terrain model. The MPRS also allowed the commander and staff to rotate and manipulate the terrain model, providing multiple perspectives for planning and allowing various topographical features to be analyzed as part of the tactical decision making process. Terrain models and 'fly-throughs' developed by the MPRS could also be saved to VHS videotape for display on a remote color television set.[8]

Although not organically equipped, the ARSST Mission Planning Rehearsal System was also configured for connectivity with a UHF satellite communications radio, allowing input to be provided from the Tactical Data Delivery System/Tactical Data Intelligence Exchange System-B (TDDS/TADIXS-B), the Tactical Information Broadcast System (TIBS), National Imagery, Tactical Digital Link A and B (TADIL-A/B), and commercial Standard Positioning System (SPS) Global Positioning System sources.

The MPRS processing unit was originally based on a Silicon Graphics IRIS INDIGO station, with 96 Megabytes RAM. For storage and data retrieval, the system was equipped with two disk drives (1.3 Gigabytes internal and 3.5 Gigabytes external), an 8mm tape drive, and a CD-ROM drive. Products developed by the MPRS could be stored on a video tape, viewed on the system's color monitor, or delivered in hard copy format using a Tektronix color printer.[9]

A training package for the operation of the MPRS was developed by the Army Space Support Team in December 1994. This training package included twelve training blocs and a test section. Under the program of instruction, students learned how to prepare the MPRS for operation, import imagery and elevation data files, create MPRS projects, conduct analysis, and produce videotapes of the rehearsal.[10]

INMARSAT Communications Terminals

The third system provided to the ARSST as part of the Commercial Space Package was the International Maritime Satellite Organization (INMARSAT) communications terminal. During Army deployments to Saudi Arabia, Iraq, Turkey, Somalia, Zaire, and Haiti, INMARSAT terminals had been used to augment the military communications system and, in many cases, had been used when military systems were unavailable or proved to be unresponsive. The ARSST was equipped with INMARSAT terminals to provide a responsive and easily deployable early-entry communications system for future Army operations.

Two types of INMARSAT communications terminals were provided to the ARSST. The first, a Standard B terminal, was designed to support ARSST deployments to a Corps headquarters. This suitcase-sized terminal was capable of full duplex data transmission at speeds of up to 64 Kbps.[11] ARSST personnel were trained to set up and operate a Standard B terminal within 5 minutes.

The second type of INMARSAT terminal, the Standard M, was a much lighter system and was intended for deployment in support of both Corps and Division headquarters. The Standard M was capable of 2.4 Kbps voice and data transmission.[12] As with the Standard B, ARSST personnel were trained to setup and operate the Standard M terminal within 5 minutes.[13]

The ARSST was equipped with both INMARSAT Standard B and M terminals because the two types of terminals offered a tradeoff between system weight and speed of transmission (See Figure A2-2, below). While the Standard M was lighter than the Standard B (30 pounds versus 66 pounds), its transmission speeds were far inferior (2.4 Kbps secure/unsecure data and fax versus 64 Kbps unsecure data or 9.6 Kbps secure voice/data/fax). Moreover, the Standard M terminal's slower transmission speeds translated into airtime costs that were up to six times higher than for the Standard B.

An issue that has repeatedly impacted upon the Army's ability to use INMARSAT is the use of the system for military operations. This issue was identified in September 1993 during the Louisiana Maneuvers General Officer Working Group when the Commercial Space Package was initially reviewed.[14] In a 25 July 1994 memorandum, the Army Spectrum Manager promulgated an Army-wide policy clarifying the use of INMARSAT terminals. Under this policy, it was noted that the INMARSAT system was designed for low-volume communications that are dedicated "exclusively for peaceful purposes." Section 3b of this policy delineated the three acceptable uses of INMARSAT by Army units in the field: [1] Emergency communications; [2] Communications in support of peacekeeping missions; and [3] Other non-aggressive general purpose communications.[15]

The Multi-Spectral Imagery Processor (MSIP)

The fourth major system acquired for the ARSST as part of the Army's Commercial Space Package was the Multi-Spectral Imagery Processor. The MSIP was designed to provide a supported unit with the capability to acquire, process, deliver, and use multi-spectral imagery from space systems.

The most common sources of multi-spectral imagery products for the MSIP were Landsat Thematic Mapper (TM) and French SPOT satellite data. In addition, the MSIP was capable of processing imaging radar data and national imagery files. Sensors onboard these satellites were capable of receiving and measuring various wavelengths and frequencies associated with natural and man-made objects on the ground. By selectively filtering the wavelengths and sampling over a broad range of frequencies, the satellites could group the samplings into various bands and transmit images. An analyst could then combine this data to produce descriptive colors, or "signatures," which correlate to various entities on the ground and which can be used to enhance certain features. For example, "True Color" combinations (bands 1, 2, and 3) approximate the way the human eye perceives this image from the position of the satellite. The combination of bands 4, 3, and 2 is known as "False Color," in which the vegetation band (band 4) is assigned to the red color gun. In this combination, vegetation appears red with the brighter red color indicating thicker, denser vegetation than the darker red. These colors also indicate differences between deciduous and coniferous forests, which is important information when doing a trafficability analysis.

The Multi-Spectral Imagery Processor system also had the capability to merge different data types. For example, the multi-spectral resolution of the Landsat Thematic Mapper is 30 meters per pixel while the black and white spatial resolution of imagery from SPOT is much higher at 10 meters per pixel. By combining the two data types, the MSIP could produce imagery that had the spatial resolution of SPOT and the multi-spectral characteristics of Landsat. Another MSIP capability was spatial modeling, in which two or more products are integrated into a new product. For example, combining overhead satellite imagery with DMA Digital Terrain Elevation Data (DTED) produced three-dimensional perspective views. Essentially the process "draped" the satellite imagery over the wire-frame map of the DTED to lend a realistic feel for the terrain.[16]

As initially procured by the Army, the Multi-Spectral Imagery Processor was composed of a SUN Sparc station 10 (or equivalent) with 64 Megabytes RAM, two disk drives (424 Megabyte internal, 2.6 Gigabyte external), a CD-ROM drive, and an 8mm tape drive. Imagery output was displayed on standard color monitors, with two hardcopy printing options available: a Linotronics printer for lithographic reproduction (for use at Corps level only) and a Tektronix Phaser II (for use at both Corps and Division level).[17]

A training support package for the MSIP was developed by the ARSST in December 1994. This training program included eleven primary training blocs and a test section. During the first part of the training course, the principles of multi-spectral imagery collection and processing were reviewed by the students. Then, students were taught how to prepare the MSIP for operation, initialize the MSIP, load and convert data, and rectify, enhance, and classify images. Training on the system culminated with a series of modeling and terrain analysis exercises.[18]

Upgraded and New ARSST Equipment

In January 1996, the Army Space Support Team conducted a formal review of lessons learned during its first year of operations. At this review, a number of recommendations were made regarding the need for new equipment and systems. First, ARSST personnel expressed a need for the capability to receive large data files in remote locations. Second, they emphasized the requirement for better communications and interface capabilities with other deployed space support teams. Third, they agreed that all communications security equipment assigned to the ARSST had to be MIL-Standard. Fourth, they noted a need for a streamlined equipment maintenance process. Finally, ARSST personnel emphasized that a balance had to be struck to ensure that the cost of equipment did not outweigh its benefits to the warfighter.[19]

In the time period from 1996 to 1998, the Army Space Support Team would seek to meet these objectives by upgrading the original Commercial Space Package systems, acquiring enhanced systems and capabilities, and experimenting with new software and hardware. Key ARSST systems are described below.

The Space Support Platform (SSP)

The Space Support Platform was one of the key hardware and software upgrade efforts initiated by the ARSST. The SSP sought to integrate the capabilities of the Multi-Spectral Imagery Processor and the Mission Planning Rehearsal System and, in the process, create a much more powerful tool. By linking the MSIP and the MPRS into a single system, the ARSST hoped to reduce the time required to transform imagery files into mission planning tools, incorporate a commercial Geographic Information System (GIS) capability into the existing MPRS tool, and allow a supported unit's graphics and planning information to be integrated into the SSP. With the resulting system, the ARSST would be able to display operational graphics and tables in discernible layers, validate topographic rectification, allow the interaction and compatibility of various overlays and plans to be assessed, and provide a tool for assessing terrain effects on alternative courses of action.[20]

The Space Support Platform itself was originally based on an SGI Max Impact workstation with 40 Gigabytes of retrievable memory, a 250 MHz processor, 384 Megabytes of RAM, a CD-ROM drive, and 8mm and 4mm tape drives. Software mounted on the Space Support Platform included *IMAGINE*, *EDGE*, *WINGS*, *OMNI*, and *TSOC*.[21] *IMAGINE* software was integrated into the SSP to provide a terrain analysis capability. *IMAGINE* was used to convert raw aerial photographs and overhead imagery into formatted maps. In addition, the software could integrate imagery with Digital Terrain Elevation Data to develop three-dimensional terrain models. *EDGE* provided the ARSST with the ability to model and simulate both space and ground assets. With *EDGE*, ARSST personnel could develop three-dimensional 'fly-throughs' of a potential area of operation for a supported unit. In addition, *EDGE* allowed additional information (such as electronic intelligence data) to be superimposed on the three-dimensional terrain model.[22] A similar three-dimensional terrain modeling and fly-through capability was provided by *WINGS*. *TSOC* was designed to provide satellite tracking analysis and to permit space support team elements deployed in-theater to work together. *OMNI* was developed as a GPS accuracy planning tool.

The Space Support Platform Plus (SSP+)

As technology continued to evolve rapidly, offering improved commercial off-the-shelf space products, the ARSST continued to upgrade the original Space Support Platform. The new Space Support Platform Plus (SSP+) built upon the lessons learned by the ARSST in the field — while taking advantage of new technologies and software — to provide an improved space support system.

In upgrading the original SSP to the new SSP+, the ARSST established a series of system requirements. Specifications developed for the new SSP+ included an upgrade to a Silicon Graphics Octane Dual CPU system (R10000, 250 MHz), a minimum of 512 Megabytes RAM (1 Gigabyte preferred), 4 Megabyte-texture memory, and VHS video output option. Storage on the system was to be based on two 9-Gigabyte internal drives and an external 128 Gigabyte drive. The system was also to include one internal and two external UltraWide SCSI chains. As for peripherals, the SSP+ was to be equipped with a 8mm external tape drive and a Read/(Re)Write external CD-ROM. The system was to have a minimum complement of IRIX operating system software, an Internet browser, EDGE 3.3 or greater, ERDAS *IMAGINE* 8.3 or greater, and TSOC 3.2 or greater. In addition, the SSP+ would also benefit from a larger color monitor.[23]

Both the SSP and the SSP+ provide a number of common space support capabilities. First, both systems can be used to develop two-dimensional maps, to include grid overlays. Second, both systems can be used to produce two- and three-dimensional snapshots and montages. Third, the two systems can generate image maps and topographical blowups. Fourth, both the SSP and the SSP+ can be used to conduct three-dimensional fly-throughs of an area of operations. Fifth, the two systems can be used to generate GPS satellite availability and coverage information. Finally, both of the systems can display the orbits and earth coverage of satellites.

The Multi-Source Tactical System (MSTS)

The Multi-Source Tactical System was designed as a tool for processing battlefield information and providing situational awareness to the supported commander. The

MSTS allows a three-dimensional view of the battlefield to be developed, with applicable intelligence and operational data overlaid on the terrain.[24] Sources of information for the MSTS include unclassified and classified imagery (from commercial satellites, airborne sensors, or national assets) and intelligence data from TIBS and TRAP.[25]

The ARSST has used the MSTS to track missile events for supported units.[26] In addition, the ARSST has had some success in using the MSTS to support unit planning and operations. For example, during the 1st Infantry Division BCTP in 1998, the Division suffered heavy losses of helicopters in the initial stages of the exercise. With the Multi-Source Tactical System, the anti-air threat could be accurately tracked. After this capability was demonstrated to Division planners, no further helicopters were 'destroyed' during the BCTP.[27]

The Laptop Visualization Device (LVD)

The Laptop Visualization Device was designed to provide advanced terrain analysis and mission planning support through a commercial off-the-shelf laptop computer. The LVD is based upon three software modules. The Route Planner Module is used to develop a terrain model and a fly-through of the requested terrain. The Route Builder Module converts this information into a movie that can be played on the LVD system. The Route Viewer Module is used to view the output and, ultimately, help supported units develop and evaluate tactical courses of action.[28]

The LVD itself is based upon a laptop computer system, with 24 Megabtyes of RAM and a 540 Megabyte hard drive. For connectivity, the LVD is equipped with a 14.4 baud modem and an Ethernet connection. The LVD has been used by the ARSST in a number of exercises and deployments, to include ULCHI FOCUS LENS 97 and a 5th Special Forces Group Army Warfighter Exercise conducted from February to March 1997.

The All Source Analysis System—Warlord (ASAS Warlord)

The All Source Analysis System was developed as an all-source intelligence fusion tool to support tactical decision making. The ASAS is based upon a series of hardware and software modules, providing message and graphics input, intelligence processing and reporting, target identification and nomination, and communications processing and interfacing capabilities. These modules allow intelligence input to be received from a number of sources, to include unit reconnaissance elements, electronic intelligence systems, airborne sensors, human intelligence and counterintelligence sources, and national intelligence assets. The ASAS can process, correlate, and fuse hundreds of reports per hour, ensuring that information is provided in a timely fashion to supported commanders and staffs. ASAS systems have been fielded to separate brigades and regiments, Division Headquarters, Corps Headquarters, and Military Intelligence Brigades.[29]

The ASAS Warlord system is a rapid-prototype system intended to provide All Source Analysis System capabilities in a lighter and more mobile platform. The ARSST uses the ASAS Warlord to provide information to a supported unit's intelligence staff.[30]

ARSST Communications

A key space support requirement that has been repeatedly emphasized by ARSST personnel is the need for a communications capability that permits a team in the field to acquire large data files rapidly and access the full spectrum of USARSPACE (Forward) capabilities while deployed in the field. The Army Space Support Team has conducted a series of experiments to address this issue, using systems ranging from INMARSAT terminals, the Secret Internet Protocol Router Network (SIPRNET), the Global Broadcast System (GBS), and cellular phones.

In 1997, U.S. Army Space Command commissioned an independent study of ARSST communications connectivity options and approaches. This study, delivered in February 1998, identified four categories of communications requirements for the Army Space Support Team: [1] Messaging or low data rate communications; [2] Voice communications; [3] SIPRNET web browsing; and [4] Downloading of large digital files (such as imagery data). A variety of commercial and military systems were evaluated against these ARSST requirements on the basis of system availability, performance, and operational factors.

The authors of this independent study made four recommendations for addressing ARSST communications requirements. First, they concluded that the only way to meet current ARSST high data rate communications requirements at the present time was to use organic military assets. For this reason, it was recommended that planning to obtain access to these capabilities be made a top priority prior to ARSST deployment. Second, they noted that the Iridium system would provide a "limited, but secure, voice connectivity worldwide in an easily carried package" once deployed. For this reason, it was recommended that the ARSST obtain the military version of the Iridium handset as soon as it becomes available. Third, it was recommended that the likelihood of an ARSST deployment to a remote location (not serviced by organic communications) be conducted to determine if an interim communications solution using GBS might be required. Finally, it was recommended that U.S. Army Space Command continue to monitor the commercial market to determine what systems might best fulfill long-term requirements.[31]

In the 1998 draft Concept of Operations for the Army Space Support Cell and the Army Space Support Team, three different communications architectures were described. The first architecture presented was based upon a deployment in support of the annual ULCHI FOCUS LENS exercise in Korea. This architecture employed the ARCTIC BOX as the central communications node. Under this approach, Theater Automated Command and Control Information Management

System (TACCIMS) information would be routed through the SIPRNET and the Network Encryption System (NES). The Army Space Support Cell would process information through each of the deployed ARSST teams in theater and would provide connectivity back to other U.S. Army Space Command elements in Colorado Springs.[32]

The second architecture presented was based upon ARSST support requirements in Europe. Under this approach, the Joint Broadcast Service (JBS) or the Global Broadcast Service (GBS) would be used to transmit data overseas to V Corps. Once in theater, information would be transmitted from the JBS/GBS terminal to units in the field via the SIPRNET. If JBS or GBS were not available, a communications set-up would be established instead like that developed for III Corps.[33]

The third architecture described in the ASSC concept of operations was based upon a direct SIPRNET connection. This approach was designed for ARSST deployments in support of III Corps exercises. During these missions, an ASSC and an ARSST would be collocated with the Corps Headquarters, while ARSST teams would be stationed with subordinate Divisions and Brigades.[34]

---

[1] Major Jensen, Call the COPS. (Colorado Springs, Colorado: U.S. Army Space Command, undated.).

[2] U.S. Army Space Command, Final Training Support Package for the High Resolution Satellite Receiver. 27 February 1995.

[3] Memorandum, Brigadier General Edward G. Anderson III, U.S. Army Training and Doctrine Command, to Deputy Chief of Staff, Operations, ATTN: DAMO-FD, Subject: Operational Needs Statement (ONS) for the Commercial Space Package (CSP). 18 March 1994.

[4] U.S. Army Space Command, Army Space Support Team (ARSST) Concept of Operations (CONOPS) (DRAFT). (Colorado Springs, Colorado: U.S. Army Space Command: 12 December 1994.).

[5] U.S. Army Space Command, Final Training Support Package for the High Resolution Satellite Receiver. 27 February 1995.

[6] U.S. Army Space Command, Tactical Weather System (TWS) Program of Instruction (POI). 12 September 1996.

[7] U.S. Army Space Command, Revised Draft: Training Support Package for Mission Planning Rehearsal System (MPRS). 2 December 1994.

[8] Ibid.

[9] Memorandum, Brigadier General Edward G. Anderson III, U.S. Army Training and Doctrine Command, to Deputy Chief of Staff, Operations, ATTN: DAMO-FD, Subject: Operational Needs Statement (ONS) for the Commercial Space Package (CSP). 18 March 1994. U.S. Army Space Command, Army Space

Support Team (ARSST) Concept of Operations (CONOPS) (DRAFT). (Colorado Springs, Colorado: U.S. Army Space Command: 12 December 1994.).

[10] U.S. Army Space Command, Revised Draft: Training Support Package for Mission Planning Rehearsal System (MPRS). 2 December 1994.

[11] Memorandum, Brigadier General Edward G. Anderson III, U.S. Army Training and Doctrine Command, to Deputy Chief of Staff, Operations, ATTN: DAMO-FD, Subject: Operational Needs Statement (ONS) for the Commercial Space Package (CSP). 18 March 1994.

[12] Ibid.

[13] U.S. Army Space Command, Army Space Support Team (ARSST) Concept of Operations (CONOPS) (DRAFT). (Colorado Springs, Colorado: U.S. Army Space Command: 12 December 1994.).

[14] Memorandum, Brigadier General Edward G. Anderson III, U.S. Army Training and Doctrine Command, to Deputy Chief of Staff, Operations, ATTN: DAMO-FD, Subject: Operational Needs Statement (ONS) for the Commercial Space Package (CSP). 18 March 1994.

[15] Memorandum, Earl J. Holliman, Army Spectrum Manager, Subject: Use of International Maritime Satellite (INMARSAT). 25 January 1994.

[16] U.S. Army Space Command, Revised Draft: Training Support Package for Mission Planning Rehearsal System (MPRS). 2 December 1994.

[17] Memorandum, Brigadier General Edward G. Anderson III, U.S. Army Training and Doctrine Command, to Deputy Chief of Staff, Operations, ATTN: DAMO-FD, Subject: Operational Needs Statement (ONS) for the Commercial Space Package (CSP). 18 March 1994.

[18] U.S. Army Space Command, Revised Draft: Training Support Package for the Multi-Spectral Imagery Processor (MSIP). 2 December 1994.

[19] Meeting Notes, Major Foeller, U.S. Army Space Command, "Army Space Support to the Warfighter Review," 11 January 1996.

[20] ARINC, Task Execution Plan: Army Space Support Team (ARSST) MPRS-MPIS Integration. 1996.

[21] Major Wayne Brainerd, "Space Support Platform." 1997.

[22] Brown International, "Draft Army Space Support Cell Concept of Operations." Undated.

[23] U.S. Army Space Command, "Description/Specification/Work Statement: Upgrade to the Space Support Platform Plus." Undated.

[24] Brown International, "Draft Army Space Support Cell Concept of Operations." Undated.

[25] U.S. Army Space Command (Forward), <u>The Army Tactical Missile Defense Element Handbook</u>. Undated.

[26] U.S. Army Space Command Briefing, "ARSST Systems," Undated.

[27] Dr. James Walker and James Hooper, "James Williamson Oral History Interview, ARSST Historical/Lessons Learned Study," 22 October 1998.

[28] Brown International, "Draft Army Space Support Cell Concept of Operations." Undated.

[29] Colonel Jerry V. Proctor, "All Source Analysis System Information Briefing" <u>ASAS User's Conference</u>. 6 August 1998.

[30] Brown International, "Draft Army Space Support Cell Concept of Operations." Undated.

[31] Ibid., p. viii.

[32] Brown International, "Draft Army Space Support Cell Concept of Operations." Undated.

[33] Ibid.

[34] Ibid.

APPENDIX TWO: ACRONYMS

ABC	Airborne Corps
ADRG ARC	Digitized RasterGraphics
AFSPACECOM	Air Force Space Command
AFSST	Air Force Space Support Team
ALERT	Attack and Launch Early Reporting to Theater
AOR	Area of Operations
ARSPACE	Army Space Command
ARSST	Army Space Support Team
ASA	Army Space Agency
ASAS	All Source Analysis System
ASDP	Army Space Demonstration Program
ASEDP	Army Space Exploitation Demonstration Program
ASI	Army Space Institute
ASIOE	Associated Support Items of Equipment
ASPLO	Army Space Liaison Officer
ASSC	Army Space Support Cell
ASTAC	Army Space Tactical Demonstration program
ATCCS	Army Tactical Command & Control System
AUEL	Automated Unit Equipment List
BCBL	Battle Command Battle Laboratory
BCTP	Battle Command Training Program
BDA	Battle Damage Assessment
BLUFOR	Blue Force
BOD	Board of Directors
C2	Command and Control

C4I	Command, Control, Communications, Computers and Intelligence
CASCOM	Combined Arms Support Command
CCB	Configuration Control Board
CCI	Controlled Communications and Intelligence
CEL	Civilian Employment Level
CENTCOM	United States Central Command
CG	Commanding General
CINC	Commander in Chief
CINCSPACE	Commander in Chief, United States Space Command
CJCS	Chairman Joint Chiefs of Staff
CJTF	Commander, Joint Task Force
COMSEC	Communications Security
CONOPS	Concept of Operations
CONUS	Continental United States
COP	Contingency Operations Package
COPS	Contingency Operations (Space)
COTS	Commercial Off-the-Shelf
CP	Command Post
CPX	Command Post Exercise
CSH	Common Software/Hardware
CSP	Commercial Space Package
CSS	Combat Service Support
CTAT	Combined Terrain Analysis Team
CTT-H	Commander's Tactical Terminal-Hybrid
CY	Current Year
DAMO-FD	Assistant Deputy Chief of Staff for Operations and Plans, Force Development
DCSINT	Deputy Chief of Staff for Intelligence
DCSOPS	Deputy Chief of Staff for Operations and Plans

DISN	Defense Integrated Switched Network
DIV	Division
DMS	Defense Mapping School
DMSP	Defense Meteorological and Surveillance Program
DoD	Department of Defense
DSCS	Defense Satellite Communications System
DSP	Defense Support Program
DTED	Digital Terrain Elevation Data
DTLOMS	Doctrine, Training, Leader Development, Organization, Material Development, Soldiers
DTSS	Digital Topographic Support System
EAC	Echelons Above Corps
EUCOM	European Command
FAD	Funding Authorization Document
FOC	Full operational capability
FORSCOM	United States Army Forces Command
FP	Force Projection
FSST	Forward Space Support in Theater
FY	Fiscal Year
GBS	Global Broadcast System
GCCS	Global Command and Control System
GMF	Ground Mobile Forces
GOWG	General Officer Working Group
GPS	Global Positioning System
HDRSAT	High Data Rate Tactical Satellite Terminal
HSIC	Hardware Software Integration Center
HQ	Headquarters

HQDA	Headquarters, Department of the Army
HRWSR	High Resolution Weather Satellite Receiver
ICBM	Intercontinental Ballistic Missile
IDP	Issue Decision Package
IFSARE	Interferometric Synthetic Aperture Radar for Elevations
ILS	Integrated Logistics Support
IMETS	Integrated Meteorological System
INMARSAT	International Maritime Satellite Organization
INTELSAT	International Telecommunications Satellite Organization
IOC	Interim Operational Capability (for GPS)
IPB	Intelligence Preparation of the Battlefield
JBS	Joint Broadcast Service
JRTC	Joint Readiness Training Center
JSCP	Joint Strategic Capabilities Plan
JSDF	Japan Self-Defense Force
JSST	Joint Space Support Team
JTAGS	Joint Tactical Ground Station
JTF	Joint Task Force
LAM	Louisiana Maneuvers
LAM TF	Louisiana Maneuvers Task Force
LCC	Land Component Commander
LEOCOMM	Low-Earth Orbit Communications
LES	Land Earth Station
LIGHTSAT	Light satellite
LMS	Lightweight, Multipurpose Shelter
LNO	Liaison Officer
LVD	Laptop Visualization Device

MACOM	Major Command
MEF	Marine Expeditionary Force
METEOSAT	Meteorological Satellite
METT-T	Mission, Enemy, Troops, Terrain, and Time
MDEP	Management Decision Package
MI	Military Intelligence
MILSATCOM	Military Satellite Communications
MOA	Memorandum of Agreement
MPRS	Mission Planning Rehearsal System
MRC	Major Regional Conflict
MSI	Multi-Spectral Imagery
MSIP	Multi-Spectral Imagery Processor
MSTS(A)	Multi-Source Tactical System, Army
NAVSST	Navy Space Support Team
NAVSTAR	Navigation System Using Timing and Ranging
NCA	National Command Authority
NCO	Noncommissioned Officer
NES	Network Encryption System
NET	New Equipment Training
NKPA	North Korean People's Army
NOAA	National Oceanic Atmospheric Administration
NORAD	North American Aerospace Defense Command
NTC	National Training Center
OCONUS	Outside the Continental United States
OCR	Operational Capability Requirements
ODA	Operational Detachment Alpha
ODP	Officer Distribution Plan

OMA	Operations and Maintenance, Army
ONS	Operational Needs Statement
OPA	Other Procurement, Army
OPCON	Operational Control
OPLAN	Operations Plan
OPTEMPO	Operations Tempo
P3I	Planned, Process and Product Improvement
PACOM	Pacific Command
PC	Personal Computer
PE	Program Element
PEO-CCS	Program Executive Office, Command and Control Systems
PLDC	Primary Leadership Development Course
POM	Program Objective Memorandum
POS/NAV	Position/Navigation
RSI	Remotely Sensed Imagery
SA	Selective Availability (GPS)
SATCOM	Satellite Communications
SCP	Standardized Command Post
SFG	Special Forces Group
SHF	Super High Frequency
SIDS	Secondary Imagery Dissemination System
SIPRNET	Secure Internet Protocol Router Network
SLBM	Submarine-Launched Ballistic Missiles
SLGR	Small Lightweight Global Positioning System Receiver
SMDC	Space and Missile Defense Command (U.S. Army)
SMDBL	Space and Missile Defense Battle Laboratory
SOP	Standard Operating Procedure

SOUTHCOM	Southern Command
SPOT	Satellite Pour l'Observation de la Terre
SSDC	Space and Strategic Defense Command (U.S. Army)
SSP	Space Support Platform
SSP+	Space Support Platform Plus
STARTEX	Start Exercise
STOMP	Support to Theater Operations Management Plan
SWO	Staff Weather Officer
SWS	Small Weather System
TACDAR	Tactical Detection and Reporting system
TACCIMS	Theater Automated Command and Control Information Management System
TDA	Table of Distribution and Allowances
TEC	Topographic Engineering Center
TES	Tactical Events System
TERS	Tactical Events Reporting System
TF	Task Force
TIIP	Topographic Imagery Integration Program
TIROS	Television Infra-Red Observation Satellite
TM	Team
TOC	Tactical Operations Center
TPFDD	Time Phased Force Deployment Data
TPFDL	Time Phased Force Deployment List
TPIO-SPACE	TRADOC Program Integration Office for Space
TRADOC	Training and Doctrine Command
TRAP	Tactical and Related Applications
TSOC	Theater Support Operations Cell
TTEC	Topographic Technology Exploitation Cell
UCMJ	Universal Code of Military Justice

UFR	Unfunded Requirement
UJTL	Universal Joint Task List
USACOM	United States Atlantic Command
USAF	United States Air Force
USAFISA	U.S. Army Force Integration Support Activity
USAREUR	United States Army Europe
USARSPACE	United States Army Space Command
USASMDC	United States Army Space and Missile Defense Command
USASOC	United States Army Special Operations Command
USASSDC	United States Army Space and Strategic Defense Command
USCINCSPACE	See CINCSPACE
USSPACECOM	United States Space Command
USSTRATCOM	United States Strategic Command
VSP	Volume Subscription Program (INMARSAT)
VTC	Video Teleconference
WFX	Warfighting Exercise
WRAASE	Corporate Name For A German Manufacturer Of Satellite Equipment And Electronics